Wonders of Science Writing Lessons

Implementing the Structure and Style® Writing Method

Teacher's Manual

First Edition © March 2023
Institute for Excellence in Writing, L.L.C.

The purchase of this book allows its owner access to PDF downloads that accompany *Wonders of Science Writing Lessons*. See blue page for details and download instructions. Our duplicating/copying policy for these resources is specified on the copyright page for each of these downloads.

Additional copies of this Teacher's Manual may be purchased from IEW.com/WOS-T

Institute for Excellence in Writing (IEW®)
8799 N. 387 Road
Locust Grove, OK 74352
800.856.5815
info@IEW.com
IEW.com

Printed in the United States of America

IEW® and Structure and Style® are registered trademarks of the Institute for Excellence in Writing, L.L.C.

These lessons are not intended as a science curriculum replacement, but rather their purpose is to broaden subject knowledge while students learn to write.

Contributors

Sabrina Cardinale
Sharyn Gregory
Denise Kelley
Andrea Pewthers
Heidi Thomas
Julie Walker

Designer

Melanie Anderson

Illustrator

Erin Covey

Accessing Your Downloads
Teacher's Manual

The purchase of this book allows its owner access to PDF downloads of the following:

- the optional *Wonders of Science Writing Lessons* Reproducible Checklists
- the optional *Wonders of Science Writing Lessons* Vocabulary Cards
- the optional *Wonders of Science Writing Lessons* Simplified Source Texts
- the optional *Wonders of Science Writing Lessons* Advanced Additions
- the optional *Wonders of Science Writing Lessons* Exemplars

To download these e-resources, please follow the directions below:

1. Go to our website: IEW.com

2. Log in to your online customer account. If you do not have an account, you will need to create one.

3. After you are logged in, type this link into your address bar: IEW.com/WOS-TE

4. Click the checkboxes next to the names of the files you wish to place in your account.

5. Click the "Add to my files" button.

6. To access your files now and in the future, click on "Your Account" and click on the "Files" tab (one of the gray tabs).

7. Click on each file name to download the files onto your computer.

Please note: You may download and print these PDF files as needed for use within *your immediate family*. However, this information is proprietary, and we are trusting you to be on your honor not to share it with anyone. Please see the copyright page for further details.

If you have any difficulty receiving these downloads after going through the steps above, please call 800.856.5815.

Institute for Excellence in Writing
8799 N. 387 Road
Locust Grove, OK 74352

Contents

UNIT 7: INVENTIVE WRITING

UNIT 8: FORMAL ESSAY MODELS

UNIT 9: FORMAL CRITIQUE AND RESPONSE TO LITERATURE

Appendices

Welcome to *Wonders of Science Based Writing Lessons.* This Teacher's Manual shows reduced copies of the Student Book pages along with instructions to teachers and sample key word outlines. Please be aware that this manual is not an answer key. The samples provided in this book are simply possibilities of what you and your students could create.

Lesson instructions are directed to the student, but teachers should read them over with their students and help as necessary, especially with outlining and structure and style practice. It is assumed that teachers have viewed and have access to IEW's *Teaching Writing: Structure and Style* video course and own the *Seminar Workbook.* Before each new unit, teachers should review the appropriate information in that workbook and video. You can find references to the *Teaching Writing: Structure and Style* course in the teacher's notes for each new unit.

Introduction

The lessons in this book teach Structure and Style® in writing. As they move through various science themes and topics, they incrementally introduce and review the models of structure and elements of style found in the Institute for Excellence in Writing's *Teaching Writing: Structure and Style®.*

It is important to note that these lessons are not intended as a science curriculum replacement, but rather their purpose is to broaden subject knowledge while students learn to write. The primary purpose is for students to learn structure and style in writing.

Student Book Contents

- **Scope and Sequence Chart** (pages 8–9)

- **The Lesson Pages**
  This is the majority of the text. It contains the instructions, source texts, worksheets, and checklists you will need for each lesson.

- **Appendix I: Modified MLA Format**

- **Appendix II: Mechanics**
  This appendix contains a compilation of the correct mechanics of writing numbers, punctuating dates, referencing individuals, etc. that are found in many of the lessons. Well-written compositions are not only written with structure and style, but they also contain correctly spelled words and proper punctuation.

- **Appendix III: Critique Thesaurus**
  This appendix provides a list of literary terms and their synonyms that are often used when critiquing various forms of literature. This page will be used in Unit 9.

- **Appendix IV: Adding Literature**
  This appendix suggests various books and stories to be read or listened to.

- **Appendix V: Vocabulary Chart and Quizzes**
  This appendix provides a list of the vocabulary words and their definitions organized by lesson as well as quizzes to take periodically. Twenty-two lessons include new vocabulary words. Every lesson includes vocabulary practice. The goal is that these great words will become part of your natural writing vocabulary.

  Vocabulary cards are found on the blue page as a PDF download. Print them, cut them out, and place them in a plastic bag or pencil pouch for easy reference. Each week you should study the words for the current lesson and continue to review words from previous lessons.

Customizing the Checklist

The total point value of each assignment is indicated at the bottom of each checklist. This total reflects only the basic items and does not include the vocabulary words. If vocabulary words are included, add the appropriate amount of points and write the new total on the custom total line.

Important: Teachers and parents should remember IEW's EZ+1 Rule when introducing IEW stylistic techniques. The checklist should include only those elements of style that have become easy plus one new element. If students are not yet ready for a basic element on the checklist, simply have them cross it out. Subtract its point value from the total possible and write the new total on the custom total line at the bottom. If you would like to add elements to the checklist, assign each a point value and add these points to the total possible, placing the new total on the custom total line.

Reproducible checklists are available. See the blue page for download information.

Checklists

Each lesson includes a checklist that details all the requirements of the assignment. Tear the checklist out of the book so that you can use it while writing. Check off each element when you are sure it is included in your paper. With each assignment, turn in the checklist to be used by the teacher for grading. Reproducible checklists are available. See the blue page for download information.

Teacher's Manual

The Teacher's Manual includes all of the Student Book contents with added instructions for teachers, including sample key word outlines and style practice ideas. Teachers may teach directly from this manual without the need of their own copy of the Student Book.

Teaching Writing: Structure and Style

Along with the accompanying Teacher's Manual for this Student Book, it is required that the teacher of this course has access to *Teaching Writing: Structure and Style*. This product is available in DVD format or Forever Streaming. For more information, please visit IEW.com/TWSS

Adapting the Schedule

Groups who follow a schedule with fewer than thirty weeks will have to omit some lessons. Because there are several lessons for each of the nine IEW units, this is not a problem. Teach lessons that introduce new concepts and omit some of those that do not.

Grading with the Checklist

To use the checklists for grading, do not add all the points earned. Instead, if an element is present, put a check in the blank across from it. If an element is missing, write the negative point value on its line. Total the negative points and subtract them from the total possible (or your custom total).

Note: Students should have checked the boxes in front of each element they completed.

Encourage students to bring a thesaurus to class. Most students enjoy using an electronic thesaurus, but for those who prefer books, IEW offers a unique one entitled *A Word Write Now*.

This schedule is provided to emphasize to parents and students, particularly in a class setting, that teachers and students should not expect to complete an entire lesson in one day. Spreading work throughout the week will produce much better writing with much less stress. Parents teaching their own children at home should follow a similar schedule.

Suggested Weekly Schedule

All of the instructions for what to do each week are included in the Assignment Schedule located on the first page of each lesson. While there may be slight variations, most lessons are organized as follows:

Day 1

1. Review vocabulary words or past lesson concepts.

2. Learn a new structural model and/or writing concepts.

3. Read the source text, write a key word outline (KWO), and tell back the meaning of each line of notes.

Day 2

1. Review the KWO from Day 1.

2. Learn a new stylistic technique and complete practice exercises.

3. Study the vocabulary words for the current lesson and complete vocabulary exercises.

4. Begin the rough draft using the KWO. Follow the checklist.

Day 3

1. Review vocabulary words.

2. Finish writing your composition and check each item on the checklist.

3. Submit your composition to an editor with the completed checklist attached.

Day 4

1. Write or type a final draft, making any corrections your editor asked you to make.

2. Paperclip the checklist, final draft, rough draft, and KWO together. Hand them in.

The lessons are organized in such a way that all new concepts regarding structure are introduced on day 1, and new style concepts and vocabulary words are introduced on day 2.

Students will benefit from learning new structure and style concepts with a teacher. In addition, students should plan to read the source text and begin KWOs with a teacher. These instructions are also found on day 1.

The instructions on day 3 and day 4 may be completed by students more independently. However, teachers and/or parents should be available to help and to edit.

Scope and Sequence

Lesson	Subject and Structure	Style (First Introduced)	Vocabulary Words
Unit 1 1	Dead Ants introduction to structure	introduction to style	pungent, secure signal, transport
Unit 2 2	Honey Bees	-ly adverb	craft, efficiently instinctively, intently
3	Bombardier Beetles		aggressively, caustic generate, lethally
4	Monarch Migration title rule	*who/which* clause	arduous, intuitively vital, wondrous
Unit 3 5	Daedalus and Icarus		construct, glide resolutely, surreptitiously
6	Archimedes	strong verb banned words: *think/thought, go/went*	conclude, ingenious reside, substantiate
7	Jack and the Beanstalk	*because* clause	clamber, desperately germinate, vigorously
8	Rumpelstiltskin	banned words: *say/said*	alchemist, brag dash, incredulously
Unit 4 9	Steam Engines topic-clincher sentences		
10	Model T Ford	quality adjective banned words: *good, bad, big, small*	fabricate, launch momentous, significant
11	Flight	*www.asia* clause	enthralling ponderous, replicate, suspend
12	Spacesuits	#2 prepositional opener	durable, explosively monitor, penetrating
Unit 5 13	Meteorite		dilapidated, mesmerized reveal, speedily
14	Message in a Bottle	#3 -ly adverb opener	bob, cautiously pen, resourceful
15	Science Lab		ardently, detect methodically, rancid

Lesson	Subject and Structure	Style (First Introduced)	Vocabulary Words
Unit 6 16	Nikola Tesla source and fused outlines		
17	Albert Einstein, Part 1	#6 vss opener	accept, accomplish inquisitively, technical
18	Albert Einstein, Part 2 works consulted		grieved, instantly plead, solve
19	Maria Telkes additional sources required		devise, immigrate industriously, potable
Unit 7 20	Favorite Invention, Part 1 body paragraphs	#5 clausal opener *www.asia.b* clause	alter, innovative persistently, unique
21	Favorite Invention, Part 2 introduction and conclusion		certainly, consequently furthermore, similarly
22	Exploring a Place Outdoors, Part 1		explore, investigate meander, scrutinize
23	Exploring a Place Outdoors, Part 2		
Unit 8 24	Albert Einstein, Part 3	#1 subject opener #4 -ing opener	achievement, advantage benefit, contribution
25	A Prominent Scientist, Part 1 additional sources required		
26	A Prominent Scientist, Part 2		
Unit 9 27	George Washington Carver, Part 1		antagonist, climax protagonist, theme
28	George Washington Carver, Part 2		
29	Nathaniel Bowditch, Part 1 character analysis		
30	Nathaniel Bowditch, Part 2		

Institute for Excellence in Writing

Lesson 1: Dead Ants

Structure:	Unit 1: Note Making and Outlines
Style:	Introduction to Structure and Style
Subject:	Dead Ants

Watch the sections for Unit 1: Note Making and Outlines. At IEW.com/twss-help reference the TWSS Viewing Guides.

Lesson 1: Dead Ants

UNIT 1: NOTE MAKING AND OUTLINES

Lesson 1: Dead Ants

Goals

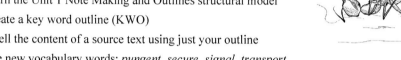

- to learn the Unit 1 Note Making and Outlines structural model
- to create a key word outline (KWO)
- to retell the content of a source text using just your outline
- to use new vocabulary words: *pungent, secure, signal, transport*

Assignment Schedule

Day 1

1. Read Introduction to Structure and Style and New Structure—Note Making and Outlines.

2. Read "Dead Ants." Read it again and write a key word outline (KWO).

Day 2

1. Review your KWO from Day 1.

2. Look at the vocabulary cards for Lesson 1. Complete Vocabulary Practice.

3. Try to add at least one vocabulary word to your KWO.

Day 3

1. Prepare to give an oral report using your KWO. Read. Think. Look up. Speak. Practice telling back the information one line at a time. Read a line; then, look up and talk about it. Then read the next line, look up, and talk about it. Continue through the outline this way.

2. Practice until the presentation of the paragraph is smooth. It is important to realize that you are not trying to memorize the exact words of the source text. You are trying to remember the ideas and communicate those ideas in your own words.

Day 4

1. Review the vocabulary words.

2. After practicing, use your KWO and give an oral report to a friend or family member as explained on Day 3. If applicable, be prepared to give the oral report in class.

Literature Suggestions

If you wish to incorporate literature into the curriculum, see a suggested list of books in Appendix IV.

Students will benefit from reading the source text and beginning KWOs with a teacher. Teachers should plan to teach New Structure, New Style, and introduce the vocabulary words. These items are always found in Day 1 and Day 2 of the Assignment Schedule.

Vocabulary

Print the vocabulary cards for Lesson 1. Hold up the cards. Read each definition and ask your students to guess which word it matches by looking at the pictures.

Introduction to Structure and Style

In this book you will learn many ways to make your writing more exciting and more enjoyable to read. You will learn to write with *structure* and with *style*.

Structure

What is structure? The dictionary defines structure as "the arrangement of and relations between the parts or elements of something complex."

What has structure? Think of a house. What had to happen before the house was built? The architect had to draw the blueprints, the plans, for the builders to follow. The builders had to follow the plans so that each contractor could arrive on time. You cannot put the walls up before the foundation is poured. You certainly cannot put the roof on before the frame is finished. Each step must be completed in order so that the house has proper structure.

Writing a paper, in some ways, is similar to building a house. A paper contains many facts and ideas. If you were just to begin writing without planning, your facts and ideas would probably not be arranged in the most logical way. Your composition would not be structured well and would not communicate your thoughts effectively. In this course you will "draw plans" for everything before you write. Your "plans" will be outlines, and they will follow a particular model of structure for each type of composition.

Style

What comes to your mind when you hear the word style? Many people think of clothes. Clothes come in a variety of styles. One would dress differently to attend a wedding than to go to a baseball game. That is because formal events require a formal style of clothing, whereas casual settings do not.

Similarly, there are also different styles of language. Below are two sentences that communicate the same information in different styles. Which do you like better?

> He mixed the liquids.

> After the scientist combined the two elements, he cautiously stirred the mixture as green smoke filled the room.

You probably like the second sentence better because it is more descriptive. When you write, you must realize that the readers are not with you and cannot see, hear, or feel what is in your mind. This means that you must fill in the details and paint vivid pictures with your words. Descriptive words will help readers see, hear, feel, and experience the scene you are writing about as the second sentence does. The IEW elements of style will give you the tools you need to do just this.

New Structure

Note Making and Outlines

In Unit 1 you will practice choosing key words to form an outline—a key word outline (KWO). A KWO is one way to take notes. Key words indicate the main idea of a sentence. By writing down these important words, you can remember the main idea of a text.

Read the source text. Then locate two or three important words in each sentence that indicate the main idea. Transfer those words to the KWO. Write the key words for the first fact of the KWO on the Roman numeral line. Write no more than three words on each line.

Symbols, numbers, and abbreviations are "free." Symbols take less time to draw than it would take to write the word. Abbreviations are commonly accepted shortened forms of words. Can you guess what each of the following might stand for?

As you form the KWO, separate key words, symbols, numbers, and abbreviations with commas.

After you have completed the KWO, you must test it to ensure the words you chose will help you remember the main idea of the sentence. For this reason whenever you finish writing a KWO, put the source text aside and use your outline to retell the paragraph line by line, sentence by sentence.

Encourage students to use symbols, numbers, and abbreviations.
A symbol is legal if it can be written in less time than it takes to write the word.

Symbols $\bigcirc$ = speak/tell   ➜ = to/across/next   ✿ = flower

Numbers   123 = numbers

Abbreviations H_2O = water   ea. = each   X = no/none

UNIT 1: NOTE MAKING AND OUTLINES

Source Text

Dead Ants

When an ant dies, it produces a chemical called oleic acid. The smell of the oleic acid alerts the other ants in the colony. They then carry the dead ant to the midden. The midden is the garbage dump that is also known as the ant cemetery. If oleic acid is placed onto a live ant, the other ants will try to carry the live ant to the midden. This is because most ants do not have eyes or ears, so they rely on their sense of smell. Burying their dead is called necrophoresis. It helps prevent the spread of disease in their nest. Oleic acid allows the ants to deal with their dead while keeping the colony safe.

Mechanics _____

Contractions are not used in academic writing.

    Institute for Excellence in Writing

The KWOs in the Teacher's Manual are only samples. Every class and each student will have unique outlines.

Sample   Lesson 1: Dead Ants

Key Word Outline

On the lines below, write no more than three key words from each sentence of the source text. Choose words that will best help you remember the meaning of the sentence. Use symbols, numbers, and abbreviations freely. They do not count as words. However, be sure you can remember what they mean.

I.   A, die →, oleic acid

1.   smell, OA, alerts, colony

2.   carry, dead A →, midden

3.   dump = ant cemetery

4.   OA, placed, live A →, midden

5.   A, X eyes, X ears, smell

6.   bury, dead = necrophoresis

7.   prevent, disease, nest

8.   OA, keep, colony, safe

Cover the source text and tell the meaning of each line of notes in your own words.
If a note is unclear, check the source text and add what you need to in order to make it clear.

Writing the KWO

Symbols, numbers, and abbreviations are free. Using them allows room for other key words.

Since *ants* is the title, simply write *A* when writing the KWO.

After writing *oleic acid* the first time, simply write *OA*.

X = no/none

In a classroom setting, write class ideas on a whiteboard. Students may copy these or use their own ideas.

Tell Back

Telling back the KWO is an important step in the prewriting process.

Read.
Think.
Look up.
Speak.

Andrew Pudewa teaches, "You may look at your notes, and you may speak to your audience, but you may not do both at the same time."

Vocabulary

Students study vocabulary to become better thinkers, speakers, and writers.

Allow students to use derivatives of words.

Vocabulary Practice

Listen   to someone read the vocabulary words for Lesson 1 aloud.

Speak   them aloud yourself.

Read   the definitions and sample sentences on the vocabulary cards.

Write   four sentences using one of this lesson's vocabulary words in each sentence. You may use derivatives of the words. For example, you may add an -ed, -s, or -ing to a basic vocabulary word.

pungent   *The ants took the dead body to the pungent garbage dump.*

secure   *The midden keeps the ant colony secure from disease.*

signal   *The smell of oleic acid signals the colony that there is a dead ant.*

transport   *The dead ants are transported to the midden.*

Think   about the words and their meanings so you can use them in your assignments.

Institute for Excellence in Writing

Lesson 2: Honey Bees

Structure: Unit 2: Writing from Notes
Style: -ly adverb
Subject: Honey Bees

Teaching Writing: Structure and Style

Watch the sections for Unit 2: Writing from Notes. At IEW.com/twss-help reference the TWSS Viewing Guides.

UNIT 2: WRITING FROM NOTES

Lesson 2: Honey Bees

Lesson 2: Honey Bees

Lesson 2: Honey Bees

Goals

* to learn the Unit 2 Writing from Notes structural model
* to create a key word outline (KWO)
* to write a paragraph from the KWO
* to add a new dress-up: -ly adverb
* to be introduced to the composition checklist
* to use new vocabulary words: *craft, efficiently, instinctively, intently*

Assignment Schedule

Day 1

1. Play No-Noose Hangman. Directions for this game and all other suggested games can be found in the Teacher's Manual.

2. Read Mechanics and New Structure—Writing from Notes.

3. Read "Honey Bees." Read it again and write a KWO.

Day 2

1. Review your KWO from Day 1.

2. Learn how to dress-up your writing. Read New Style and complete Style Practice.

3. Look at the vocabulary cards for Lesson 2. Complete Vocabulary Practice.

4. Using your KWO as a guide, begin writing a rough draft of your paragraph in your own words.

5. Go over the checklist. You will need to underline one -ly adverb. You may use more than one, but only underline one. Also, label the vocabulary words that you use. Put a check in the box for each requirement on the checklist you have completed.

6. See Appendix I. It explains how to format your papers.

Day 3

1. Review all vocabulary words learned thus far.

2. Finish writing your paragraph using your KWO, your Style Practice, and the checklist to guide you. Try your best not to look back at the source text.

3. Turn in your rough draft to your editor with the completed checklist attached. The back side of all checklists are blank so that they can be removed from this consumable book.

In Unit 2 students use the KWO to write a summary paragraph. As you model writing from the KWO, stress the importance of writing in your own words.

No-Noose Hangman

See Appendix VI for game directions. For this lesson use the following phrases and bonus questions:

FREE FROM HARM Bonus: What is the vocabulary word? *secure* Can you finish the definition? *or threat of danger*

THREE KEY WORDS Bonus: In addition to two or three key words, what may you write on each line of a KWO? *symbols, numbers, and abbreviations*

Exemplar

The Exemplars file contains a student's completed assignment for Lesson 2. The example is for the teacher and not intended to be used by the student.

See the blue page for download instructions.

Day 4

1. Write or type a final draft, making any corrections your editor asked you to make.

2. Paperclip the checklist, final draft, rough draft, and KWO together. Hand them in.

Study for Vocabulary Quiz 1. It will cover words from Lessons 1–2.

Mechanics

Numbers

Occasionally you will incorporate numbers into your writing. Here are rules to keep in mind:

1. Spell out numbers that can be expressed in one or two words.

   twenty, fifty-three, three hundred

2. Use numerals for numbers that are three or more words.

   123, 204

3. Spell out ordinal numbers.

   the fifth flower, the first circle

4. Use numerals with dates. Do not include st, nd, rd, or th.

   January 1, 2020

   December 25 not December 25th

5. Use numerals with symbols.

   $500   100˚C   25 mph

6. Never begin a sentence with a numeral.

   100˚C (212˚F) is the boiling temperature of water. (incorrect)

   The boiling temperature of water is 100˚C (212˚F). (correct)

New Structure

Writing from Notes

In Unit 2 you will use a key word outline (KWO) to write a paragraph. When you write from key word notes, you may use your own words, sentences, and ideas.

This is the first sentence of the source text:

> Honey bees must have nectar and water to make honey.

Your key word notes may look something like this:

> I.   HB, nectar + H_2O = honey

Practice

Using the key word notes, write a sentence that communicates the main idea of the first sentence. Use a thesaurus for help. Here is an example:

> Honey bees use flower nectar and water to make honey.

> *Honey bees instinctively make honey using nectar from a flower and water.*

The Editor

Selecting and "hiring" an editor is key to your writing success. You will need to acquire an editor to complete your assignments in this book. The purpose of the editor is to look over your work to amend anything that is not correct or complete. When you receive your paper back with the corrections marked, you will then rewrite your paper including the changes suggested by your editor. This process is very important because through the editing process you will receive useful feedback from your editor and learn correct spelling, punctuation, and proper grammar usage.

Writing from Notes

Students should not try to remember and write the exact words of the source text.

They should use their notes to understand the key ideas and write those ideas in their own words. One note may become two or more sentences, or two notes may become one sentence.

Editing

When editing, Andrew Pudewa says, "Hands on structure, hands off content."

Make the paper grammatically legal; however, refrain from meddling with content.

For tips on evaluating your students, search at IEW.com for Andrew Pudewa's article "Marking and Grading," available at no cost to you.

Source Text

Honey Bees

Honey bees must have nectar and water to make honey. When worker bees find flowers full of nectar, they fly back to the hive to tell the other bees. They do not use words or maps to show where the nectar is. They perform the waggle dance. The waggle dance looks like the number eight. The honey bee makes one circle and waggles as it turns around to make the other circle. This dance tells the other bees exactly where to find the flowers. The waggle dance is an innate behavior. No one has taught the honey bee how to do it. It just knows how.

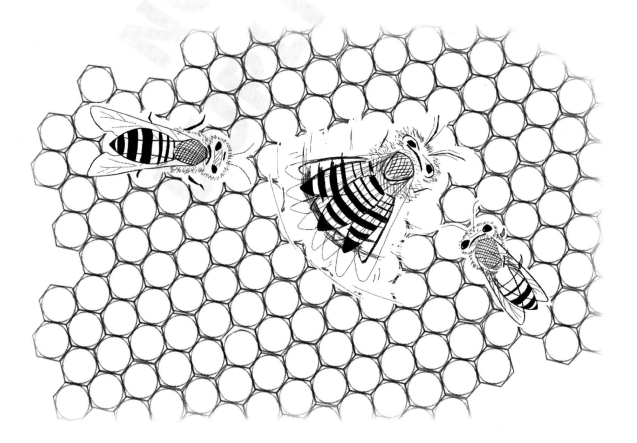

Sample

Key Word Outline

On the lines below, write no more than three key words from each sentence of the source text. Choose words that will best help you remember the meaning of the sentence.

I.   *HB, nectar + H_2O = honey*

1.   *worker, B,* 🌼 🗨 *, others*

2.   *X words, X maps →, nectar*

3.   *perform, waggle, dance*

4.   *WD, looks, 8*

5.   *◯, waggle, another, ◯*

6.   *WD, tells, others, find,* 🌼

7.   *WD, innate, behavior*

8.   *X taught, how*

9.   *just, knows*

Cover the source text and tell the meaning of each line of notes in your own words.
If a note is unclear, check the source text and add what you need to in order to make it clear.

Writing the KWO

After writing *waggle dance* the first time, simply write *WD*.

Use the scientific name for water: H_2O.

Tell Back

Require students to use the KWO to tell back the summary in complete sentences.

Help as needed.

New Style

Dress-Ups

There are many IEW elements of style. The first element you will be introduced to is called a dress-up because it will help you "dress up" your writing. The IEW dress-ups are descriptive words, phrases, or clauses that you add to a sentence. You will learn six dress-ups. To indicate that you have added a dress-up to a sentence, you should underline it. Although you may use more than one of a specific type of dress-up in a paragraph, only underline one of each type in each paragraph.

-ly Adverb Dress-Up

In this lesson you will learn the first dress-up: the -ly adverb.

An -ly adverb is an adverb that ends in -*ly*. Adverbs are words that modify verbs, adjectives, or other adverbs. Most often they tell *how* or *when* something is done.

Notice how the meaning of this sentence changes when different -ly adverbs are added:

Honey bees perform the waggle dance.

Honey bees <u>eagerly</u> perform the waggle dance.

Honey bees <u>instinctively</u> perform the waggle dance.

Now you choose an -ly adverb.

Honey bees _____*carefully*_____ perform the waggle dance.

 From now on, include an -ly adverb in each paragraph you write. Mark the -ly adverb by underlining it.

-ly Adverb

Students benefit from looking at word lists like those listed on this page. A longer list of -ly adverbs can be found on the *Portable Walls for Structure and Style® Students* as well as the IEW Writing Tools App.

From this point forward students should include one -ly adverb in each paragraph they write. Although more than one -ly adverb may be placed in a paragraph, only one should be underlined.

This dress-up now appears on the checklist.

-ly Adverbs

angrily

anxiously

boldly

carefully

eagerly

excitedly

fearfully

foolishly

futilely

hopefully

humbly

hysterically

innocently

intrepidly

joyfully

longingly

mysteriously

probably

savagely

sheepishly

smugly

stubbornly

suspiciously

tirelessly

woefully

Institute for Excellence in Writing

Style Practice

-ly Adverb Dress-Up

You must include an -ly adverb in the paragraph you write for this lesson. You may look at the list on the previous page or at a longer list found on the *Portable Walls for Structure and Style® Students* or on the IEW Writing Tools App. Some of your vocabulary words may be helpful as well. Write a few ideas on the lines below.

Note: A vocabulary word that is an -ly adverb may count as an -ly adverb and a vocabulary word.

What -ly adverbs could express . . .

1. how the worker bees fly back to the hive?

    speedily, directly, intently, swiftly

2. how the honey bees find the flowers?

    easily, effortlessly, successfully, fervently

3. how the bees make honey?

    instinctively, expertly, cleverly, skillfully

4. how the dance tells other bees where to find the flowers?

    directly, instantly, helpfully, efficiently

Look   at your KWO and consider -ly adverbs to include in your composition.

Suggested Answers

To model strong word choices, the suggested answers have come from a thesaurus.

Vocabulary

Students may use vocabulary words from any lesson if they so desire. *Efficiently, instinctively, and intently* are vocabulary words.

Vocabulary Practice

Listen   to someone read the vocabulary words for Lesson 2 aloud.

Speak   them aloud yourself.

Read   the definitions and sample sentences on the vocabulary cards.

Write   the part of speech and the definition beside each word.

craft   *verb; to make or produce with care, skill, or ingenuity*

Vocabulary

If students do not know the part of speech, encourage them to use a dictionary.

efficiently   *adverb; producing desired results with little or no waste*

instinctively   *adverb; a strong natural tendency or ability*

intently   *adverb; very concentrated in attention; focused*

Think   about the words and their meanings so you can use them in your assignments.

Before students begin to write, preview the checklist. This ensures that the students understand expectations.

Unit 2 Composition Checklist
Lesson 2: Honey Bees

Writing
from
Notes

Name: _____

IEW — Institute for Excellence in Writing

STRUCTURE

☐ MLA format (see Appendix I) _____ 6 pts

☐ title centered _____ 5 pts

☐ checklist on top, final draft, rough draft, key word outline _____ 5 pts

STYLE

¶1 **Dress-Ups** (underline one of each) (5 pts each)

☐ -ly adverb _____ 5 pts

MECHANICS

☐ capitalization _____ 1 pt

☐ end marks and punctuation _____ 1 pt

☐ complete sentences _____ 1 pt

☐ correct spelling _____ 1 pt

VOCABULARY

☐ vocabulary words – label *(voc)* in left margin or after sentence

Total: _____ 25 pts

Custom Total: _____ pts

Checklist

If your students are handwriting their assignments, disregard the MLA requirement on the checklist.

In each lesson students are directed to give their editors a rough draft with the completed checklist attached. The back sides of all checklists are blank so they can be removed from this consumable book.

Teachers are free to adjust a checklist by requiring only the stylistic techniques that have become easy, plus one new one. EZ+1

Instruct students to tear the checklist out of the book so that they can use it while writing.
Train students to check what they do and do what they check.

Intentionally blank so the checklist can be removed.

Lesson 3: Bombardier Beetles

Structure:	Unit 2: Writing from Notes
Style:	no new style
Subject:	Bombardier Beetles

Lesson 3: Bombardier Beetles

UNIT 2: WRITING FROM NOTES

Lesson 3: Bombardier Beetles

Goals

* to practice the Units 1 and 2 structural models
* to create a 1-paragraph KWO
* to write a 1-paragraph summary
* to take Vocabulary Quiz 1
* to use new vocabulary words: *aggressively, caustic, generate, lethally*

Assignment Schedule

Day 1

1. Play Around the World.
2. Take Vocabulary Quiz 1.
3. Read "Bombardier Beetles." Read it again and write a KWO.

Day 2

1. Review your KWO from Day 1.
2. Complete Style Practice.
3. Look at the vocabulary cards for Lesson 3. Complete Vocabulary Practice.
4. Using your KWO as a guide, begin writing a rough draft in your own words.
5. Go over the checklist. Put a check in the box for each requirement you have completed.

Day 3

1. Review all vocabulary words learned thus far.
2. Finish writing your paragraph. Try your best not to look back at the source text.
3. Turn in your rough draft to your editor with the completed checklist attached.

Day 4

1. Write or type a final draft, making any corrections your editor asked you to make.
2. Paperclip the checklist, final draft, rough draft, and KWO together. Hand them in.

Around the World

See Appendix VI for game directions. Use the vocabulary chart on page 304, Lessons 1–2. Because there are only eight words, it is fine to repeat. You are helping students prepare for the quiz.

Motivate

When students turn in their final drafts, read some of their compositions aloud. Clap for them! It motivates writers to hear their pieces being read aloud. This is why we write—for an audience.

Source Text

Bombardier Beetles

Bombardier beetles have a unique way to scare off predators. They spray hot acid at their enemies. Bombardier beetles have two compartments inside their abdomens. Each compartment contains a different chemical. When a beetle detects an enemy, it releases a protein that triggers the chemicals to mix together and make formic acid. The acid can get as hot as 100°C (212°F). The beetle shoots the acid out the tip of its abdomen with a loud popping noise. It has enough acid to make twenty sprays. The spray can kill small insects and injure larger predators including humans.

Mechanics _____

Write temperatures in degrees Celsius with Fahrenheit in parentheses. Express temperatures with the ° symbol rather than the word. Use C for Celsius and F for Fahrenheit.

Do not use spaces or periods between the temperature, symbol, and abbreviation.

Sample

Key Word Outline

On the lines below, write no more than three key words from each sentence of the source text. Choose words that will best help you remember the meaning of the sentence.

I.   *BB, unique, scare, predators*

1.   *spray, acid, enemies*

2.   *BB, 2, compartments, abdomen*

3.   *ea., compartment, different, chemical*

4.   *👀, enemy, mix = formic acid*

5.   *acid, hot, 100°C/212°F*

6.   *shoots, abdomen, POP*

7.   *enough, acid, 20, sprays*

8.   *spray, kill, injure*

Cover the source text and tell the meaning of each line of notes in your own words.
If a note is unclear, check the source text and add what you need to in order to make it clear.

> **Reminder**
>
> Students should write two or three key words per line. Compound nouns such as *formic acid* count as one key word.

Style Practice

-ly Adverb Dress-Up

You must include an -ly adverb in the paragraph you write for this lesson. Write a few ideas on the line below each sentence. Choose your favorite to write on the blank in the sentence. You may look at the list found on page 22, the *Portable Walls for Structure and Style Students*, or the IEW Writing Tools App. Some of your vocabulary words may be helpful as well.

1. Bombardier beetles ___*forcefully*_____ spray hot acid.

   -ly adverbs ___*aggressively, forcefully, powerfully, instinctively*_____

2. The spray ___*instantly*_____ injures predators.

   -ly adverbs ___*effectively, potently, successfully, instantly*_____

   Look   at your KWO and consider -ly adverbs to include in your composition.

Vocabulary Practice

Listen   to someone read the vocabulary words for Lesson 3 aloud.

Speak   them aloud yourself.

Read   the definitions and sample sentences on the vocabulary cards.

Write   the correct words in the blanks. You may use derivatives of the words.

   Bombardier beetles ___*generate*___ spray from the acid in their abdomens.

   The beetle shoots the ___*caustic*_____ acid at predators.

   Enemies are ___*lethally*_____ injured by the spray.

   Bombardier beetles ___*aggressively*_____ use hot acid to scare off predators.

Think   about the words and their meanings so you can use them in your assignments.

Unit 2 Composition Checklist
Lesson 3: Bombardier Beetles

Writing
from
Notes

Name: _____

Institute for **Excellence** In **Writing**
Listen. Speak. Read. Write. Think!

STRUCTURE

☐ MLA format (see Appendix I) _____ 6 pts

☐ title centered _____ 5 pts

☐ checklist on top, final draft, rough draft, key word outline _____ 5 pts

STYLE

¶1 **Dress-Ups** (underline one of each) (5 pts each)

☐ -ly adverb _____ 5 pts

MECHANICS

☐ capitalization _____ 1 pt

☐ end marks and punctuation _____ 1 pt

☐ complete sentences _____ 1 pt

☐ correct spelling _____ 1 pt

VOCABULARY

☐ vocabulary words – label *(voc)* in left margin or after sentence

Total: _____ 25 pts

Custom Total: _____ pts

Checklist

If your students are handwriting their assignments, disregard the MLA requirement on the checklist.

Teachers are free to adjust a checklist by requiring only the stylistic techniques that have become easy, plus one new one. EZ+1

Intentionally blank so the checklist can be removed.

Lesson 4: Monarch Migration

Structure: Unit 2: Writing from Notes
                      title rule

Style: *who/which* clause

Subject: Monarch Migration

UNIT 2: WRITING FROM NOTES

Lesson 4: Monarch Migration

Goals

- to practice the Units 1 and 2 structural models
- to create a 2-paragraph KWO
- to write a 2-paragraph summary
- to add a dress-up: *who/which* clause
- to create a title
- to use new vocabulary words: *arduous, intuitively, vital, wondrous*

Assignment Schedule

Day 1

1. Read "Monarch Migration." Read it again and write a KWO.

2. Read New Structure—Titles.

Day 2

1. Review your KWO from Day 1.

2. Learn a new dress-up, the *who/which* clause. Read New Style and complete Style Practice.

3. Look at the vocabulary cards for Lesson 4. Complete Vocabulary Practice.

4. Using your KWO and Style Practice to guide you, begin writing a rough draft in your own words.

5. Go over the checklist. Put a check in the box for each requirement you have completed.

Day 3

1. Review all vocabulary words learned thus far.

2. Finish writing your 2-paragraph summary. Include an -ly adverb dress-up and a *who/which* clause dress-up in each paragraph.

3. Turn in your rough draft to your editor with the completed checklist attached.

Day 4

1. Write or type a final draft, making any corrections your editor asked you to make.

2. Paperclip the checklist, final draft, rough draft, and KWO together. Hand them in.

Source Text

Monarch Migration

Monarch butterflies are the only butterflies that complete a round-trip migration. They travel up to three thousand miles from North America to Mexico. Monarchs can travel hundreds of miles in one day on air currents at speeds of fifteen to twenty-five miles per hour. Although they have never traveled to Mexico, they go to the same mountains and hibernate in the same trees as the migratory generations before them. These amazing butterflies use the sun and a magnetic compass in their antennae to help them navigate the long flight. The trip south and then back north can take nearly a year, so it is not the same butterfly that completes the entire journey.

The monarch's lifespan depends on when it hatches. Several generations hatch during the spring and summer months and live for two to six weeks. When it becomes cold, the migratory generation hatches and heads south toward warmer weather. The migratory generation's lifespan is nine months. As they fly south, they stop at butterfly gardens for nectar and shelter. These butterfly waysides, which are cultivated by helpful humans, are critical for survival. The butterflies finally arrive in Mexico, hibernate for six to eight months, and then lay eggs and die. The new generation of monarchs hatches and travels northward, living only two to six weeks. A fresh generation finishes the difficult round-trip journey.

Note

The plural of *antenna* is *antennae* when the word refers to the protuberances found on the heads of insects.

The plural noun *antennas* refers to electrical instruments.

Mechanics

Capitalize *north*, *south*, *east*, and *west* when they refer to a region or proper name. Do not capitalize these words when they indicate direction. Do not capitalize words like *northern* or *northward*.

Sample

Key Word Outline

Each Roman numeral represents one paragraph.

I. _____ *MB, only, round-trip, migration*

  1. _____ *3,000 mi, North America → Mexico*

  2. _____ *100s mi/day, currents, 15–25 mph*

  3. _____ *X Mex., travel, mt., hibernate, , generations*

  4. _____ * + magnetic , antennae, navigate*

  5. _____ *1yr, X same, MB, entire, journey*

II. _____ *lifespan, depends, hatches*

  1. _____ *generations, spring, summer, 2–6 wks*

  2. _____ *cold, migratory, hatch, S, *

  3. _____ *migratory, MB, lifespan, 9, mos*

  4. _____ *fly, S, (STOP), gardens, shelter*

  5. _____ *waysides, critical, survival*

  6. _____ *Mex., hibernate, 6–8 mos, lay , die*

  7. _____ *new, hatch, travel, N, 2–6 wks*

  8. _____ *fresh, G., finishes, journey*

> **Reminder**
>
> Students should write two or three key words per line. Proper nouns such as North America count as one key word.
>
> Students should use symbols, numbers, and abbreviations.
>
> The standard abbreviation for *Mexico* is *Mex.* *Miles* is abbreviated *mi*; *mountains* is *mt.*; *weeks* is *wks*; *months* is *mos*.

Cover the source text and tell the meaning of each line of notes in your own words.
If a note is unclear, check the source text and add what you need to in order to make it clear.

New Structure

Titles

An interesting title grabs a reader's attention. To make an intriguing title, repeat one to three key words from the final sentence.

The last sentence of "Dead Ants" (Lesson 1 source text) states, "Oleic acid allows the ants to deal with their dead while keeping the colony safe." A variety of different titles can be written using the key words.

> **Title repeats one to three key words from final sentence.**

Dealing with Their Dead

A Safe Colony

Ant Acid

Titles have simple rules for capitalization:

Capitalize the first word and the last word.

Capitalize all other words except articles (a, an, the), coordinating conjunctions (for, and, nor, but, or, yet, so), and prepositions (such as in, over, on, without).

Practice

You do not know what your final sentence for this writing assignment will be. However, you can practice forming titles using the source text. The final sentence of the source text with key words in bold is below. Create an intriguing title that includes one to three of these words. Write two or three ideas.

A fresh **generation** finishes the **difficult round-trip journey**.

The Difficult Journey

Journey of Generations

Finishing the Round-Trip

From now on, make a title for your compositions by repeating one to three key words from the final sentence. If you develop your title first, ensure you follow the title rule by incorporating key words from the title into your final sentence.

Titles

To form a title, key words in a last sentence sometimes need to be changed. That is fine. If students ask, offer suggestions.

Nonessential Clauses - provide information that, while inter
Change the main point of a sentence. Information that i
the meaning of the sentence. Commas

Essential clause - Describes a clause that is an impor
because it modifies a key word. N

New Style

Who/Which Clause Dress-Up

In this lesson you will learn another dress-up: *who/which* clause.

A *who/which* clause is a clause that provides description or additional information.

> Humans, <u>who</u> provide critical support, create butterfly gardens.

> Monarch antennae, <u>which</u> have a magnetic compass, help them navigate.

Notice:

1. A *who/which* clause begins with the word *who* or *which*.

   Use *who* when referring to people and *which* when referring to things.

   To indicate a *who/which* clause, underline only the first word of the clause: *who* or *which*.

2. The *who/which* clause gives information about a noun—a person, place, thing, or idea.

   Humans, <u>who</u> provide critical support, create butterfly gardens.

   Monarch *antennae,* <u>which</u> have a magnetic compass, help them navigate.

3. The *who/which* clause is added to a sentence that is already complete.

   ✳ If you remove the *who/which* clause, a sentence must remain. ✳

   Humans, <u>who</u> provide critical support, *create butterfly gardens.* (sentence)

   If you only insert the word *who* or *which*, you will have a fragment.

   Humans, <u>who</u> provide critical support. (fragment)

   ❜ A nonessential *who/which* clause is set off with commas; an essential clause has no commas.

   The migratory generation, <u>which</u> flies south to Mexico, lives nine months.
   (nonessential, commas)

   Humans <u>who</u> create butterfly gardens help monarchs survive. (essential, no commas)

Practice

Add a *who/which* clause to each sentence. Punctuate and mark correctly.

1. People _____ *<u>who</u> want to help butterflies* _____

   _____ provide wayside stations with nectar and shelter.

2. Monarch butterflies *, <u>which</u> can travel hundreds of miles in one day ,* _____

   _____ head south in the winter.

> From now on, include a *who/which* clause in each paragraph you write.
> Mark the *who/which* clause by underlining the word *who* or *which*.

non
take no
they are ess

*Humans <u>who</u> crea
butterfly gardens help
monarchs survive.*

Not all humans help
monarchs survive.
The *who* clause
is essential to the
sentence.

For younger
students simply
encourage them
to place commas
around all
who/which clauses
and only later
teach essential
and nonessential
who/which
clauses.

Read the sentences
and orally fill in the
blanks several times.
When students
understand the
pattern of the
who/which clause,
direct them to write.

Style Practice

-ly Adverb Dress-Up

You must include an -ly adverb in each paragraph you write for this lesson. Write a few ideas on the lines below. Use a thesaurus or your vocabulary words.

1. What -ly adverbs could express how humans cultivate wayside gardens?

   carefully, attentively, diligently, faithfully

2. What -ly adverbs could express how monarch butterflies travel hundreds of miles in one day?

   steadily, intuitively, deliberately, purposefully

Look   at your KWO and consider -ly adverbs to include in your composition.

Vocabulary Practice

Listen   to someone read the vocabulary words for Lesson 4 aloud.

Speak   them aloud yourself.

Read   the definitions and sample sentences on the vocabulary cards.

Write   the words that match the definitions.

intuitively   with an instinctive inner sense

arduous   requiring strenuous effort; difficult and tiring

wondrous   inspiring a feeling of wonder or delight; marvelous

vital   necessary to the existence or well-being of something

Think   about the words and their meanings.
Which vocabulary words could you use in this assignment?

   efficiently, instinctively, arduous, vital, wondrous

Institute for Excellence in Writing

Unit 2 Composition Checklist
Lesson 4: Monarch Migration

Writing
from
Notes

Name: _____

Institute for
Excellence in
Writing

STRUCTURE

☐ MLA format (see Appendix I) _____ 6 pts

☐ title centered and repeats 1–3 key words from final sentence _____ 5 pts

☐ checklist on top, final draft, rough draft, key word outline _____ 5 pts

STYLE

¶1 ¶2 Dress-Ups (underline one of each)   (5 pts each)

☐ ☐ -ly adverb _____ 10 pts

☐ ☐ *who/which* clause _____ 10 pts

MECHANICS

☐ capitalization _____ 1 pt

☐ end marks and punctuation _____ 1 pt

☐ complete sentences _____ 1 pt

☐ correct spelling _____ 1 pt

VOCABULARY

☐ vocabulary words – label *(voc)* in left **margin** or after sentence

Total: _____ 40 pts

Custom Total: _____ pts

Checklist

The two boxes under style indicate two paragraphs. Students should include and mark an -ly adverb and a *who/which* clause in each paragraph.

Teachers are free to adjust a checklist by requiring only the stylistic techniques that have become easy, plus one new one. EZ+1

Intentionally blank so the checklist can be removed.

Lesson 5: Daedalus and Icarus

Teaching Writing: Structure and Style

Structure: Unit 3: Retelling Narrative Stories

Style: no new style

Subject: a story from Greek mythology

Watch the sections for Unit 3: Retelling Narrative Stories. At IEW.com/twss-help reference the TWSS Viewing Guides.

UNIT 3: RETELLING NARRATIVE STORIES

[handwritten: deh · duh · luhs   i · kr · uhs]

Lesson 5: Daedalus and Icarus

Goals

- to learn the Unit 3 Retelling Narrative Stories structural model
- to create a 3-paragraph KWO using the Unit 3 Story Sequence Chart
- to write a 3-paragraph story
- to use new vocabulary words: *construct, glide, resolutely, surreptitiously*

Assignment Schedule

Day 1

1. Complete the Review.

2. Read New Structure—Retelling Narrative Stories.

3. Read "Daedalus and Icarus." Then write a KWO by answering the Story Sequence Chart questions. As you answer each question, place two or three key words on each line of the KWO. Use symbols, numbers, and abbreviations when possible. Each Roman numeral on the KWO represents a paragraph, so your completed story will be three paragraphs in length.

4. Cover the source text and tell the meaning of each line of notes in your own words. If a note is unclear, add what you need to in order to make it clear.

Day 2

1. Review your KWO from Day 1.

2. Complete Developing the Setting.

3. Complete Style Practice.

4. Look at the vocabulary cards for Lesson 5. Complete Vocabulary Practice.

5. Using your KWO as a guide, begin writing a rough draft in your own words.

6. Go over the checklist. Put a check in the box for each requirement you have completed. There are three boxes for both dress-ups because all three paragraphs should include both dress-ups.

Day 3

1. Review all vocabulary words learned thus far.

2. Finish writing your 3-paragraph story.

3. Turn in your rough draft to your editor with the completed checklist attached.

In this new unit students begin by reading a story. No longer are key words taken from each sentence; rather, key words are now found in developing key ideas.

★ Key ideas are formed by answering questions related to the Story Sequence Chart. For example, you will ask, "Who are the characters?" Form key words from the answer.

The same outlining rules apply: two or three key words per line; symbols, numbers, and abbreviations are free.

Exemplar

The Exemplars file contains a student's completed assignment for Lesson 5. The example is for the teacher and not intended to be used by the student.

See the blue page for download instructions.

Day 4

1. Write or type a final draft, making any corrections your editor asked you to make.

2. Paperclip the checklist, final draft, rough draft, and KWO together. Hand them in.

Review

Play No-Noose Hangman.

How should you create an intriguing title?

Read one of the sentences with a *who/which* clause in your summary about monarch migration.

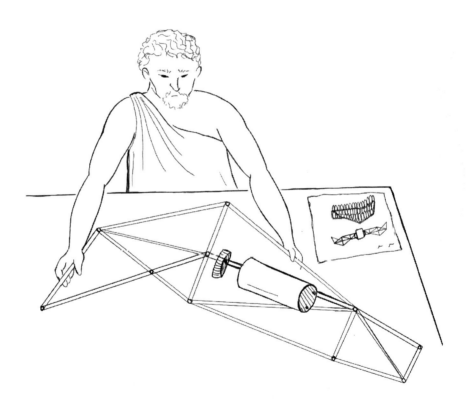

Review

Title repeats one to three key words from final sentence.

No-Noose Hangman

For this lesson use the following phrases and bonus questions:

TITLE FROM FINAL SENTENCE

Bonus: Explain the title rule. *The title repeats 1–3 key words from the final sentence.*

FOCUSED

Bonus: What is the vocabulary word? *intently*

DIFFICULT AND TIRING

Bonus: What is the vocabulary word? *arduous*

New Structure

Retelling Narrative Stories

In Unit 3 you will focus on story writing. Every story, regardless of how long it is, contains the same basic elements: characters and setting, conflict or problem, climax and resolution. As a result, you will use a new method of note taking. To create an outline for a story, you will not choose words from each sentence like you did in Units 1 and 2. Instead, you will choose key words by asking questions about a story using the Story Sequence Chart.

The Story Sequence Chart

The Story Sequence Chart has three Roman numerals. That is because the assignments in Unit 3 are each three paragraphs long. Each paragraph has a distinct purpose. The first paragraph tells about the people or animals in the story and when and where they live. The second paragraph tells about the conflict or problem that occurs within the story. The third paragraph begins with the climax, the turning point in the story, and ends with the resolution, the events that occur after the climax.

I. Characters and Setting

Who is in the story?
What are they like?
When does it happen?
Where do they live/go?

II. Conflict or Problem

What do they need/want?
What do they think?
What do they say and do?

III. Climax and Resolution

How is the problem/need resolved?
What happens after?
What is learned?

Read the source text and then use the Story Sequence Chart to analyze the story. Begin with the characters and setting. Ask the questions within each section in any order. For example, in Section I it does not matter whether you introduce the characters or the setting first.

The answers to the questions become the details for the outline. As you answer a question, write two or three key words on the KWO. Use symbols, numbers, and abbreviations when possible. You do not have to answer every question. You may need more than one line to answer one question, or you may be able to answer two questions on one line. Keep your answers brief. You can add more details when you write your own version of the story.

Source Text

Daedalus and Icarus

Long ago on the island of Crete lived Daedalus and his son Icarus. Daedalus, a craftsman, worked for King Minos and built many beautiful things for him, including a grand palace and a complicated labyrinth. King Minos became upset with Daedalus when he dishonored the queen, and the king locked him and his son in a tower. Escape would be difficult because they were surrounded by water.

Daedalus watched a flock of birds, and he got an idea. The clever craftsman crafted two sets of wooden wings. He told Icarus to gather feathers. They spent years collecting feathers and attaching them to the wooden wings with wax.

When the wings were almost complete, Daedalus gave Icarus two rules to follow. He told Icarus not to fly too close to the sun. It would melt the wax. He also told him not to fly too close to the sea. Its spray would weigh him down.

Finally, the day came for their escape. They flapped their wooden wings and took off toward freedom. Forgetting his father's instructions, Icarus soared higher and higher. When he flew too close to the sun, the wax began to melt. Feathers began to fall off the wooden frames. Since Icarus could no longer fly, he fell into the sea. When Daedalus realized Icarus had fallen into the sea, he continued alone. If only Icarus had listened to his father, both could have successfully escaped.

Mechanics _____

Titles that precede a name must be capitalized. Do not capitalize titles that follow a name or are not used with a name.

Before completing the KWO, remind students that this is a new unit and that key words are found differently. Key words are no longer found by looking at each sentence. Key words are found by using the Story Sequence Chart to ask and answer questions. Not all of the questions on this page need to be answered. Within each section, questions may be asked in any order that helps the story flow.

The KWOs in the Teacher's Manual are only samples. Every class and each student will have unique outlines.

Sample   Lesson 5: Daedalus and Icarus

Key Word Outline—Story Sequence Chart

Characters and Setting

| I. | long ago, isl, Crete |

> When does the story happen?
>
> Who is in the story?
>
> What are they like?
>
> Where do they live or go?

1. Daedalus, craftsman, clever
2. construct, palace, labyrinth
3. Icarus, son, foolish
4. King Minos, 😕, D, dishonored, wife
(5.) punishment, D + I, locked, tower

Conflict or Problem

II. escape, difficult, surrounded, H_2O

> What does the main character want or need?
>
> What do the main characters do, say, think, and feel?
>
> What happens before the climax?

1. D, 👀 birds, idea, fly
2. build, wings, wood
3. yrs, D + I, collected, feathers, wax
4. done, 2 rules, X fly, ☀, H_2O
(5.)

Climax and Resolution

III. wings, flapped, freedom

> What leads to the conflict being solved (the climax)?
>
> What happens as a result?
>
> What is learned? (message, moral)

1. I, forgot, instructions
2. close, ☀, wax, melted
3. feathers, fell, X fly
4. I, fell, sea
(5.) D, alone, I, X listen

Title repeats 1–3 key words from final sentence.

I. Characters and Setting

In this paragraph answer questions about the Island of Crete, Daedalus and Icarus, and the tower.

II. Conflict or Problem

In this paragraph answer questions about the main conflict: Daedalus and Icarus are locked in a tower and need a plan to escape.

III. Climax and Resolution

In this paragraph begin with the climax, which is when Daedalus and Icarus flap their wings and fly toward freedom.

Each Roman numeral indicates a different paragraph. Encourage students to use the KWO to tell back the story in complete sentences. Model the process as needed.

One of the goals of developing the setting is to make the readers feel as if they are there. Encourage students to describe the setting in a way that helps the readers see, hear, and feel things by creating a strong image and feeling.

Developing the Setting

We often tell when we write.

> The tower was on an island.

Instead of *telling* the readers, *show* them. Choose a subject and add a verb. Use a thesaurus.

> The tower *isolated*.

> " **Create a strong image and feeling.** "

Once you have your basic sentence, add details. Ask yourself questions—who, what, when, where, why, and how—about the subject and verb. Build the answers into your sentence.

> What did it isolate? *the prisoners The tower isolated the prisoners.*

Continue asking questions. What was the tower like? What part of the tower isolated? How did the prisoners feel? As you answer each question, add to your sentence.

> *The locked cell in the lofty* tower isolated *the lonely and desperate prisoners.*

Practice

As you begin your story, look for places to provide details that create a strong image and feeling.

1. The story begins on the island. Begin with the subject (who/what) and verb (show what the subject is doing). *Example: Craftsman built.*

   Artisan crafted.

   Ask questions and add to your basic sentence. *Example: Daedalus, a skilled craftsman, built an ornate palace on the secluded island.*

   On the idyllic island of Sicily, the artisan skillfully crafted a complicated and

   mysterious labyrinth.

2. The second setting of the story is in a tower. Begin with a subject (who/what) and verb (what the subject is doing). *Example: King locked.*

   King shoved.

   Ask questions and add to your basic sentence. *Example: The angry king locked Daedalus and Icarus in the secluded tower, slamming the heavy iron gates as he left.*

   Furious with Daedalus and Icarus, the king shoved the two craftsmen in the

   isolated and impenetrable tower.

Suggested Answers

The suggested answers are more sophisticated than most students will write. They are purposefully written to provide a model of strong word choices.

Style Practice

Who/Which Clause Dress-Up

Combine the statements using the word *who* or *which*. Punctuate and mark correctly.

1. Daedalus was locked in a tower. Daedalus had dishonored the queen.

   Daedalus, <u>who</u> had dishonored the queen, was locked in a tower.

2. Daedalus had an idea. Daedalus watched a flock of birds.

   Daedalus, <u>who</u> watched a flock of birds, had an idea.

3. Icarus fell into the sea. Icarus flew too close to the sun.

   Icarus, <u>who</u> flew too close to the sun, fell into the sea.

-ly Adverb Dress-Up

Write a few ideas for an -ly adverb dress-up on the line below each sentence.
Choose your favorite to write on the blank in the sentence.

1. The craftsman _____ *surreptitiously* _____ built two sets of wings.

   -ly adverbs _____ *cleverly, carefully, surreptitiously, precisely* _____

2. Icarus _____ *tirelessly* _____ collected feathers.

   -ly adverbs _____ *steadily, resolutely, tirelessly, diligently* _____

3. Icarus _____ *arrogantly* _____ flew too close to the sun.

   -ly adverbs _____ *arrogantly, unknowingly, willfully, tragically* _____

   Look   at your KWO and consider dress-ups to include in your composition.

UNIT 3: RETELLING NARRATIVE STORIES

Vocabulary Practice

Listen to someone read the vocabulary words for Lesson 5 aloud.

Speak them aloud yourself.

Read the definitions and sample sentences on the vocabulary cards.

Write four sentences using one of this lesson's vocabulary words in each sentence.

construct   *Icarus and his father constructed two sets of wings.*

_____

glide   *King Minos watched Daedalus and Icarus glide to safety.*

_____

resolutely   *Daedalus resolutely continued without Icarus.*

_____

surreptitiously   *Daedalus surreptitiously made a plan to escape.*

_____

_____

Think about the words and their meanings so you can use them in your assignments.

Vocabulary

The sample sentences are only suggestions. If students ask for help, offer an idea. Listen as they read their sentences aloud.

Allow students to use derivatives of words.

Institute for Excellence in Writing

Unit 3 Composition Checklist
Lesson 5: Daedalus and Icarus

Retelling
Narrative
Stories

Name: _____

Institute for
Excellence in
Writing

STRUCTURE

☐ MLA format (see Appendix I) _____ 5 pts

☐ title centered and repeats 1–3 key words from final sentence _____ 5 pts

☐ story follows Story Sequence Chart _____ 6 pts

☐ each paragraph contains at least four sentences _____ 6 pts

☐ checklist on top, final draft, rough draft, key word outline _____ 5 pts

STYLE

¶1 ¶2 ¶3 **Dress-Ups** (underline one of each)   (3 pts each)

☐ ☐ ☐ -ly adverb _____ 9 pts

☐ ☐ ☐ *who/which* clause _____ 9 pts

MECHANICS

☐ capitalization _____ 1 pt

☐ end marks and punctuation _____ 1 pt

☐ complete sentences _____ 1 pt

☐ correct spelling _____ 2 pts

VOCABULARY

☐ vocabulary words – label *(voc)* in left margin or after sentence

Total: _____ 50 pts

Custom Total: _____ pts

Motivate

Because positive reinforcement is a wonderful motivator, consider incorporating a ticket system as described on page 319. When you return graded papers, give a ticket for each vocabulary word used.

Checklist

Teachers are free to adjust a checklist by requiring only the stylistic techniques that have become easy, plus one new one. EZ+1

Intentionally blank so the checklist can be removed.

Lesson 6: Archimedes

Structure:	Unit 3: Retelling Narrative Stories
Style:	strong verb, banned words: *think/thought, go/went*
Subject:	a story about an inventor from ancient Greece

Lesson 6: Archimedes

UNIT 3: RETELLING NARRATIVE STORIES

Lesson 6: Archimedes

Goals

- to practice the Unit 3 structural model
- to create a 3-paragraph KWO using the Unit 3 Story Sequence Chart
- to write a 3-paragraph story
- to add a new dress-up: strong verb
- to ban weak verbs: *think/thought, go/went*
- to use new vocabulary words: *conclude, ingenious, reside, substantiate*

Assignment Schedule

Day 1

1. Complete the Review.

2. Read Mechanics.

3. Read "Archimedes." Then write a KWO by answering the Story Sequence Chart questions with two or three key words per line.

4. Cover the source text and tell the meaning of each line of notes in your own words. If a note is unclear, add what you need to in order to make it clear.

Day 2

1. Review your KWO from Day 1.

2. Complete Developing the Setting and Characters.

3. Learn a new dress-up, the strong verb. Read New Style and complete Style Practice.

4. Look at the vocabulary cards for Lesson 6. Complete Vocabulary Practice.

5. Using your KWO as a guide, begin writing a rough draft in your own words.

6. Go over the checklist. Put a check in the box for each requirement you have completed.

Day 3

1. Review all vocabulary words learned thus far.

2. Finish writing your 3-paragraph story.

3. Turn in your rough draft to your editor with the completed checklist attached.

UNIT 3: RETELLING NARRATIVE STORIES

Day 4

1. Write or type a final draft, making any corrections your editor asked you to make.

2. Paperclip the checklist, final draft, rough draft, and KWO together. Hand them in.

Study for Vocabulary Quiz 2. It will cover words from Lessons 1–6.

Review

Play a vocabulary game from the Teacher's Manual.

The first paragraph of your story includes what two things?

The second paragraph of your story identifies what?

The third paragraph of your story begins with the climax. What is a climax?

Institute for Excellence in Writing

Mechanics

Direct Quotes

Notice the words in quotation marks in the source text. When characters talk in a story, use quotation marks to indicate the exact words that the characters say.

Separate the speaking verb from the direct quote with a comma. If the direct quote is an exclamation or question, follow it with an exclamation mark or question mark.

speaking verb, "Quote."   speaking verb, "Quote!"   speaking verb, "Quote?"

"Quote," speaking verb   "Quote!" speaking verb   "Quote?" speaking verb

Commas and periods always go inside the closing quotation marks. Exclamation marks and question marks go inside closing quotation marks when they are part of the material quoted; otherwise, they go outside.

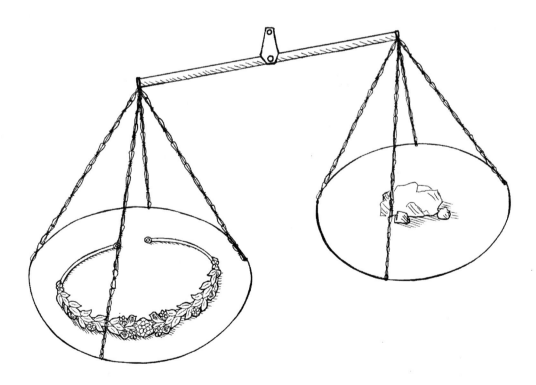

Source Text

Archimedes

Once on the island of Sicily there lived an inventor named Archimedes. He invented machines that could move heavy things, lift water, and even fight wars. Everyone wanted him to help solve their problems, including the king of Sicily.

One day King Hieron summoned Archimedes. "I think I have been cheated," the king told Archimedes. "You must prove it!" The king had given a goldsmith a block of pure gold to make a new crown. He suspected that some of the gold had been replaced with cheaper metal.

Archimedes spent hours trying to think of a way to prove that the crown was not made of pure gold. He designed experiments and drew diagrams, but nothing worked. He decided that he should take a break and relax.

Archimedes filled a bathtub full of water. As he stepped into the tub, water spilled over the edge. He realized that the amount of water that spilled over the edge of the tub was equal to the weight of his body. He would put the crown in a tub of water and compare the amount (volume) of water that spilled over to the weight (mass) of the gold that should be in the crown. He jumped up, grabbed his towel, and ran through the streets. "Eureka!" he shouted. "I have it!" Archimedes conducted his experiment, and the king's suspicions proved correct. The crown was not pure gold.

On the left are the story sequence questions that students ask about the story as they create the KWO. Use the helpful hints to guide students to answer the questions. Within each section, ask the questions in any order to help the story make sense.

Sample

Key Word Outline—Story Sequence Chart

Characters and Setting

I. _____ island, Sicily, Archimedes

> When does the story happen?
>
> Who is in the story?
>
> What are they like?
>
> Where do they live or go?

1. _____ A, inventor, smart

2. _____ machines, move, ↑, fight

3. _____ helped, 🏃 🏃, solved, problems

4. _____ everyone + king, knew, A

(5.) _____

I. Characters and Setting

In this paragraph answer questions about when and where the story takes place. Tell about Archimedes and how he helps the people of Sicily, including the king.

Conflict or Problem

II. _____ K, summoned, A, "help, cheated!"

> What does the main character want or need?
>
> What do the main characters do, say, think, and feel?
>
> What happens before the climax?

1. _____ A, needed, proof

2. _____ goldsmith, ✐, pure, gold

3. _____ X gold, cheap, metal

4. _____ A, thought, experiment, diagrams

(5.) _____ take, break, relax

II. Conflict or Problem

In this paragraph answer questions about the main problem: Archimedes must prove that the crown is not pure gold.

Climax and Resolution

III. _____ A, filled, bathtub, stepped, ↓

> What leads to the conflict being solved (the climax)?
>
> What happens as a result?
>
> What is learned? (message, moral)

1. _____ H_2O, spilled, out

2. _____ H_2O = weight, body

3. _____ crown, ↓, H_2O, compare

4. _____ jumped, towel, "Eureka"

(5.) _____ crown, X gold, proof

III. Climax and Resolution

In the final paragraph begin with the climax, which is when Archimedes stepped into the bathtub.

Note

The chemical symbol for gold is Au. It is derived from the Latin word aurum, meaning gold.

Title repeats 1–3 key words from final sentence.

One of the goals of developing the setting is to make the readers feel as if they are there. Another goal is to create a mood for the story. For example, a happy story might begin with the sun shining and birds singing, whereas a sad story might begin with a dreary, cloudy day.

Developing the Setting and Characters

We often tell when we write.

> Archimedes was an inventor.

Instead of *telling* the readers, *show* them. Choose a subject and add a verb. Use a thesaurus.

> Archimedes *invented.*

" **Create a strong image and feeling.** "

Once you have your basic sentence, add details. Ask yourself questions—who, what, when, where, why, and how—about the subject and verb. Build the answers into your sentence.

> What did he invent? *contraptions Archimedes invented contraptions.*

Continue asking questions. Where did he invent? What kind of contraptions? What was it like where he invented? How did he invent? As you answer each question, add to your sentence.

> *Surrounded by charts and diagrams,* Archimedes *tenaciously* invented *useful contraptions in his cluttered and dusty workshop.*

Practice

As you begin your story, look for places to provide details that create a strong image and feeling.

1. The story begins with the king calling for Archimedes. Begin with the subject (who/what) and verb (show what the subject is doing).
   Example: *King called.*

   King summoned.

   Ask questions and add to your basic sentence. ***Example:*** *Worried that his new crown was not pure gold, the king called Archimedes into his chambers for help.*

   Clutching his new crown, the greedy king frantically summoned Archimedes and

   demanded that he immediately prove the crown was fake.

2. The second setting of the story is in Archimedes's workshop. Begin with a subject (who/what) and verb (what the subject is doing). ***Example:*** *Archimedes thought.*

   Archimedes contemplated.

   Ask questions and add to your basic sentence. ***Example:*** *Hurriedly pacing back and forth, Archimedes thought of all the possible ways he could solve the king's dilemma.*

   Stepping back from scratched out formulas and scattered files, Archimedes

   contemplated a new idea that could be the answer he frantically sought.

New Style

Strong Verb Dress-Up

In this lesson you will learn another dress-up: strong verb.

Every sentence has a verb, but not all verbs are strong verbs. Strong verbs show action. The strongest verbs show action that is easy to picture. They help a reader picture what someone or something is doing. Here is the verb test. If a word fits in one of the blanks, it is a verb.

I will _____   Yesterday, I _____

Use the verb test. Underline the word if it is a verb.

table   <u>bolted</u>   teacher   <u>glide</u>   <u>sing</u>   <u>devour</u>

Banned Words

Boring verbs should be avoided in writing. For this reason you will not be allowed to use certain verbs in the writing you do for this class. These will be called *banned words*.

Archimedes *thought* of a way to prove that the crown was not pure gold.

Does the word *thought* help you imagine the pressure he was feeling? What strong verbs might be more descriptive than *thought*? On the line below, add to the list of synonyms for *think/thought*.

Synonyms for *think/thought* ___ *pondered, considered, deliberated*   *investigated, explored* ___

Here is another example of a boring verb:

Archimedes *went* to tell the king.

Does the word *went* help you imagine his excitement? What strong verbs might be more descriptive than *went*? On the line below, add to the list of synonyms for *go/went*. Notice how changing the verb changes what you imagine when you read the sentence.

Synonyms for *go/went* ___ *hurried, raced, charged*   *dashed, sprinted* ___

From now on in these lessons, the words *think/thought* and *go/went* are banned. To avoid these banned words, use a thesaurus or your vocabulary words or look at the lists of substitutes on the *Portable Walls for Structure and Style Students* or the IEW Writing Tools App.

 From now on, include a strong verb in each paragraph you write. Mark the strong verb by underlining it.

⊘ BANNED WORDS   VERBS: THINK/THOUGHT, GO/WENT

Strong Verb

This is the third dress-up introduced in this book. This means three dress-ups now appear on the checklist, and three dress-ups should be underlined in each paragraph written for this lesson.

The pace for adding stylistic techniques can be adjusted if a student needs time to practice previous dress-ups. Adjust the checklist if necessary.

Style Practice

-ly Adverb Dress-Up

Write a few ideas for an -ly adverb dress-up on the lines below.

1. What -ly adverbs could express how the king summoned Archimedes?

   *frantically, furiously, insistently, formally*

2. What -ly adverbs could express how Archimedes worked to prove the crown was fake?

   *fervently, relentlessly, doggedly, tenaciously*

Who/Which Clause Dress-Up

Add a *who/which* clause. Punctuate and mark correctly.

The king _____ _*who ruled Sicily*_ _____

_____ worried he had been tricked.

Look   at your KWO and consider dress-ups to include in your composition.

Vocabulary Practice

Listen   to someone read the vocabulary words for Lesson 6 aloud.

Speak   them aloud yourself.

Read   the definitions and sample sentences on the vocabulary cards.

Write   the correct words in the blanks.

Archimedes _*reside (d)*_ on the island of Sicily.

Archimedes's _*ingenious*_ experiment proved the king's suspicions.

Archimedes _*conclude (d)*_ that the crown was not pure gold.

The evidence gathered in his experiment _*substantiate (d)*_ his hypothesis.

Think   about the words and their meanings so you can use them in your assignments.

Unit 3 Composition Checklist
Lesson 6: Archimedes

Retelling
Narrative
Stories

Name: _____

IEW

Institute for
Excellence in
Writing

STRUCTURE

☐ MLA format (see Appendix I) _____ 5 pts

☐ title centered and repeats 1–3 key words from final sentence _____ 5 pts

☐ story follows Story Sequence Chart _____ 6 pts

☐ each paragraph contains at least four **sentences** _____ 6 pts

☐ checklist on top, final draft, rough draft, **key** word outline _____ 5 pts

STYLE

¶1 ¶2 ¶3 **Dress-Ups** (underline one of each)   (3 pts each)

☐ ☐ ☐ -ly adverb _____ 9 pts

☐ ☐ ☐ *who/which* clause _____ 9 pts

☐ ☐ ☐ strong verb _____ 9 pts

CHECK FOR BANNED WORDS (-1 pt for each use): think/thought, go/went _____ pts

MECHANICS

☐ capitalization _____ 1 pt

☐ end marks and punctuation _____ 1 pt

☐ complete sentences _____ 2 pts

☐ correct spelling _____ 2 pts

VOCABULARY

☐ vocabulary words – label *(voc)* in left margin or after sentence

Total: _____ 60 pts

Custom Total: _____ pts

Motivate

If you are using the ticket system as described on page 319, give a ticket for each vocabulary word used when you return graded papers.

Checklist

Teachers are free to adjust a checklist by requiring only the stylistic techniques that have become easy, plus one new one. EZ+1

Intentionally blank so the checklist can be removed.

Lesson 7: Jack and the Beanstalk

Structure:	Unit 3: Retelling Narrative Stories
Style:	*because* clause
Subject:	an English fairy tale

UNIT 3: RETELLING NARRATIVE STORIES

Lesson 7: Jack and the Beanstalk

Goals

- to practice the Unit 3 structural model
- to create a 3-paragraph KWO using the Unit 3 Story Sequence Chart
- to write a 3-paragraph story
- to add a new dress-up: *because* clause
- to take Vocabulary Quiz 2
- to use new vocabulary words: *clamber, desperately, germinate, vigorously*

Assignment Schedule

Day 1

1. Take Vocabulary Quiz 2.
2. Complete the Review.
3. Read "Jack and the Beanstalk."
4. Write a KWO by answering the Story Sequence Chart questions.
5. Cover the source text and tell the meaning of each line of notes in your own words. If a note is unclear, add what you need to in order to make it clear.

Day 2

1. Review your KWO from Day 1.
2. Complete Developing the Setting and Characters.
3. Learn a new dress-up, the *because* clause. Read New Style and complete Style Practice.
4. Look at the vocabulary cards for Lesson 7. Complete Vocabulary Practice.
5. Using your KWO as a guide, begin writing a rough draft in your own words.
6. Go over the checklist. Put a check in the box for each requirement you have completed.

Day 3

1. Review all vocabulary words learned thus far.
2. Finish writing your 3-paragraph story.
3. Turn in your rough draft to your editor with the completed checklist attached.

Day 4

1. Write or type a final draft, making any corrections your editor asked you to make.
2. Paperclip the checklist, final draft, rough draft, and KWO together. Hand them in.

Review

Play No-Noose Hangman.

Add punctuation where it is needed in this sentence.

> I am such a fool   Jack's mother cried.

No-Noose Hangman

For this lesson use the following phrases and bonus questions:

COMMAS AND PERIODS ALWAYS INSIDE

Bonus: What are commas and periods always inside of? *closing quotation marks*

Once solved review quotation rules on page 53.

Review

"I am such a fool," Jack's mother cried.

OR

"I am such a fool!" Jack's mother cried.

Source Text

Jack and the Beanstalk

Based on the Tale Told by Clifton Johnson (1924) Abridged

Long ago a wicked giant attacked a knight's castle. He killed the knight and stole everything that the knight owned, including his goose that laid golden eggs. The knight's wife and his son Jack were left to live in a small cottage with only a milk cow. They lived in poverty. One day Jack's mother decided to sell their cow. On her way to the market, a man approached her and offered five magic beans for the cow. Jack's mother laughed loudly. "I am not a fool," she told the man. The man was persistent, and soon Jack's mother returned home with five beans in her pocket.

As soon as Jack's mother entered the house, she realized that the man had tricked her. She threw the beans into the fire and told Jack about her foolishness. Jack consoled his mother and assured her that everything would be all right. He noticed that one of the beans had rolled out of the fire and decided to plant it. He found the sunniest spot in the garden and dug a hole. After planting the bean, he watered it. He knew that it would take several days before it germinated and sprouted.

The next morning he was surprised to find that the bean had grown into a beanstalk. It was as tall as he was! Every day the beanstalk grew taller and taller until he could no longer see its top. Jack wondered how tall it actually was, so he started climbing the stalk. Soon he found himself in the clouds. As he looked around, he saw a castle in the distance. Deciding to explore, he carefully climbed off the beanstalk.

Much to Jack's surprise, a fierce giant came out of the castle. Jack trembled with fear and hid until the giant had left. Jack entered the castle. He saw many beautiful things, but his eyes settled on a goose surrounded by golden eggs. He knew from his mother's stories that this must be the giant that had killed his father and stole all of their belongings. "I will take back what is ours," Jack declared as he grabbed the goose and headed toward the beanstalk.

The giant suddenly appeared behind Jack and shouted, "Hey! Where are you taking my goose?" Terrified, Jack ran back to the beanstalk and climbed down it.

Once he reached the ground, he called to his mother. "Bring the axe," he shouted. He chopped and chopped the thick beanstalk. When he saw the giant's feet coming through the clouds, he chopped faster. Finally, the beanstalk began to sway back and forth. It fell with a huge crash. The giant was no more. Once again, Jack and his mother had their goose that laid golden eggs, and they both lived happily ever after.

Sample

Key Word Outline—Story Sequence Chart

Characters and Setting

| When does the story happen? |
| Who is in the story? |
| What are they like? |
| Where do they live or go? |

I. _____ long, ago, - - giant

1. _____ kill, knight

2. _____ took, goose, gold ⊙⊙

3. _____ wife, son, Jack, X $$

4. _____ w, foolish, $, cow, 5 beans

(5.) _____ Jack, hopeful, planted

Conflict or Problem

| What does the main character want or need? |
| What do the main characters do, say, think, and feel? |
| What happens before the climax? |

II. _____ beanstalk, tall, J, climb

1. _____ castle, giant, explored

2. _____ 👀 goose, golden, eggs

3. _____ took, back, "ours"

4. _____ grabbed, goose, → beanstalk

(5.) _____

Climax and Resolution

| What leads to the conflict being solved (the climax)? |
| What happens as a result? |
| What is learned? (message, moral) |

III. _____ giant, appeared, yelling

1. _____ terrified, J, climbed ↓

2. _____ mother, axe, chopped

3. _____ 👀 giant, beanstalk, swayed

4. _____ fell, crash, X giant

(5.) _____ Jack, ⚲, lived, happily

Title repeats 1–3 key words from final sentence.

I. Characters and Setting

In this paragraph describe the cottage. Tell about the giant, Jack's family, and the magic beans.

II. Conflict or Problem

In this paragraph answer questions about the main conflict: Jack and his mother were poor because their golden goose had been taken. Jack needed to reclaim it.

III. Climax and Resolution

In the final paragraph begin with the climax, which is when the giant discovered that Jack had grabbed the goose.

Just as writers develop the setting, they develop the characters. In this story encourage students to describe how evil the giant was. Explain how devastating it was to have everything taken away by the giant. Describe the poverty of Jack and his mother.

Developing the Setting and Characters

This story has been retold by many people for centuries. As you write your version, describe the setting in more detail.

> ## Create a strong image and feeling.

Practice

As you begin your story, look for places to provide details that create a strong image and feeling.

1. The story takes place in a poor village. Begin with the subject (who/what) and verb (show what the subject is doing). ***Example:*** *Jack's mother decided.*

    Jack's mother realized.

    Ask questions and add to your basic sentence. ***Example:*** *Looking in the empty cupboards, Jack's poor mother decided that it was time to sell their only cow.*

    Jack's mother eventually realized that she had to sell the cow in order to fill their

    empty stomachs.

2. Describe the bean. Follow the established pattern. ***Example:*** *The bean grew. Rescued from the fire, the tiny bean grew into a towering stalk.*

    The bean sprouted. With Jack's tender care, the discarded bean sprouted

    and instantaneously climbed towards the sunny sky.

3. Describe Jack. Follow the established pattern.

    Jack scaled. Grabbing a thick branch, Jack scaled his way limb by limb through the

    clouds until he reached the top of the beanstalk.

4. Describe the giant. Follow the established pattern.

    The giant roared. The hideous giant angrily roared as he clambered down the

    beanstalk in pursuit of his prized golden goose.

Four dress-ups now appear on the checklist, and four dress-ups should be underlined in each paragraph written for this lesson. The pace for adding stylistic techniques can be adjusted if a student needs time to practice previous dress-ups. Adjust the checklist if necessary.

New Style

Because **Clause Dress-Up**

In this lesson you will learn another new dress-up: *because* clause. A *because* clause helps your readers better understand what you write because a *because* clause explains why.

Jack and his mother were poor because a giant had stolen from them.

Jack's mother sold the cow because she needed money.

Notice:

1. A *because* clause begins with the word *because*.

   To indicate a *because* clause, underline only the first word of the clause: *because*.

2. A *because* clause contains a subject and a verb.

   Jack and his mother were poor because *a giant had stolen* from them.

   Jack's mother sold the cow because *she needed* money.

3. A *because* clause is added to a sentence that is already complete.

   Jack and his mother were poor because a giant had stolen from them.

   Jack's mother sold the cow because she needed money.

   ❯ If a *because* clause follows a complete sentence, no comma is needed. If the *because* clause is at the beginning of the sentence, a comma is required.

   The giant chased Jack because he had taken the golden goose. (no comma)

   Furiously, because Jack had taken the golden goose, the giant chased him. (comma)

Practice

Add a *because* clause to each sentence. Notice that the word *because* is underlined.

1. The magic bean sprouted because *Jack provided all it needed to germinate.*

   _____

2. Jack and his mother lived happily ever after because *the golden goose returned home.*

   _____

From now on, include a *because* clause in each paragraph you write.
Mark the *because* clause by underlining the word *because*.

Because Clause

The *because* clause gives writers the chance to reason about cause and effect. Lead students through the information about the *because* clause.

For younger students simply encourage them to place the *because* clause after a sentence that is already complete.

Read the sentences and orally fill in the blanks several times. When students understand the pattern of the *because* clause, then direct them to write.

Style Practice

Strong Verb Dress-Up and -ly Adverb Dress-Up

On the first line below the sentence, write strong verbs that could replace the italicized banned verb. On the second line write ideas for -ly adverbs that you could use with the strong verbs.

The giant *went*.

strong verbs   *clambered, pursued, chased, hunted*

-ly adverbs   *angrily, clumsily, breathlessly, desperately*

Who/Which Clause Dress-Up

Add a *who/which* clause. Punctuate and mark correctly.

The giant _____ *, who stole the golden goose,*

_____ lived in a castle built upon the clouds.

Look   at your KWO and consider dress-ups to include in your composition.

Vocabulary Practice

Listen   to someone read the vocabulary words for Lesson 7 aloud.

Speak   them aloud yourself.

Read   the definitions and sample sentences on the vocabulary cards.

Write   the words that match the definitions.

_____ *germinate*   to begin to grow or develop

_____ *desperately*   showing great worry

_____ *vigorously*   using force and energy

_____ *clamber*   to climb in an awkward way

Think   about the words and their meanings so you can use them in your assignments.

Unit 3 Composition Checklist
Lesson 7: Jack and the Beanstalk

Retelling
Narrative
Stories

Name: _____

IEW | Institute for
Excellence in
Writing

STRUCTURE

☐ MLA format (see Appendix I) _____ 5 pts

☐ title centered and repeats 1–3 key words from final sentence _____ 5 pts

☐ story follows Story Sequence Chart _____ 6 pts

☐ each paragraph contains at least four sentences _____ 6 pts

☐ checklist on top, final draft, rough draft, key word outline _____ 5 pts

STYLE

¶1 ¶2 ¶3 Dress-Ups (underline one of each) (3 pts each)

☐ ☐ ☐ -ly adverb _____ 9 pts

☐ ☐ ☐ *who/which* clause _____ 9 pts

☐ ☐ ☐ strong verb _____ 9 pts

☐ ☐ ☐ *because* clause _____ 9 pts

CHECK FOR BANNED WORDS (-1 pt for each use): think/thought, go/went _____ pts

MECHANICS

☐ capitalization _____ 1 pt

☐ end marks and punctuation _____ 1 pt

☐ complete sentences _____ 2 pts

☐ correct spelling _____ 3 pts

VOCABULARY

☐ vocabulary words – label *(voc)* in left margin or after sentence

Total: _____ 70 pts

Custom Total: _____ pts

Motivate

Consider giving double tickets for each vocabulary word a student uses in this story. Just a little extra motivation can yield amazing results.

Checklist

Teachers are free to adjust a checklist by requiring only the stylistic techniques that have become easy, plus one new one. EZ+1

Intentionally blank so the checklist can be removed.

Lesson 8: Rumpelstiltskin

Structure:	Unit 3: Retelling Narrative Stories
Style:	banned words: *say/said*
Subject:	a German fairy tale

UNIT 3: RETELLING NARRATIVE STORIES

Lesson 8: Rumpelstiltskin

Goals

- to practice the Unit 3 structural model
- to create a 3-paragraph KWO using the Unit 3 Story Sequence Chart
- to write a 3-paragraph story
- to ban weak verbs: *say/said*
- to use new vocabulary words: *alchemist, brag, dash, incredulously*

Assignment Schedule

Day 1

1. Complete the Review.
2. Read "Rumpelstiltskin."
3. Read Story Variation. If you desire to write a variation of the story, answer the questions at the bottom of the page.
4. Complete the KWO by answering the Story Sequence Chart questions. If you decided to change your characters, use the ideas you wrote at the bottom of Story Variation.
5. Cover the source text and tell the meaning of each line of notes in your own words. If a note is unclear, add what you need to in order to make it clear.

Day 2

1. Review your KWO from Day 1.
2. Complete Style Practice.
3. Look at the vocabulary cards for Lesson 8. Complete Vocabulary Practice.
4. Using your KWO as a guide, begin writing a rough draft in your own words.
5. Go over the checklist. Put a check in the box for each requirement you have completed.

Day 3

1. Review all vocabulary words learned thus far.
2. Finish writing your 3-paragraph story.
3. Turn in your rough draft to your editor with the completed checklist attached.

Day 4

1. Write or type a final draft, making any corrections your editor asked you to make.
2. Paperclip the checklist, final draft, rough draft, and KWO together. Hand them in.

Source Text

Rumpelstiltskin

Question Game

See Appendix
VII for game
directions.

Choose from the
questions on
pages 329–331.
For this lesson the
following would
work well: 1, 2,
5, 7, 8, 9, 33, 35,
and vocabulary
words.

Once there was a farmer who had a beautiful and clever daughter. He was very proud of her. One day he told the king that his daughter could spin gold out of straw. He knew that the king was greedy and had alchemists across the land trying to turn ordinary items into gold. The king immediately sent for the girl and showed her a large pile of straw. He gave her a spinning-wheel and said, "If you can spin this into gold by morning, I will make you my queen." The poor girl tried to tell the king that her father's words were not true, but the king did not listen.

The girl sat down and cried. In time, an odd-looking little man appeared and asked why she was crying.

She replied, "I must spin this straw into gold, but I cannot."

When the strange little man offered to do it for her, she explained that she had nothing to give in return.

"Then promise me the first child that you may have when you are queen," the little man suggested.

Although she did not believe she would become the queen, she agreed because she did not know what else to do. The little man sat down at the wheel and sang. Soon the large pile of straw became a large pile of gold. In the morning the king saw the pile of gold. As he had promised, he married the farmer's daughter.

Time passed, and the new queen forgot about the little man, and she forgot her promise. At the birth of her first child, the little man appeared to collect what she had promised. She cried and offered to give him all the wealth of the kingdom if he would let her keep her baby. Finally, he said, "I will give you three days, and if during that time you tell me my name, you can keep your child."

The queen lay awake all night, thinking of all the odd names that she had ever heard. In the morning she sent messengers everywhere to find new names. For two days she called out the names she had found, but none were correct. On the third day, one of the messengers returned with news. He told the queen that he saw a funny little man dancing and heard the man say, "Rumpelstiltskin is my name!"

When the queen heard this, she jumped for joy. The little man appeared, and she began her list of names. After she had recited several names, she asked, "Can your name be Rumpelstiltskin?"

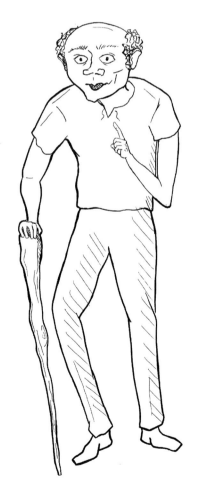

Rumpelstiltskin yelled and stomped his feet in rage. He could not believe that someone had guessed his secret. Rumpelstiltskin tried to back out of his agreement with the queen. He was lonely and wanted to raise the child as his own. The queen stood her ground and told him he had to honor his promise. Rumpelstiltskin ran into the woods and was never seen again.

Story Variation

When you write this story, you may change the characters and some of the details. The story occurs because the farmer's daughter agrees to give away her first-born child. Because she had not considered the consequence of her agreement, she faces losing her baby. As you complete the first portion of the Story Sequence Chart, one of the questions you will answer is *who is in the story?* Instead of answering *the king, the farmer's daughter, and Rumpelstiltskin,* change the characters.

Use the questions on the Story Sequence Chart to further develop for variation.

1. Describe the setting. Is it a farm, a castle, or a city?

   Answers will vary as each student will make up his or her setting.

2. Who are the two main characters in your story? Describe them.

3. What condition could one character agree to because he or she was feeling pressured to accomplish an impossible task?

4. How does the character find a way out of the agreement?

Sample

Key Word Outline—Story Sequence Chart

Characters and Setting

> When does the story happen?
>
> Who is in the story?
>
> What are they like?
>
> Where do they live or go?

I. _____ *king, greedy, alchemists*

   1. _____ *farmer, daughter, clever*

   2. _____ ⟨speech⟩ *K, D, straw, →, gold*

   3. _____ *K, "make, gold," queen*

   4. _____ *D, "cannot," father, X true*

  (5.) _____ *strange, man, ?, crying*

Conflict or Problem

> What does the main character want or need?
>
> What do the main characters do, say, think, and feel?
>
> What happens before the climax?

II. _____ *D, cannot, straw →, gold*

   1. _____ *man, help, D, X give*

   2. _____ *man, 1st, baby, mine*

   3. _____ *D, agreed, became, queen*

   4. _____ *man, ⟨speech⟩ name, X baby*

  (5.) _____ *messenger, ⟨speech⟩ Q, "Rumpelstiltskin"*

Climax and Resolution

> What leads to the conflict being solved (the climax)?
>
> What happens as a result?
>
> What is learned? (message, moral)

III. _____ *Q, man, name = "Rumpelstiltskin"*

   1. _____ *R, angry, X agreement*

   2. _____ *R, lonely, wanted, child*

   3. _____ *Q, made, R, honor, promise*

   4. _____ *R, ran, X seen*

  (5.) _____

Title repeats 1–3 key words from final sentence.

I. Characters and Setting

As students write about the setting and characters, remember that they may use the characters and setting from the source text or create their own.

II. Conflict or Problem

In this paragraph answer the questions about the main conflict: the farmer's daughter agrees to give up her first child in order to become queen.

III. Climax and Resolution

In the final paragraph begin with the climax, which is when the queen guesses the man's name is Rumpelstiltskin.

Style Practice

Strong Verb Dress-Up

The words *think/thought* and *go/went* are already banned. In this lesson another word is banned: *say/said*. In each pair of sentences below, a verb is in italics. Underline the verb that is stronger because it is easier to picture.

1. The king *said* that she would become queen.

   The king <u>*promised*</u> that she would become queen.

2. I will *say* his name and save my child.

   I will <u>*declare*</u> his name and save my child.

From now on in these lessons, the words *say/said* are also banned. To avoid these banned words, use a thesaurus or your vocabulary words or look at the lists of substitutes on the *Portable Walls for Structure and Style Students* or the IEW Writing Tools App.

Strong Verb Dress-Up and -ly Adverb Dress-Up

Look at your KWO and write ideas for each.

1. List strong verbs and -ly adverbs to include in your first paragraph.

   strong verbs ___*bragged, confessed, wept*___

   -ly adverbs ___*boastfully, despairingly, fervently*___

2. List strong verbs and -ly adverbs to include in your second paragraph.

   strong verbs ___*promised, assisted, proposed*___

   -ly adverbs ___*adamantly, sincerely, frantically*___

3. List strong verbs and -ly adverbs to include in your third paragraph.

   strong verbs ___*stomped, desired, dashed*___

   -ly adverbs ___*insistently, earnestly, incredulously*___

⊘ BANNED WORDS   VERBS: THINK/THOUGHT, GO/WENT, SAY/SAID

Who/Which **Clause Dress-Up**

Add a *who/which* clause to each sentence. Punctuate and mark correctly.

1. The farmer told the king _____ *, who wanted more riches,* _____

    _____ that his daughter could spin straw into gold.

2. The farmer's daughter _____ *, who could not spin straw into gold,* _____

    _____ cried out in desperation.

3. The queen's messenger _____ *, who searched for three days,* _____

    _____ discovered the secret name.

Because **Clause Dress-Up**

Add a *because* clause to each sentence. Underline the word *because*.

1. The king married the farmer's daughter <u>because</u> _*she turned straw into piles of gold.*_

    _____

2. The queen bargained with the little man <u>because</u> _*she wanted to keep her baby.*_

    _____

3. Rumpelstiltskin ran away <u>because</u> _*the queen had guessed his name.*_

    _____

    Look   at your KWO and consider clauses to include in your composition.

Vocabulary Practice

Listen   to someone read the vocabulary words for Lesson 8 aloud.

Speak   them aloud yourself.

Read   the definitions and sample sentences on the vocabulary cards.

Write   four sentences using one of this lesson's vocabulary words in each sentence.

alchemist   *The alchemist worked day and night to find the right formula to turn iron into gold.*

brag   *People became tired of listening to the farmer brag about his daughter.*

dash   *The queen watched Rumpelstiltskin angrily dash into the forest.*

incredulously   *The little man incredulously stared at the queen when she guessed his name.*

Think   about the words and their meanings so you can use them in your assignments.

Unit 3 Composition Checklist
Lesson 8: Rumpelstiltskin

Retelling
Narrative
Stories

IEW | Institute for Excellence in Writing
Listen, Speak, Read, Write, Think!

Name: _____

STRUCTURE

☐ MLA format (see Appendix I) _____ 5 pts

☐ title centered and repeats 1–3 key words from final sentence _____ 5 pts

☐ story follows Story Sequence Chart _____ 6 pts

☐ each paragraph contains at least four sentences _____ 6 pts

☐ checklist on top, final draft, rough draft, key word outline _____ 5 pts

STYLE

¶1 ¶2 ¶3 Dress-Ups (underline one of each)   (3 pts each)

☐ ☐ ☐ -ly adverb _____ 9 pts

☐ ☐ ☐ *who/which* clause _____ 9 pts

☐ ☐ ☐ strong verb _____ 9 pts

☐ ☐ ☐ *because* clause _____ 9 pts

CHECK FOR BANNED WORDS (-1 pt for each use): think/thought, go/went, say/said _____ pts

MECHANICS

☐ capitalization _____ 1 pt

☐ end marks and punctuation _____ 1 pt

☐ complete sentences _____ 2 pts

☐ correct spelling _____ 3 pts

VOCABULARY

☐ vocabulary words – label *(voc)* in left margin or after sentence

Total: _____ 70 pts

Custom Total: _____ pts

Motivate

For the last assignment written in this unit, consider giving double tickets for each vocabulary word a student uses in this story. Just a little extra motivation can yield amazing results.

Checklist

Teachers are free to adjust a checklist by requiring only the stylistic techniques that have become easy, plus one new one. EZ+1

Intentionally blank so the checklist can be removed.

Lesson 9: Steam Engines

Structure: Unit 4: Summarizing a Reference
                        topic-clincher sentences

Style: no new style

Subject: steam engines

Teaching Writing: Structure and Style

Watch the sections for Unit 4: Summarizing a Reference. At IEW.com/twss-help reference the TWSS Viewing Guides.

UNIT 4: SUMMARIZING A REFERENCE

Lesson 9: Steam Engines

Goals

- to learn the Unit 4 Summarizing a Reference structural model
- to learn and use the topic-clincher rule
- to create a KWO
- to write a 1-paragraph report
- to review vocabulary words

Assignment Schedule

Day 1

1. Play Vocabulary Lightning.
2. Read New Structure—Summarizing a Reference.
3. Memorize the topic-clincher rule.
4. Read "Steam Engines" and write a KWO.

Day 2

1. Review your KWO from Day 1 and complete Structure Practice.
2. Complete Style Practice.
3. Complete Vocabulary Practice. There are no new words for this lesson.
4. Using your KWO as a guide, begin writing a rough draft in your own words.
5. Go over the checklist. Put a check in the box for each requirement you have completed.

Day 3

1. Review all vocabulary words learned thus far.
2. Finish writing your report. Follow the topic-clincher rule. Highlight or bold two or three key words that repeat or reflect in the topic and clincher sentences.
3. Turn in your rough draft to your editor with the completed checklist attached.

Day 4

1. Write or type a final draft, making any corrections your editor asked you to make.
2. Paperclip the checklist, final draft, rough draft, and KWO together. Hand them in.

In this new unit the KWO is formed by taking key words from interesting and important facts found in a source text. Initially, teachers will likely need to assist students as they limit their notes. Model the process. Let students choose facts they think are interesting or important, limiting them to 5–7 total facts.

In this unit students learn to organize writing by beginning each paragraph with a topic sentence and ending each with a clincher sentence.

Exemplar

The Exemplars file contains a student's completed assignment for Lesson 9. The example is for the teacher and not intended to be used by the student.

See the blue page for download instructions.

Read this page to introduce Unit 4: Summarizing a Reference. Talk about the difference between the compositions students wrote for Unit 3 (3-paragraph narrative stories using the Story Sequence Chart) and the compositions they will write for Unit 4 (1-paragraph reports about a single topic). Read about the topic and clincher sentences and their purpose.

New Structure

Summarizing a Reference *5-7 Facts!!*

In Unit 4 you will write reports by summarizing a reference. When you write a short report, most often you turn to an encyclopedia, textbook, or Internet article for information. These sources typically have much more information than you need. It is important to understand that you will not try to note every fact from the source text. Instead, you will choose five to seven interesting or important facts and "*SOME*-a-rize."

When you write a report, your facts must be organized into paragraphs. Each paragraph will begin with a topic sentence, contain facts, and end with a clincher sentence.

1 topic = 1 paragraph

Topic Sentence

The topic sentence tells what the paragraph is about. For this reason, it is the first sentence of the paragraph. Every paragraph should have one clear topic. When you write the KWO, ask yourself, "What will the paragraph be about?" As you answer, write two or three key words on the Roman numeral line.

Facts

On the other lines of the KWO, write facts that support the topic. To find facts, read the source text and look for five to seven things that you find interesting or important. To help you remember each fact that you choose, write two or three key words about the fact on the KWO. If needed, you may use two lines to write one fact, or you may combine facts so that you have two facts on one line. Remember to include symbols, numbers, and abbreviations.

Clincher Sentence

The clincher sentence reminds the reader what the paragraph was about. For this reason, it is the last sentence of the paragraph. The KWO ends with the word *clincher*. Do not place key words on the clincher line. Instead when you form your rough draft, repeat (same word) or reflect (synonym of the word) two or three key words from the topic line.

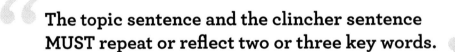

The topic sentence and the clincher sentence MUST repeat or reflect two or three key words.

Motivate

Help students learn the topic-clincher rule. If teaching to a classroom of students, advise students to be ready to recite the rule in order to enter class next time.

Sample Paragraph

The following paragraph is a short report about Denis Papin. Of course, there is too much information about this man to be placed in a single paragraph. Therefore, the author has chosen a specific topic about Papin to write about.

In 1679 French physicist Denis **Papin** created a bone **digester** which used high-pressure **steam**. The digester was made to take the fat out of bones and make it hard enough to be ground into bone meal. Papin's pressure cooker would cook the bones with water at a high temperature in a tightly sealed container. Pressure would build up inside the digester, and a valve had to be added to release steam so that it would not explode. Papin watched how the valve opened and closed as the amount of steam increased or decreased. Papin thought that steam could be used to make an engine and shared his work with other scientists. **Steam** engines were developed because of **Papin's** creation of the bone **digester**.

Notice:

1. The topic sentence tells what the paragraph is about. The key words in bold are the main idea words of the topic sentence.

2. The sentences that follow the topic sentence each provide a fact that supports, proves, or illustrates how Papin's digester used steam.

3. The clincher sentence states the same main idea as the topic sentence. The key words in bold repeat or reflect the same key words found in the topic sentence.

4. One can easily see that the topic-clincher rule was followed because the following words are bold: *Papin, digester, steam, Steam, Papin's, digester.*

Source Text

Steam Engines

The invention of the steam engine made it easier to move people and goods from place to place. Before the steam engine, people used horses, mules, and oxen to pull carts and wagons. Ships used manpower or wind power. These were not reliable sources of power. Animals needed rest and feed stops. They did not move fast, and they could be stubborn. Wind might not blow for days at a time, leaving ships stranded in the middle of the ocean. In 1679 French physicist Denis Papin invented a pressure cooker. When he watched the pressurized steam raise the lid off the pot, he had the idea that steam could be used to move things. However, it was not until one hundred years later that Scottish inventor James Watt made a steam engine with enough power to move trains and boats. To produce steam to power the engines, water was boiled using a coal fire. Pressurized steam then caused the piston connected to the machine's wheels to move up and down. This action turned the wheels, and the vehicle moved forward. The earliest steam engines did the work of five hundred horses. Today they can do the work of five to seven thousand horses. In fact, the term horsepower was first used to compare the work of a steam engine to how many horses it took to make the same amount of power. The steam engine made it possible to move larger loads of goods and greater numbers of people from place to place.

Locate Key Words

Guide students to find 5–7 facts. Reread the first sentence. Ask your students, "Is that interesting or important?" If they answer yes, place a check mark by the fact or sentence.

Allow students to choose facts that they find interesting or important. Very likely their facts will differ from the ones chosen in this Teacher's Manual.

Before completing the KWO, remind students that this is a new unit and that key words are found differently. What goes on the Roman numeral line? (*key words for the topic*) Lines 1–5 (6/7) are for key words from facts, not from each sentence. Ask which facts interest them. Help them limit the number of facts they choose. If students are young, stop at five facts. Do not put key words for a clincher on the KWO. Direct students to write the clincher sentence when they write the paragraph.

The KWOs in the Teacher's Manual are only samples. Every class and each student will have unique outlines.

Sample   Lesson 9: Steam Engines

Key Word Outline

Decide the topic of your paragraph. For this lesson the topic has been given to you and noted in key words on the Roman numeral line (the topic line) of the KWO.

Re-read the source text and write five to seven facts to support the topic. You will have to leave some facts out. You are *SOME-a-rizing*.

I.   Topic: *S. engines, transport, easier*

1.   *before, SE, animals +* ⛵ *, manpower*

2.   *animals, X reliable, Zzz, stubborn*

3.   ⛵ *, wind, X blow, stranded*

4.   *James Watt, invented, SE, ++ power*

5.   *H_2O, boiled, steam, pistons, ↑↓*

(6.) *pistons, turn, wheels, SE →*

(7.) *1 SE = 500 horses, move, goods*

Clincher

Use the KWO to tell each line of notes in your own words. For the clincher, repeat or reflect the words on the topic line.

Structure Practice

Topic Sentence

The topic sentence must tell what your paragraph is about. Use the key words on the topic line (or synonyms of those words) to write a topic sentence. There are several different possibilities for communicating the topic of the paragraph, even from the same key words.

> The **steam engine** made **transportation easier**.

Clincher

Discuss ideas for a clincher using two to three key words that repeat or reflect words written on the topic sentence line.

Here are sample clincher sentences:

*It was **easier** to transport goods because of the **steam engine**.*

***Steam engines** transport goods and people more **efficiently**.*

In the second example, *efficiently* reflects the word *easier.*

Style Practice

Strong Verb Dress-Up and -ly Adverb Dress-Up

On the first line below the sentence, write strong verbs that could replace the italicized banned verb. On the second line write ideas for -ly adverbs that you could use with the strong verbs.

Denis Papin *thought* that an engine could be made with steam power.

strong verbs   _hypothesized, theorized, speculated, surmised_

-ly adverbs   _cleverly, attentively, deliberately, conscientiously_

Who/Which Clause Dress-Up

Add a *who/which* clause. Punctuate and mark correctly.

Pressurized steam moves the pistons   _, which were attached to the train's wheels._

Because Clause Dress-Up

Add a *because* clause. Underline the word *because*.

Animals were not a reliable source of power <u>because</u>   _they needed to stop frequently._

Look   at your KWO and consider dress-ups to include in your composition.

Vocabulary Practice

Think   about the words and their meanings.

Which vocabulary words could you use in this assignment?

transport, efficiently, generate, construct, glide

Unit 4 Composition Checklist
Lesson 9: Steam Engines

Summarizing
a Reference

Name: _____

IEW | Institute for Excellence in Writing

STRUCTURE

- ☐ MLA format (see Appendix I) _____ 2 pts
- ☐ title centered and repeats 1–3 key words from final sentence _____ 3 pts
- ☐ topic-clincher sentences repeat or reflect 2–3 key words (highlight or bold) _____ 3 pts
- ☐ checklist on top, final draft, rough draft, key word outline _____ 1 pt

STYLE

¶1 Dress-Ups (underline one of each)   (3 pts each)

- ☐ -ly adverb _____ 3 pts
- ☐ *who/which* clause _____ 3 pts
- ☐ strong verb _____ 3 pts
- ☐ *because* clause _____ 3 pts

CHECK FOR BANNED WORDS (-1 pt for each use): think/thought, go/went, say/said _____ pts

MECHANICS

- ☐ capitalization _____ 1 pt
- ☐ end marks and punctuation _____ 1 pt
- ☐ complete sentences _____ 1 pt
- ☐ correct spelling _____ 1 pt

VOCABULARY

- ☐ vocabulary words – label *(voc)* in left margin or after sentence

Total: _____ 25 pts

Custom Total: _____ pts

Checklist

Notice that the checklist requires students to highlight or bold topic-clincher key words.

Dress-ups should continue to be underlined.

Teachers are free to adjust a checklist by requiring only the stylistic techniques that have become easy, plus one new one. EZ+1

UNIT 4: SUMMARIZING A REFERENCE

Intentionally blank so the checklist can be removed.

Institute for Excellence in Writing

Lesson 10: Model T Ford

Structure: Unit 4: Summarizing a Reference

Style: quality adjective, banned words: *good, bad, big, small*

Subject: Model T

Lesson 10: Model T Ford

UNIT 4: SUMMARIZING A REFERENCE

Lesson 10: Model T Ford

Goals

- to practice the Unit 4 structural model
- to create a KWO
- to write a 1-paragraph report
- to add a new dress-up: quality adjective
- to ban weak adjectives: *good, bad, big, small*
- to use new vocabulary words: *fabricate, launch, momentous, significant*

Assignment Schedule

Day 1

1. Play a vocabulary game from the Teacher's Manual.
2. Read "Model T Ford" and write a KWO.

Day 2

1. Review your KWO from Day 1 and complete Structure Practice.
2. Learn a new dress-up, the quality adjective. Read New Style and complete Style Practice.
3. Look at the vocabulary cards for Lesson 10. Complete Vocabulary Practice.
4. Using your KWO as a guide, begin writing a rough draft in your own words.
5. Go over the checklist. Put a check in the box for each requirement you have completed.

Day 3

1. Review all vocabulary words learned thus far.
2. Finish writing your report. Follow the topic-clincher rule. Highlight or bold two or three key words that repeat or reflect in the topic and clincher sentences.
3. Turn in your rough draft to your editor with the completed checklist attached.

Day 4

1. Write or type a final draft, making any corrections your editor asked you to make.
2. Paperclip the checklist, final draft, rough draft, and KWO together. Hand them in.

Source Text

Model T Ford

Henry Ford found a way to produce cars that everyone could afford. When Ford introduced the Model T automobile, he said, "I will build a car for the great multitude." His new factory assembly line system made it possible for many people to own a car. In 1908 when Ford started selling the Model T, there were only eight thousand cars on American roads. The average car cost about $2,500, which was five times more than most workers made in a year. The Model T cost $850. This was much less, but it was still more than double the average person's salary. The factory could only build eleven cars per month, so few cars were available. Ford put the first moving assembly line in his factory in 1913. A conveyor belt pulled the vehicle down the line, and the workers built the car piece-by-piece. Ford needed to build the car as fast as possible. The Model T came only in black because black paint dried fastest. By 1914 it took just ninety-three minutes to build one Model T. Ford Motor Company now built as many cars in a day as the company used to build in a month. Increasing the number of cars available helped lower the car's price to $300. From 1917 to 1923, the company sold more than fifteen million Model Ts, which was over half the cars in the world. Ford Motor Company provided affordable cars.

Mechanics _____

The names of adults are referenced by their first and last name the first time they are mentioned. After the first time, they are only referenced by their last name.

Sample

Key Word Outline

Decide the topic of your paragraph. Note it in key words on the topic line of the KWO.
Re-read the source text and write five to seven facts to support the topic.

I.   Topic: *Ford, Model T, affordable*

   1.   *avg, cost, $2,500, 5x, salary*

   2.   *MT, $800, still, 2x, salary*

   3.   *1913, assembly, MT, conveyor, belt*

   4.   *MT, black, dry, fast*

   5.   *1914, 93 min, build, MT*

 (6.)   *#, cars, ↑, price, ↓, $300*

 (7.)   *> ½, cars, world, MT*

Clincher

Use the KWO to tell each line of notes in your own words. For the clincher, repeat or reflect the words on the topic line.

> ### Writing the KWO
>
> Students will likely need continued help. Model the process by writing a sample KWO on the whiteboard for them to see. Help students limit which interesting or important facts they choose.

Structure Practice

Topic Sentence

Use the key words that you wrote on the KWO topic line (or synonyms of those words) to write a topic sentence for your paragraph.

   *Henry **Ford** built the **affordable Model T**.*

New Style

Quality Adjective Dress-Up

In this lesson you will learn another dress-up: quality adjective.

An adjective is a describing word. An adjective describes a noun—a person, place, thing, or idea. Here is the adjective test. If the word fits in the blank, it is an adjective.

the _____ pen or person

Use the adjective test. Underline six adjectives below.

dog	chew	<u>ravishing</u>	<u>elegant</u>	<u>hideous</u>
<u>brave</u>	<u>zealous</u>	<u>prominent</u>	pair	table

Banned Words

Boring adjectives like boring verbs should be avoided in writing. For this reason you will not be allowed to use certain adjectives in the writing you do for this class.

Good, bad, big, and *small* are not very descriptive; they are ordinary. Quality adjectives like *Useful, harmful, significant,* and *trivial* add more detail and provide a strong image and feeling.

What quality adjectives might be more descriptive than *good, bad, big,* and *small?* On the lines below, add to the list of synonyms.

Synonyms for *good*   ___superior, magnificent___   *useful, splendid*

Synonyms for *bad*   ___regrettable, disgusting___   *inferior, dreadful*

Synonyms for *big*   ___major, momentous___   *sizable, immense*

Synonyms for *small*   ___miniature, inconsequential___   *meager, compact*

From now on in these lessons, the words *good, bad, big,* and *small* are banned. To help yourself avoid these banned words, use a thesaurus or your vocabulary words or look at the -ly adverb list on the *Portable Walls for Structure and Style Students* or the IEW Writing Tools App. Dropping the -ly from the words on the -ly adverb list will transform them into adjectives.

 From now on, include a quality adjective in each paragraph you write.
Mark the quality adjective by underlining it.

⊘ **BANNED WORDS**   THINK/THOUGHT, GO/WENT, SAY/SAID   ADJECTIVES: GOOD, BAD, BIG, SMALL

Institute for Excellence in Writing

Style Practice

-ly Adverb Dress-Up

Write a few ideas for an -ly adverb dress-up on the line below each sentence.
Choose your favorite to write on the blank in the sentence.

1. The black paint _____*promptly*_____ dried.

    -ly adverbs _____*rapidly, promptly, completely, conveniently*_____

2. A conveyor belt _____*efficiently*_____ pulled the car down the line.

    -ly adverbs _____*methodically, efficiently, steadily, slowly*_____

3. Factory workers _____*skillfully*_____ built the Model T in ninety-three minutes.

    -ly adverbs _____*adeptly, efficiently, skillfully, surprisingly*_____

Strong Verb Dress-Up

Do not use the exact words found in the text. On the line below each sentence, write strong verbs that are synonyms of the italicized words. Use a thesaurus.

1. Ford *found* a way to produce affordable cars.

    strong verbs _____*discovered, created, developed*_____

2. Ford *put* an assembly line in his factory.

    strong verbs _____*placed, installed, established*_____

3. Ford Motor Company *built* eleven cars in one day.

    strong verbs _____*manufactured, constructed, assembled*_____

Who/Which Clause Dress-Up

Add a *who/which* clause. Punctuate and mark correctly.

In 1908 the average car ___*, which cost $2,500,*_____

_____ was not affordable.

Because Clause Dress-Up

Add a *because* clause. Underline the word *because*.

By 1914 most people could afford a Model T <u>because</u> ___*it only cost $300.*_____

_____

Look   at your KWO and consider clauses to include in your composition.

Vocabulary Practice

Listen   to someone read the vocabulary words for Lesson 10 aloud.

Speak   them aloud yourself.

Read   the definitions and sample sentences on the vocabulary cards.

Write   the correct words in the blanks.

Ford made a _____*momentous*_____ announcement.

Ford Motor Company ____*launch (ed)*____ the first moving assembly line.

Cars were _____*fabricate (d)*_____ on an assembly line.

In 1908 $2,500 was a ____*significant*____ amount of money to pay for a car.

Think   about the words and their meanings so you can use them in your assignments.

Unit 4 Composition Checklist
Lesson 10: Model T Ford

Summarizing
a Reference

Name: _____

IEW Institute for **Excellence** in **Writing**
Listen. Speak. Read. Write. Think.

STRUCTURE

☐ MLA format (see Appendix I) _____ 2 pts

☐ title centered and repeats 1–3 key words from final sentence _____ 3 pts

☐ topic-clincher sentences repeat or reflect 2–3 key words (highlight or bold) _____ 5 pts

☐ checklist on top, final draft, rough draft, key word outline _____ 1 pt

STYLE

¶1 Dress-Ups (underline one of each)   (3 pts each)

☐ -ly adverb _____ 3 pts

☐ *who/which* clause _____ 3 pts

☐ strong verb _____ 3 pts

☐ *because* clause _____ 3 pts

☐ quality adjective _____ 3 pts

CHECK FOR BANNED WORDS (-1 pt for each use): think/thought, go/went, say/said, good, bad, big, small _____ pts

MECHANICS

☐ capitalization _____ 1 pt

☐ end marks and punctuation _____ 1 pt

☐ complete sentences _____ 1 pt

☐ correct spelling _____ 1 pt

VOCABULARY

☐ vocabulary words – label *(voc)* in left margin or after sentence

Total: _____ 30 pts

Custom Total: _____ pts

Checklist

Point out all the banned words on the checklist. Each of these words must be avoided when writing.

Teachers are free to adjust a checklist by requiring only the stylistic techniques that have become easy, plus one new one. EZ+1

Intentionally blank so the checklist can be removed.

Lesson 11: Flight

Structure: Unit 4: Summarizing a Reference
Style: *www.asia* clause
Subject: flight

UNIT 4: SUMMARIZING A REFERENCE

Lesson 11: Flight

Goals

* to practice the Unit 4 structural model
* to create a KWO
* to write a 2-paragraph report
* to add a new dress-up: *www.asia* clause
* to use new vocabulary words: *enthralling, ponderous, replicate, suspend*

Assignment Schedule

Day 1

1. Play Two Strikes and You're Out.
2. Read Structure—Identifying the Topic.
3. Read "Flight" and write a KWO.

Day 2

1. Review your KWO from Day 1.
2. Learn a new dress-up, the *www.asia* clause. Read New Style and complete Style Practice.
3. Look at the vocabulary cards for Lesson 11. Complete Vocabulary Practice.
4. Using your KWO as a guide, begin writing a rough draft in your own words.
5. Go over the checklist. Put a check in the box for each requirement you have completed.

Day 3

1. Review all vocabulary words learned thus far.
2. Finish writing your 2-paragraph report. Follow the topic-clincher rule in each paragraph.
3. Turn in your rough draft to your editor with the completed checklist attached.

Day 4

1. Write or type a final draft, making any corrections your editor asked you to make.
2. Paperclip the checklist, final draft, rough draft, and KWO together. Hand them in.

Structure

Identifying the Topic

Subject

The subject is the thing you research—the thing you write about. A subject of a paper may be a person, place, event, animal, or issue.

Topic

The topic is the division of the thing you research—a thing within the subject.

If the subject is house, the possible topics (divisions) may be rooms, layout, history, construction, flooring, location, etc.

If the subject is cats, the possible topics (divisions) may be characteristics, senses, behavior, lifespan, breeds, play, domestication, etc.

If the subject is airplanes, the possible topics (divisions) may be history, materials, construction, aerodynamics, technology, etc.

if 1 topic = 1 paragraph
then 2 topics = 2 paragraphs

Topic Sentence

The topic sentence tells what the paragraph is about. When you write your KWO, you begin by placing key words on the topic line. When writing multi-paragraph compositions, follow the pattern: *subject, topic,* one more word *about the topic.*

If you write a paragraph about the kitchen in your house, the key words on the topic line of the KWO may be *house, kitchen, mess*y. Every fact on the outline and sentence in the paragraph then supports or proves the topic: the kitchen in the house is messy.

As another option, the key words on the topic line of the KWO may be *house, kitchen, activity.* Every fact on the outline and sentence in the paragraph then supports or proves the topic: the kitchen in the house is filled with activity.

The three key words you place on the topic line determine the facts that you search for during the research process.

Practice

Read the source text and then fill in these blanks.

1. The subject for this lesson is ___*flight*_____

2. Possible topics include _____*birds, inventors, humans, flying machines*_____

3. On the KWO indicate the topics on the topic lines following this pattern: *subject, topic,* one more word *about the topic.*

Subjects and Topics

Help students find topics by reading a paragraph and asking, "What is this paragraph about?" The answers provided are suggestions, and students' answers may vary.

Source Text

Flight

Since the beginning of time, humans have wanted to fly. Many myths and religions are filled with stories of people taking flight. The myth of Daedalus and Icarus from 1400 B.C. is one of the most well-known tales of man soaring the skies. Archaeologists have discovered cave drawings of people with wings dating back 4,300 years. Humans have tried to imitate birds by jumping off cathedrals and towers with flapping wings. They have attempted to fly by dangling off large kites. It was not until inventors started studying birds that they discovered the aerodynamics of flight.

In the 1400s Italian artist and inventor Leonardo da Vinci drew pictures of his ideas for flying machines in notebooks. By watching birds fly, he learned that the flapping of wings moves the bird forward and then up. The air moving over the wings at high speeds lifts the birds into the air. Da Vinci first thought that any man-made flying machine would need flapping wings. He drew many pictures of flying machines with wings that flapped.

The Wright Brothers built and flew the first airplane in 1903. Before then scientists could not figure out how to make a heavy plane move fast enough to lift it off the ground. The brothers were able to build a light engine that had enough power to push an airplane forward and lift it into the air. However, they could not control the plane. It kept crashing. Just like da Vinci, Orville and Wilbur Wright watched birds to find a solution. They saw that birds angled their wings for balance

> *Reminder*
>
> If students wish to include "the most well-known tales of man soaring the skies," they must copy it exactly as it appears in the source text and place the phrase in quotation marks.

Mechanics _____

When you add an *s* to a number to make it plural, do not add an apostrophe.

and control. They added a movable board called a rudder to copy the birds' wings. It worked. Their first flight lasted twelve seconds and went 180 feet, which was half the length of a football field.

When engineers tried to build a flying machine that could hover in the air and go in and out of tight spaces, they watched hummingbirds. Hummingbirds are the only birds that can fly backwards, forwards, and sideways. They can also hover. The secret lies in their muscles and bones. They have large wing muscles that can flap fifty to eighty times per second. A short arm bone in their wings allows them to flap their wings in a figure eight by using wrist flicks. The muscles and bones help the hummingbird hover as well as fly sideways and backwards at speeds over thirty miles per hour. A drone copies hummingbird flight by using propellers that spin quickly and that tilt in all directions. Some drones are equipped with cameras to collect data. These nimble machines enable humans to see into the eye of a storm and other inaccessible places without risking their lives.

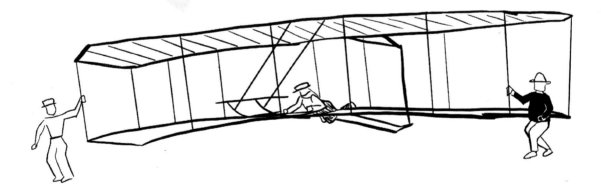

Guide students to look for 5–7 interesting or important facts that support the chosen topic and to ignore the other facts. Supporting facts can be found in any portion of the source text. Students are not limited to using facts found in a specific paragraph.

Sample

Key Word Outline

For this lesson the topic of each KWO has been started for you. Next to the first Roman numeral, write *flight (subject), birds (topic),* _____ (add one more word *about the topic*). Re-read the source text and write five to seven facts to support the first topic.

Next to the second Roman numeral, write *flight (subject), inventors (topic),* _____ (add one more word *about the topic*). Re-read the source text and write five to seven facts to support the second topic.

I. Topic: _____ *flight, birds, natural*

  1. _____ *flap, wings, bird →, ↑*

  2. _____ *++ air, wings, lift ↗*

  3. _____ *⟨ , wings, balance + control*

  4. _____ *hummingbird, lrg, wing muscles, 50–80/sec.*

  5. _____ *muscles + bones, hover, ← →, 30 mph*

  (6.) _____

  (7.) _____

  Clincher

II. Topic: _____ *flight, inventors, copy*

  1. _____ *↟ imitate, 〰, jumping, buildings, ◇*

  2. _____ *scientist, study, 〰, aerodynamics*

  3. _____ *Leonardo da Vinci, drew, pic, 〰*

  4. _____ *flap, wings, launch, → ↑*

  5. _____ *WB, 1st, light, engine, X control*

  (6.) _____ *WB, rudder = ↗〰, balance + control*

  (7.) _____ *engineers, drone, 👀 hummingbird*

  Clincher

Use the KWO to tell each line of notes in your own words. For the clincher, repeat or reflect the words on the topic line.

A *www.asia* clause contains both a subject and a verb.

As a model is not a clause because *As a model* does not contain a subject and verb.

As a model is a prepositional phrase.

As scientists studied the model is a clause because *As scientists studied the model* contains a subject (*scientists*) and verb (*studied*).

Recite the *www.asia* words over and over with students.

www.asia Clause
_____

For younger students simply encourage them to place the *www. asia* clause after a sentence that is already complete.

New Style

www.asia Clause Dress-Up

In this lesson you will learn the sixth and final dress-up: *www.asia* clause.

This clause is just like a *because* clause except it begins with one of these words: *when, while, where, as, since, if, although.* Memorize these words. An acronym can help: *www.asia.*

> The Wright brothers could control the plane <u>when</u> they added a rudder.
>
> Hummingbirds can hover <u>while</u> they fly in and out of tight spaces.

Notice:

1. A *www.asia* clause begins with *when, while, where, as, since, if, although.*

   To indicate a *www.asia* clause, underline only the first word of the clause: *when, while, where, as, since, if, although.*

2. A *www.asia* clause contains a subject and a verb.

   > The Wright brothers could control the plane <u>when</u> *they added* a rudder.
   >
   > Hummingbirds can hover <u>while</u> *they fly* in and out of tight spaces.

3. A *www.asia* clause is added to a sentence that is already complete.

   > *The Wright brothers could control the plane* <u>when</u> they added a rudder.
   >
   > *Hummingbirds can hover* <u>while</u> they fly in and out of tight spaces.

> If a *www.asia* clause follows a complete sentence, no comma is needed.
> If the *www.asia* clause is at the beginning of the sentence, a comma is required.
>
> Hummingbirds can hover <u>while</u> they fly in and out of tight spaces. (no comma)
>
> Sometimes <u>while</u> they hover, drones take pictures and collect data. (comma)

www.asia

when

while

where

as

since

if

although

Read the sentences and orally fill in the blanks several times. When students understand the pattern of the *www.asia* clause, then direct them to write.

Practice

Add a *www.asia* clause. Underline the first word of the clause.

Drones may take pictures <u>*when they fly into tight spaces.*</u>

 From now on, include a *www.asia* clause in each paragraph you write.
Mark the *www.asia* clause by underlining the first word of the clause.

Style Practice

www.asia Clause Dress-Up

Write a sentence with a *www.asia* clause that you could use in your composition. Remember to add the clause to a sentence that is already complete. Punctuate and mark correctly.

Inventors discovered the aerodynamics of flight <u>when</u> they began studying birds.

Because Clause Dress-Up

Write a sentence with a *because* clause that you could use in your composition. Remember to add the clause to a sentence that is already complete. Punctuate and mark correctly.

The Wright Brothers' plane flew <u>because</u> they built a powerful, lightweight engine.

Who/Which Clause Dress-Up

Write a sentence with a *who/which* clause that you could use in your composition. Punctuate and mark correctly.

A hummingbird, <u>which</u> can flap its wings rapidly, can fly backwards, forwards,

and sideways.

Quality Adjective Dress-Up

Next to each noun, write ideas for adjectives that create a strong image. Avoid banned adjectives.

1. hummingbirds _____ *graceful, energetic, minuscule, enthralling*

2. inventor/engineer _____ *curious, studious, brilliant, accomplished*

Name and describe two additional things scientists might see, hear, or feel.

the powerful flapping wings

the wooden, angled, movable rudder

Suggested Answers

The suggested answers are more sophisticated than most students will write. They are purposefully written to provide a model of strong word choices.

Vocabulary Practice

Listen   to someone read the vocabulary words for Lesson 11 aloud.

Speak   them aloud yourself.

Read   the definitions and sample sentences on the vocabulary cards.

Write   the part of speech and the definition beside each word.

enthralling   *adjective; capturing and holding one's attention*

ponderous   *adjective; slow and clumsy because of great weight*

replicate   *verb; to make a close or exact copy*

suspend   *verb; to keep from falling or sinking by some invisible support*

Think   about the words and their meanings so you can use them in your assignments.

Unit 4 Composition Checklist
Lesson 11: Flight

Lesson 11: Flight

Summarizing
a Reference

Name: _____ _____

IEW | Institute for Excellence in Writing

STRUCTURE

☐ MLA format (see Appendix I) _____ 2 pts

☐ title centered and repeats 1–3 key words from final sentence _____ 2 pts

☐ topic-clincher sentences repeat or reflect 2–3 key words (highlight or bold) _____ 6 pts

☐ checklist on top, final draft, rough draft, key word outline _____ 5 pts

STYLE

¶1 ¶2 **Dress-Ups** (underline one of each)   (3 pts each)

☐ ☐ -ly adverb _____ 6 pts

☐ ☐ *who/which* clause _____ 6 pts

☐ ☐ strong verb _____ 6 pts

☐ ☐ *because* clause _____ 6 pts

☐ ☐ quality adjective _____ 6 pts

☐ ☐ *www.asia* clause _____ 6 pts

CHECK FOR BANNED WORDS (-1 pt for each use): think/thought, go/went, say/said, good, bad, big, small _____ pts

MECHANICS

☐ capitalization _____ 1 pt

☐ end marks and punctuation _____ 1 pt

☐ complete sentences _____ 1 pt

☐ correct spelling _____ 1 pt

VOCABULARY

☐ vocabulary words – label *(voc)* in left margin or after sentence

Total: _____ 55 pts

Custom Total: _____ pts

Checklist

Teachers are free to adjust a checklist by requiring only the stylistic techniques that have become easy, plus one new one. EZ+1

UNIT 4: SUMMARIZING A REFERENCE

Intentionally blank so the checklist can be removed.

Lesson 12: Spacesuits

Structure: Unit 4: Summarizing a Reference

Style: #2 prepositional opener

Subject: spacesuits

Lesson 12: Spacesuits

UNIT 4: SUMMARIZING A REFERENCE

Lesson 12: Spacesuits

Goals

- to practice the Unit 4 structural model
- to create a KWO
- to write a 2-paragraph report
- to learn about variety in sentence openers
- to add a new sentence opener: #2 prepositional opener
- to use new vocabulary words: *durable, explosively, monitor, penetrating*

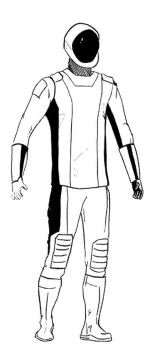

Assignment Schedule

Day 1

1. Complete the Review.
2. Read "Spacesuits" and complete Structure Practice.
3. Write a KWO.

Day 2

1. Review your KWO from Day 1.
2. Learn about sentence openers. Read New Style and complete Style Practice.
3. Look at the vocabulary cards for Lesson 12. Complete Vocabulary Practice.
4. Using your KWO as a guide, begin writing a rough draft in your own words.
5. Go over the checklist. Put a check in the box for each requirement you have completed.

Day 3

1. Review all vocabulary words learned thus far.
2. Finish writing your 2-paragraph report. Follow the topic-clincher rule in each paragraph.
3. Turn in your rough draft to your editor with the completed checklist attached.

Day 4

1. Write or type a final draft, making any corrections your editor asked you to make.
2. Paperclip the checklist, final draft, rough draft, and KWO together. Hand them in.

> Study for Vocabulary Quiz 3. It will cover words from Lessons 1–12.

Review

Review

The subject is the thing you research.

A topic is a division or part of the subject.

There are numerous correct answers for numbers 2 and 3.

1. What is the difference between a subject and a topic?

2. If ant is your subject, list four possible topics.

    anatomy   *colonies*

    life cycle   *communication*

3. If the moon is your subject, list four possible topics.

    phases   *characteristics*

    geology   *eclipses*

4. When you write your topic on the KWO, what pattern do you follow?

    subject   , *topic*   , *one more word about the topic*

5. Read a topic sentence from your report about flight.

Structure Practice

Identifying the Topic

Read the source text and then fill in these blanks.

1. The subject for this lesson is *spacesuits*

2. Possible topics include *purpose, parts, benefits, flight suit, spacewalk suit*

3. On the KWO indicate the topics on the topic lines following this pattern: *subject*, *topic*, one more word *about the topic*.

Source Text

Spacesuits

For centuries people have dreamed about traveling to space. Then, in 1961 the dream became a reality when Yuri Gagarin from the Soviet Union circled the Earth for a 108-minute orbital flight. Since that time more than five hundred men and women have orbited the Earth. Traveling in space is different from traveling in an automobile or even an airplane. Because the vacuum of space contains no gravity and no air to breathe, astronauts wear special suits that allow them to live and work in space.

Space travel stresses the human body. When a spaceship is launched, it travels from 0 to 17,500 miles per hour in only 8½ minutes. During that time astronauts experience three times the force of gravity on their bodies. It feels like a pile of bricks is on their chests. The availability of oxygen decreases the farther they travel from Earth. When the spaceship returns to Earth, the astronauts begin to feel the pull of gravity again. As the spaceship re-enters the Earth's atmosphere, temperatures approach 1700°C (3092°F). In order to survive a launch and re-entry, astronauts must wear pressurized flight suits to keep their bodies from swelling. Special compartments within the suits collect and contain sweat and other body waste. This special suit, which includes a helmet, gloves, and boots, allows men and women to survive the extreme pressure and temperature changes.

When astronauts leave the spacecraft, they wear a spacewalk suit called an extravehicular mobility unit (EMU). In space, temperatures range from 120°C (248°F) in the sunlight to minus 160°C (256°F) when it is dark. The spacewalk suit regulates body temperatures, warming and cooling astronauts as needed. While astronauts are outside the space craft, they not only face extreme temperatures, but they also encounter space dust. Space dust may not sound dangerous, but it travels at speeds of forty-four miles per second. Traveling as fast as a bullet, these particles can cause major damage. For this reason, the spacewalk helmet is made of a strong plastic found in bulletproof glass and has a sun visor and sun shades. Spacewalk suits also provide oxygen and eliminate carbon dioxide. The spacewalk suit has twenty layers that protect against heat, cold, pressure, and space dust.

Astronauts perform many tasks both inside and outside the spacecraft, so their suits need to let them move freely. The flight suit is more flexible and easy to move in than the spacewalk suit. The astronauts wear a cooling garment under the flight suit that looks like long underwear covered with tubes. The spacewalk suit also includes a cooling undergarment with three hundred feet of tubes that contain chilled water. Astronauts also need a communication system in order to send and receive messages from their command center. The flight suit has a lightweight helmet that reduces noise and connects to the communication systems. The spacewalk suit has a life support backpack. The backpack contains the water and pump for the cooling garment, oxygen to breathe and pressurize the suit, and a two-way radio for communication. Without these special clothes, astronauts could not orbit the Earth or visit the moon.

After topics have been chosen, guide students to look for 5–7 interesting or important facts that support the chosen topic and to ignore the other facts. Supporting facts can be found in any portion of the source text. Students are not limited to using facts found in a specific paragraph.

Sample

Key Word Outline

Next to the first Roman numeral, write *subject*, *topic*, one more word *about the topic*. Re-read the source text and write five to seven facts to support the first topic.

Next to the second Roman numeral, write *subject*, *topic*, one more word *about the topic*. Re-read the source text and write five to seven facts to support the second topic.

I.   Topic: _____ *spacesuits, flight suit, inside* _____

   1. _____ *pressurized, reduce, swelling* _____

   2. _____ *compartments, sweat + waste* _____

   3. _____ *flexible, cooling garment* _____

   4. _____ *long underwear, ++ tubes* _____

   5. _____ *lightweight, helmet, communicate* _____

 (6.) _____ *gloves, boots* _____

 (7.) _____

Clincher

II. Topic: _____ *spacesuits, spacewalk suit, outside* _____

   1. _____ *extravehicular, mobility, unit, EMU* _____

   2. _____ *20 layers, cooling, 300 ft tubes, H_2O* _____

   3. _____ *regulate temp, 250/-250°F, warm, cool* _____

   4. _____ *protect, space dust, 44 mps* _____

   5. _____ *helmet, bulletproof, glass* _____

 (6.) _____ *provide O_2, eliminate CO_2* _____

 (7.) _____ *life support, backpack,* _____

Clincher

Use the KWO to tell each line of notes in your own words. For the clincher, repeat or reflect the words on the topic line.

The students now know all the dress-ups. Remember, dress-ups are placed within a sentence to dress-up the writing. Students indicate a dress-up has been placed in a sentence by underlining it. Now it is time to teach your students sentence openers. Sentence openers teach sentence variety. Students indicate a sentence opener has been used by inserting a number in front of it.

UNIT 4: SUMMARIZING A REFERENCE

New Style

Sentence Openers

You are already familiar with dress-ups. In this lesson you will learn a second element of style: sentence openers.

Sentence openers are descriptive words, phrases, or clauses that you add to the beginning of a sentence. You will learn six openers—six ways to open or begin a sentence. Using various sentence openers will help your writing sound more sophisticated. To indicate that you have begun a sentence with an opener, you should number it. You can number it by putting a number in the left margin on the same line as the sentence or by putting a number in brackets directly before the sentence. Although you may use more than one specific type of sentence opener in a paragraph, only number one of each type in each paragraph.

To help you appreciate this stylistic device, read the following two versions of a paragraph about cosmonaut Yuri Gagarin. (Cosmonauts are people trained and certified by the Russian Space Agency.)

Version 1

Russian cosmonaut Yuri Gagarin was the first person to leave Earth's orbit and fly in space. His flight on April 12, 1961, lasted 108 minutes, reached the height of 203 miles, and orbited Earth one time. He flew on the Soviet Vostok 1 spacecraft. Scientists were not certain how weightlessness would affect the astronaut, so the capsule had few controls. Flight engineers flew the craft from the ground. The Vostok 1 did not have engines to slow reentry for a safe landing. Yuri Gagarin ejected four miles above Earth and parachuted to the ground. Yuri Gagarin gained international recognition upon his return to Earth.

Version 2

Russian cosmonaut Yuri Gagarin was the first person to leave Earth's orbit and fly in space on April 12, 1961. At completion this flight lasted 108 minutes, reached the height of 203 miles, and orbited Earth one time. Since scientists were not certain how weightlessness aboard the Soviet Vostok 1 spacecraft would affect the astronaut, the capsule had few controls. Operating the craft remotely, flight engineers on Earth flew the craft. The Vostok 1 did not have engines to slow reentry for landing. Safely Yuri Gagarin ejected four miles above Earth and parachuted to the ground. Upon his return to Earth, Yuri Gagarin gained international recognition.

In the paragraphs above you should have noticed that in Version 1 all the sentences begin with the subject. This makes the paragraph boring to read. When you begin your sentences with different types of openers, your writing sounds more sophisticated because your sentences begin with something other than the subject.

We call a sentence that opens with a subject the #1 subject opener. Most young writers' sentences begin with a subject. We explain the #1 subject opener to the students after they know all of the other openers.

New Style

#2 Prepositional Opener

In this lesson you will learn the first sentence opener: the #2 prepositional opener. (You will learn more sentence openers later that will be given other numbers.) The prepositional opener is a prepositional phrase placed at the beginning of a sentence.

> [2] At completion his flight lasted 108 minutes, reached the height of 203 miles, and orbited Earth one time.

> [2] Upon his return to Earth, Yuri Gagarin gained international recognition.

Notice:

1. A prepositional phrase contains at least two words and begins with a preposition.

2. A prepositional phrase ends with a noun. A prepositional phrase never contains a verb.

    There might be other words between the preposition and the noun, but there is never a verb in a prepositional phrase. Here are some examples of prepositional phrases:

    at launch   during reentry   after the flight

3. To indicate that a sentence begins with a prepositional opener, label it with a 2 in the left margin or place a [2] right before the sentence.

❝ If the prepositional phrase has five words or more, follow it with a comma. If two or more phrases open a sentence, place a comma after the last phrase. A comma is optional but usually not recommended with shorter phrases.

Practice

Write a sentence with a #2 prepositional opener. Follow the pattern: preposition + noun (no verb). Label it with a [2]. Do not underline the phrase.

[2] In 1961 Yuri Gagarin flew the first mission to space.

✎ From now on, include a #2 prepositional opener in each paragraph you write. Label it with a 2 in the margin or place a [2] before the sentence.

Prepositions

above
across
around
after
by
during
for
from
in
inside
into
near
of
off
on
outside
over
past
through
to
under
up
with
without

#2 Prepositional Opener

Encourage students to memorize the pattern: preposition + noun (no verb).

When short prepositional openers work transitionally, they will need a comma.

For example, In addition, On the other hand,

If a student writes a prepositional opener that is also a transitional opener, explain the comma is needed because the phrase is working as a transition.

Students benefit from looking at word lists like those listed on this page. A longer list of prepositions can be found on the *Portable Walls for Structure and Style Students* as well as the IEW Writing Tools App.

As students write prepositional openers, remind them to follow the pattern: preposition + noun (no verb).

If a verb is included, the student likely wrote an adverb clause. For example, *As the astronauts landed* includes a subject *(astronauts)* and verb *(landed)*. *As the astronauts landed* is a *www.asia* clause. *As protective garments*, however, is not a clause because *As protective garments* does not contain a subject and verb. *As protective garments* is a prepositional phrase.

Style Practice

#2 Prepositional Opener

Begin each sentence with a #2 prepositional opener. Follow the comma rule on page 113.

1. _____ *[2] As protective garments* _____ spacesuits shield astronauts from space dust.

2. _____ *[2] Under the flight suit* _____ the astronauts wear a cooling garment.

3. _____ *[2] Upon reentry* _____ temperatures can reach 3000˚F.

Look   at your KWO and consider openers to include in your composition.

Quality Adjective Dress-Up

Next to each noun, write ideas for adjectives that create a strong image. Avoid banned adjectives.

1. the astronaut   *brave, fearless, daring, bold*

2. the spacesuit   *durable, specialized, sturdy, advanced*

Name and describe two additional things the astronauts might see, hear, or feel.

_____ *crushing, unbearable, intense gravity*

_____ *damaging, razor-sharp, penetrating space dust*

Strong Verb Dress-Up and -ly Adverb Dress-Up

On the first line below each sentence, write strong verbs that could replace the italicized weak verb. On the second line write ideas for -ly adverbs that you could use with the strong verbs.

1. The spacesuits *give* the astronauts everything they need to survive in space.

   strong verbs   *supply, furnish, provide*

   -ly adverbs   *fully, completely, entirely*

2. When the spaceship *goes* to space, the astronauts must rely on their spacesuits.

   strong verbs   *travels, journeys, speeds*

   -ly adverbs   *swiftly, explosively, steadily*

Institute for Excellence in Writing

Because Clause Dress-Up

Add a *because* clause to each sentence. Underline the word *because*.

1. The spacewalk suit has twenty layers <u>because</u> *it must protect the astronauts from space dust.*

2. The flight suit is pressurized <u>because</u> *the lack of gravity causes the astronauts' bodies to swell.*

www.asia Clause Dress-Up

Add a *www.asia* clause to each sentence. Underline the first word of the clause.

1. Spacesuits contain a cooling garment <u>*since temperatures can be extremely hot in outer space.*</u>

2. Astronauts wear flight suits inside the space craft <u>*when the spaceship leaves and returns to Earth.*</u>

Who/Which Clause Dress-Up

Combine the statements using the word *who* or *which*. Punctuate and mark correctly.

1. The spacewalk suit has a life support backpack. The backpack contains a two-way radio.

   The spacewalk suit has a life support backpack, <u>which</u> contains a two-way radio.

2. Space suits provide protection for astronauts. Astronauts perform risky tasks in space.

   Space suits provide protection for astronauts, <u>who</u> perform risky tasks in space.

Look   at your KWO and consider clauses to include in your composition.

Vocabulary Practice

Listen   to someone read the vocabulary words for Lesson 12 aloud.

Speak   them aloud yourself.

Read   the definitions and sample sentences on the vocabulary cards.

Write   the words that match the definitions.

penetrating   able to pierce or pass into or through

durable   able to withstand damage

monitor   to watch, keep track of

explosively   in a way that is very sudden and powerful

Think   about the words and their meanings.
Which vocabulary words could you use in this assignment?

secure, transport, arduous, vital, glide, vigorously, launch,

momentous, enthralling

Unit 4 Composition Checklist
Lesson 12: Spacesuits

Summarizing
a Reference

Name: _____

IEW | Institute for Excellence in Writing

STRUCTURE

☐ MLA format (see Appendix I) _____ 1 pt

☐ title centered and repeats 1–3 key words from final sentence _____ 2 pts

☐ topic-clincher sentences repeat or reflect 2–3 key words (highlight or bold) _____ 6 pts

☐ checklist on top, final draft, rough draft, key word outline _____ 5 pts

STYLE

¶1 ¶2 Dress-Ups (underline one of each)   (3 pts each)

☐ ☐ -ly adverb _____ 6 pts

☐ ☐ *who/which* clause _____ 6 pts

☐ ☐ strong verb _____ 6 pts

☐ ☐ *because* clause _____ 6 pts

☐ ☐ quality adjective _____ 6 pts

☐ ☐ *www.asia* clause _____ 6 pts

Sentence Openers (number; one of each as possible)   (3 pts each)

☐ ☐ [2] prepositional _____ 6 pts

CHECK FOR BANNED WORDS (-1 pt for each use): think/thought, go/went, say/said, good, bad, big, small _____ pts

MECHANICS

☐ capitalization _____ 1 pt

☐ end marks and punctuation _____ 1 pt

☐ complete sentences _____ 1 pt

☐ correct spelling _____ 1 pt

VOCABULARY

☐ vocabulary words – label *(voc)* in left margin or after sentence

Total: _____ 60 pts

Custom Total: _____ pts

Checklist

Because students are writing a 2-paragraph report, they should underline twelve words, six dress-ups in each paragraph.

In addition, students should include and mark one prepositional phrase opener in each paragraph.

Teachers are free to adjust a checklist by requiring only the stylistic techniques that have become easy, plus one new one. EZ+1

UNIT 4: SUMMARIZING A REFERENCE

Intentionally blank so the checklist can be removed.

Institute for Excellence in Writing

Lesson 13: Meteorite

Structure:	Unit 5: Writing from Pictures
Style:	no new style
Subject:	a series of pictures about a meteorite

Teaching Writing: Structure and Style

Watch the sections for Unit 5: Writing from Pictures. At IEW.com/twss-help reference the TWSS Viewing Guides.

UNIT 5: WRITING FROM PICTURES

Lesson 13: Meteorite

Lesson 13: Meteorite

Goals

- to learn the Unit 5 Writing from Pictures structural model
- to create a KWO from a series of three pictures
- to write a 3-paragraph composition from the KWO
- to learn to ask questions to get ideas for writing
- to take Vocabulary Quiz 3
- to use new vocabulary words: *dilapidated, mesmerized, reveal, speedily*

Assignment Schedule

Day 1

1. Take Vocabulary Quiz 3.
2. Complete the Review.
3. Read New Structure—Writing from Pictures.
4. Write your KWO.

Day 2

1. Review your KWO from Day 1 and complete Structure Practice.
2. Complete Style Practice.
3. Look at the vocabulary cards for Lesson 13. Complete Vocabulary Practice.
4. Using your KWO as a guide, begin writing your 3-paragraph rough draft.
5. Go over the checklist. Put a check in the box for each requirement you have completed.

Day 3

1. Review all vocabulary words learned thus far.
2. Finish writing your 3-paragraph composition. Ensure that the clincher sentence of each paragraph repeats or reflects two or three key words of the central fact of the picture.
3. Turn in your rough draft to your editor with the completed checklist attached.

Day 4

1. Write or type a final draft, making any corrections your editor asked you to make.
2. Paperclip the checklist, final draft, rough draft, and KWO together. Hand them in.

In this new unit the KWO is formed by looking at three pictures and asking good questions related to the pictures. The key words are formed from the answers to the questions.

This unit is not storytelling but rather event description. Help students form the topic sentence by focusing on the central fact of each picture. Develop the outline by asking questions to describe the event.

Exemplar

The Exemplars file contains a student's completed assignment for Lesson 13. The example is for the teacher and not intended to be used by the student.

See the blue page for download instructions.

Review

A #2 prepositional opener begins with a _____, ends with a _____, and never includes a _____.

How do you indicate a #2 prepositional opener?

Read a sentence that begins with a #2 prepositional opener from your report about spacesuits.

Play Preposition Round Robin.

Scientific Information

The technical term for space rock is meteoroid. If a meteoroid enters the earth's atmosphere and burns up, the fireball or shooting star is called a meteor. If the meteor hits the ground, it is called a meteorite.

New Structure

Writing from Pictures

In Unit 5 instead of using source texts, you will write three paragraphs from a series of three pictures. Although it may seem as if you are telling a story, your task is to describe each event.

Each paragraph will begin with a central fact, contain details, and end with a clincher sentence.

if 1 topic = 1 paragraph

then 3 topics = 3 paragraphs

Central Fact

The central fact tells what you see in the picture. It is the topic sentence of the paragraph. Think of this sentence as the caption that describes the picture. When you write the KWO, ask yourself "What do I see in the picture?" As you answer, write three key words on the Roman numeral line.

Details

On the other lines of the KWO, explain in more detail what is happening and how it came to be that way. Where do you find out what is happening? Just like Unit 3, ask yourself questions. Brain-helping questions are listed on the KWO. These helpful questions include

Who is in the picture? **What** is the history of this picture? **Where** exactly is this? **How** is this being done or said? **Why** is this situation happening? **When** did this begin? What are they **doing**? **thinking**? **feeling**? **saying**? What happened just **before** the picture? What might happen **after** this picture? What might be just **outside** the picture?

The answers to your questions become the details for the outline. As you answer a question, place two or three key words on the KWO. Use symbols, numbers, and abbreviations when possible. You do not have to answer every question or ask in the order they are written. Keep your answers brief. You can add more details when you write your paragraphs.

Clincher Sentence

The clincher sentence reminds the reader what you see in the picture. Because it is the clincher sentence, it must repeat or reflect two or three key words placed on the central fact line. What rule does that remind you of?

The topic sentence and the clincher sentence MUST repeat or reflect two or three key words.

Look at the series of pictures. Encourage students to use their imaginations. Although the lesson is titled Meteorite, some students may prefer to write about something else flying through the sky. The first picture shows a boy and girl watching something in the sky. What are their names? The second picture shows something in the sky above a house. What is it? It may be a meteor or a UFO or a baseball or something else. How close is it? Will it hit the ground? Will it destroy anything? If it lands on the ground, will anyone find it? The third picture shows a crater in the ground. How was it formed? How large is the crater? Is anything in the crater? After you discuss the pictures, emphasize that students should write what they see in the picture on the central fact line. Stick with the facts, the things you see. Then, teach students to ask questions to determine what to place for notes on the rest of the KWO. Every class and each student will have unique outlines.

Reminder

This is a 3-paragraph assignment. Each paragraph will begin with the central fact, a topic sentence which describes the picture. The clincher also describes the picture. If students add conversation, do not make them indent if the speakers change.

Source

Meteorite

I.

II.

III.

A topic sentence tells the reader what the rest of the paragraph is about. In Unit 5 the topic is the picture. To write the topic sentence of the paragraph, students write a sentence that contains the two or three words they placed on the topic line of the KWO. Following the topic-clincher rule, the clincher sentence also uses those same two or three words or synonyms of them. The topic sentence and the clincher sentence become captions for the picture.

Sample   Lesson 13: Meteorite

Key Word Outline

I.   Central fact: _____ Kevin + Katie, 👀 , shooting ✰ _____

   1. _____ newlyweds, NM, just moved _____

   2. _____ graduated, college, 👀 job _____

   3. _____ struggled, X $$, ++ bills _____

   4. _____ travel, car, fix 🏠 _____

   5. _____ wished, ✰ , $$ + better, life _____

Clincher repeats or reflects 2–3 key words of central fact.

II. Central fact: _____ shooting ✰ , zoomed, house _____

   1. _____ fire ball, bright, white _____

   2. _____ beautiful, huge, ++ close _____

   3. _____ concerned, hit, 🏠 , damage? _____

   4. _____ dilapidated, ++ problems, X $$, fix _____

   5. _____ mesmerized, sonic boom _____

Clincher repeats or reflects 2–3 key words of central fact.

III. Central fact: _____ ground, crater = huge _____

   1. _____ after, ✰ disappeared, sky _____

   2. _____ landed, field, glowed _____

   3. _____ relieved, X hit, 🏠 _____

   4. _____ daytime, dug, treasure _____

   5. _____ gold, wish, true! _____

Clincher repeats or reflects 2–3 key words of central fact.
Title repeats 1–3 key words from final sentence.

?

who?

what?

when?

where?

why?

how?

doing?

thinking?

feeling?

saying?

before?

after?

outside?

Structure Practice

Topic Sentence

Use your KWO to guide you as you write your composition. Begin by looking at the words on the central fact line, the words that indicate what you see in the picture.

If you wrote *Kevin + Katie,* 👀 *, shooting* ⭐ on the central fact line next to the first picture, your topic sentence could be

Kevin and **Katie** stood in their yard and **watched** a **shooting star** in the night sky.

Use the key words that you wrote on the KWO next to the first central fact (the topic line) to write a sentence that tells what you see in the picture. Remember to highlight or bold the key words.

Answers will vary.

Continue your composition by forming sentences from the key words placed on the KWO. When you reach the clincher line, write a sentence that repeats or reflects two or three key words of the central fact. The clincher for the sample above might be

As **they watched** the **shooting star**, they wondered if their dreams would come true.

Style Practice

#2 Prepositional Opener

Begin each sentence with a #2 prepositional opener. Follow the comma rule on page 113.

1. _[2] During the night_ _____ they enjoyed star gazing.

2. _[2] Across the night sky_ _____ the strange object zoomed.

3. _[2] In the morning_ _____ they found a large crater.

Look   at your KWO and list #2 prepositional openers to include in your composition.

Quality Adjective Dress-Up

There are many things that you could describe, and you might describe the same thing differently in different paragraphs. For example, the couple might be *curious* in paragraph I, *concerned* in paragraph II, and *thrilled* in paragraph III.

Next to each noun, write ideas for adjectives that create a strong image. Avoid banned adjectives.

1. the couple _____ *curious, concerned, thrilled* _____

2. the object in the sky _____ *bright, massive, fiery* _____

3. the house _____ *dilapidated, modest, inherited* _____

4. the crater _____ *deep, wide, circular* _____

Strong Verb Dress-Up and -ly Adverb Dress-Up

Look at your KWO and write ideas for each.

1. List strong verbs and -ly adverbs to include in your first paragraph.

    strong verbs _____ *observed, struggled, wished* _____

    -ly adverbs _____ *curiously, daily, longingly* _____

2. List strong verbs and -ly adverbs to include in your second paragraph.

    strong verbs _____ *zoomed, struck, heard* _____

    -ly adverbs _____ *speedily, violently, instantly* _____

3. List strong verbs and -ly adverbs to include in your third paragraph.

    strong verbs _____ *disappeared, landed, revealed* _____

    -ly adverbs _____ *suddenly, powerfully, unexpectedly* _____

Look   at your KWO and consider clauses to include in your composition.

Vocabulary Practice

Listen   to someone read the vocabulary words for Lesson 13 aloud.

Speak   them aloud yourself.

Read   the definitions and sample sentences on the vocabulary cards.

Write   the part of speech and the definition beside each word.

dilapidated   *adjective; in bad condition because of age or lack of care*

mesmerized   *adjective; fascinated*

reveal   *verb; to make clearly known*

speedily   *adverb; moving quickly*

Think   about the words and their meanings so you can use them in your assignments.

    Institute for Excellence in Writing

Unit 5 Composition Checklist
Lesson 13: Meteorite

Writing
from
Pictures

Name: _____

Institute for
Excellence in
Writing

Listen. Speak. Read. Write. Think.

STRUCTURE

☐ MLA format (see Appendix I)   _____ 1 pt

☐ title centered and repeats 1–3 key words from final sentence   _____ 2 pts

☐ clincher sentences repeat or reflect 2–3 key words of central fact (highlight or bold) _____ 6 pts

☐ checklist on top, final draft, rough draft, key word outline   _____ 5 pts

STYLE

¶1 ¶2 ¶3 Dress-Ups (underline one of each)   (2 pts each)

☐ ☐ ☐ -ly adverb   _____ 6 pts

☐ ☐ ☐ *who/which* clause   _____ 6 pts

☐ ☐ ☐ strong verb   _____ 6 pts

☐ ☐ ☐ *because* clause   _____ 6 pts

☐ ☐ ☐ quality adjective   _____ 6 pts

☐ ☐ ☐ *www.asia* clause   _____ 6 pts

Sentence Openers (number; one of each as possible)   (2 pts each)

☐ ☐ ☐ [2] prepositional   _____ 6 pts

CHECK FOR BANNED WORDS (-1 pt for each use): think/thought, go/went, say/said,   _____ pts
good, bad, big, small

MECHANICS

☐ capitalization   _____ 1 pt

☐ end marks and punctuation   _____ 1 pt

☐ complete sentences   _____ 1 pt

☐ correct spelling   _____ 1 pt

VOCABULARY

☐ vocabulary words – label *(voc)* in left margin or after sentence

Total: _____ 60 pts
Custom Total: _____   pts

Checklist

Teachers are
free to adjust
a checklist by
requiring only
the stylistic
techniques that
have become
easy, plus one
new one. EZ+1

Intentionally blank so the checklist can be removed.

Lesson 14: Message in a Bottle

Structure: Unit 5: Writing from Pictures

Style: #3 -ly adverb opener

Subject: a series of pictures about a message in a bottle

UNIT 5: WRITING FROM PICTURES

Lesson 14: Message in a Bottle

Goals

- to practice the Unit 5 structural model
- to create a KWO from a series of three pictures
- to write a 3-paragraph composition from the KWO
- to add a new sentence opener: #3 -ly adverb opener
- to use new vocabulary words: *bob, cautiously, pen, resourceful*

Assignment Schedule

Day 1

1. Play the Question Game.
2. Review New Structure on page 121 and write your KWO.

Day 2

1. Review your KWO from Day 1 and complete Structure Practice.
2. Learn a new sentence opener, the #3 -ly adverb opener. Read New Style and complete Style Practice.
3. Look at the vocabulary cards for Lesson 14. Complete Vocabulary Practice.
4. Using your KWO as a guide, begin writing your 3-paragraph rough draft.
5. Go over the checklist. Put a check in the box for each requirement you have completed.

Day 3

1. Review all vocabulary words learned thus far.
2. Finish writing your 3-paragraph composition. Ensure that the clincher sentence of each paragraph repeats or reflects two or three key words of the central fact of the picture.
3. Turn in your rough draft to your editor with the completed checklist attached.

Day 4

1. Write or type a final draft, making any corrections your editor asked you to make.
2. Paperclip the checklist, final draft, rough draft, and KWO together. Hand them in.

Look at the series of pictures. The first picture is of a person on an empty beach writing something. What is he writing? Is it a plea for help or a treasure map or top secret information or a journal? Who is this person? What is his name? The second picture is a paper in a bottle floating in a large body of water. What body of water is it? How long has the bottle been floating? The third picture is a girl on a different beach holding the bottle and reading the paper. Who is she? How much time has passed? What is her reaction? After you discuss the pictures, remind the students to use key words to write what they see in the picture on the central fact line. Students come up with ideas that describe the event in order to write the rest of the paragraph. Asking questions is key.

UNIT 5: WRITING FROM PICTURES

Source

Message in a Bottle

I.

II.

III.

Sample

Key Word Outline

?

I.   Central fact: _____ *George, story, beach* _____

    1. _____ *father, angry, X writing* _____   who?

    2. _____ *G, X $$$, publish* _____   what?

    3. _____ *G, knows, story, excellent* _____   when?

    4. _____ ☹*, no one, cares* _____   where?

    5. _____ *story →* 🍾*, hopeful* _____   why?

Clincher repeats or reflects 2–3 key words of central fact.

how?

II.   Central fact: _____ 🍾*, story, floated → ocean* _____

    1. _____ *50 yrs,* 🍾*, bobbed, waves* _____   doing?

    2. _____ *yr after yr, X* 👀 _____   thinking?

    3. _____ *G, X hope, story, found* _____   feeling?

    4. _____ *++ yrs, dreamed, ++ stories* _____   saying?

    5. _____ 💬*grandchildren, stories, X write* _____   before?

Clincher repeats or reflects 2–3 key words of central fact.   after?

III. Central fact: _____ *Sarah, story,* 🍾*, beach* _____   outside?

    1. _____ 👀*,waded, grabbed,* 🍾*, ↑cork* _____

    2. _____ *unfolded, old, pages* _____

    3. _____ 👀*, read, shocked, ++great!* _____

    4. _____ *S, own, pub. company, excited!* 🍾 _____

    5. _____ *finally, contacted G, famous!* _____

Clincher repeats or reflects 2–3 key words of central fact.

Title repeats 1–3 key words from final sentence.

Structure Practice

Topic Sentence

Use your KWO to guide you as you write your composition. Begin by looking at the words on the central fact line, the words that indicate what you see in the picture.

If you wrote *George, story, beach* on the central fact line next to the first picture, your topic sentence could be

George began writing a **story** as he sat on the **beach.**

Use the key words that you wrote on the KWO next to the first central fact (the topic line) to write a sentence that tells what you see in the picture. Remember to highlight or bold the key words.

_____*Answers will vary.*_____

_____

Continue your composition by forming sentences from the key words placed on the KWO. When you reach the clincher line, write a sentence that repeats or reflects two or three key words of the central fact. The clincher for the sample above might be

George hoped someone would find the **story** that he had written on the **beach**.

If the opener modifies the whole sentence, you can usually say "It is _____ that ..."
adjective version (drop ly)

*↙ * Is the subject doing the verb in that manner? No comma*

"Rashly he severed the connection.
Is it rash he severed the connection?
Or did he sever it in a rash manner?

New Style

#3 -ly Adverb Opener

In this lesson you will learn another sentence opener: the #3 -ly adverb opener.

The -ly adverb opener is an -ly adverb placed at the beginning of a sentence. You have been using -ly adverbs as dress-ups. Here are examples of the -ly adverb opener:

> [3] Carefully Sarah pulled the cork out of the bottle.

> [3] Clearly, George was a skilled writer.

Notice:

1. An -ly adverb that begins a sentence is called an -ly adverb opener.
   Label it with a 3 in the left margin or place a [3] right before the sentence.

2. An -ly adverb that does not begin a sentence is called an -ly adverb dress-up.
   It is marked with an underline.

❟ If the -ly adverb opener modifies the verb, the comma is not needed.
   If the -ly adverb opener modifies the entire sentence, the comma is required.

Carefully Sarah *pulled* the cork out of the bottle. The -ly adverb modifies the verb, not the entire sentence. You cannot say it was careful that Sarah pulled the cork out of the bottle. The comma is not needed.

Clearly, *George was a skilled writer*. The -ly adverb does not modify the verb. *Clearly* modifies the entire sentence because you can say *It is clear that George was a skillful writer*. The comma is required.

Practice

Which -ly adverbs might open these sentences? Use a thesaurus or your vocabulary words or look at the -ly adverb word list on page 22, the *Portable Walls for Structure and Style Students,* or the IEW Writing Tools App. Label with a [3]. Do not underline the -ly adverb opener.

1. _____*[3] Anxiously*_____ the boy wrote a message.

2. _____*[3] Eventually,*_____ he tossed the bottle into the waves.

🖊 From now on, include two -ly adverbs—an opener and a dress-up—in each paragraph you write. Label the opener with a 3 in the margin or place a [3] before the sentence. Underline the dress-up.

Fortunately, the rain stopped.   Adversely, we can't go.
Pleasantly, the ~~wind~~ music played.
Restfully, she was sleeping.

Style Practice

#2 Prepositional Opener

Begin each sentence with a #2 prepositional opener. Follow the comma rule on page 113.

1. _____ *[2] On the beach* _____ he wrote the message.

2. _____ *[2] With a pencil in his hand,* _____ he began to write.

3. _____ *[2] After several years* _____ the bottle reached another beach.

Look at your KWO and consider openers to include in your composition.

Quality Adjective Dress-Up

Next to each noun, write ideas for adjectives that create a strong image. Avoid banned adjectives.

1. the boy _____ *young, talented, artistic, hopeful, resourceful*

2. the bottle _____ *small, ideal, glass, air-tight, perfect*

Name and describe two additional things the boy or girl might see, hear, or feel.

_____ *rough, large, powerful waves* _____

_____ *tattered, faded, torn paper* _____

Strong Verb Dress-Up and -ly Adverb Dress-Up

On the first line below each sentence, write strong verbs that could replace the italicized banned verb. On the second line write ideas for -ly adverbs that you could use with the strong verbs.

1. The boy *thought* someone would find the message.

   strong verbs _____ *hoped, believed, assumed*

   -ly adverbs _____ *hesitantly, firmly, foolishly*

2. The girl *went* in the water.

   strong verbs _____ *waded, tiptoed, plunged*

   -ly adverbs _____ *cautiously, carefully, boldly*

Suggested Answers

Not all students must complete the Style Practice exercises. Although there is nothing wrong with requiring students to complete the exercises, you may choose to assign only the exercises that students seem to struggle with the most.

Because Clause Dress-Up

Add a *because* clause to each sentence. Underline the word *because*.

1. He wrote a message <u>because</u> ___ _____ *he hoped someone would rescue him.*

2. The girl waded into the ocean <u>because</u> ____ *she wanted to grab the bottle.*

www.asia Clause Dress-Up

Add a *www.asia* clause to each sentence. Underline the first word of the clause.

1. The bottle bobbed ____ <u>*as*</u> *the waves carried it away.*

2. The boy wondered ____ <u>*if*</u> *anyone would find his message.*

Who/Which Clause Dress-Up

Combine the statements using the word *who* or *which*. Punctuate and mark correctly.

1. The girl strolled on the beach. She noticed a strange object in the water.

   The girl, <u>who</u> strolled on the beach, noticed a strange object in the water.

2. The message finally reached the shore. The message remained dry.

   The message, <u>which</u> finally reached the shore, remained dry.

Look   at your KWO and consider clauses to include in your composition.

Vocabulary Practice

Listen   to someone read the vocabulary words for Lesson 14 aloud.

Speak   them aloud yourself.

Read   the definitions and sample sentences on the vocabulary cards.

Write   the correct words in the blanks.

The boy was a __resourceful__ young man because he found a way to send a message.

He _____ _pen (ned)_ _____ a message and placed it in the bottle.

The bottle _____ _bob (bed)_ _____ on the rough waves for several weeks.

The girl _____ _cautiously_ _____ waded in the water to reach the bottle.

Think   about the words and their meanings so you can use them in your assignments.

Unit 5 Composition Checklist
Lesson 14: Message in a Bottle

Writing from Pictures

Name: _____

IEW | Institute for Excellence in Writing

STRUCTURE

☐ MLA format (see Appendix I) _____ 1 pt

☐ title centered and repeats 1–3 key words from final sentence _____ 2 pts

☐ clincher sentences repeat or reflect 2–3 key words of central fact (highlight or bold) _____ 5 pts

☐ checklist on top, final draft, rough draft, key word outline _____ 5 pts

STYLE

¶1 ¶2 ¶3 Dress-Ups (underline one of each)   (2 pts each)

☐ ☐ ☐ -ly adverb _____ 6 pts

☐ ☐ ☐ *who/which* clause _____ 6 pts

☐ ☐ ☐ strong verb _____ 6 pts

☐ ☐ ☐ *because* clause _____ 6 pts

☐ ☐ ☐ quality adjective _____ 6 pts

☐ ☐ ☐ *www.asia* clause _____ 6 pts

Sentence Openers (number; one of each as possible)   (2 pts each)

☐ ☐ ☐ [2] prepositional _____ 6 pts

☐ ☐ ☐ [3] -ly adverb _____ 6 pts

CHECK FOR BANNED WORDS (-1 pt for each use): think/thought, go/went, say/said, good, bad, big, small

MECHANICS

☐ capitalization _____ 1 pt

☐ end marks and punctuation _____ 1 pt

☐ complete sentences _____ 1 pt

☐ correct spelling _____ 1 pt

VOCABULARY

☐ vocabulary words – label *(voc)* in left margin or after sentence

Total: _____ 65 pts

Custom Total: _____ pts

Checklist

Teachers are free to adjust a checklist by requiring only the stylistic techniques that have become easy, plus one new one. EZ+1

Intentionally blank so the checklist can be removed.

Lesson 15: Science Lab

Structure:	Unit 5: Writing from Pictures
Style:	no new style
Subject:	a series of pictures about a science lab

Lesson 15: Science Lab

UNIT 5: WRITING FROM PICTURES

Lesson 15: Science Lab

Goals

- to practice the Unit 5 structural model
- to create a KWO from a series of three pictures
- to write a 3-paragraph composition from the KWO
- to use new vocabulary words: *ardently, detect, methodically, rancid*

Assignment Schedule

Day 1

1. Play Around the World or Vocabulary Lightning.
2. Write your KWO.

Day 2

1. Review your KWO from Day 1 and complete Structure Practice.
2. Complete Style Practice.
3. Look at the vocabulary cards for Lesson 15. Complete Vocabulary Practice.
4. Using your KWO as a guide, begin writing your 3-paragraph rough draft.
5. Go over the checklist. Put a check in the box for each requirement you have completed.

Day 3

1. Review all vocabulary words learned thus far.
2. Finish writing your 3-paragraph composition. Ensure that the clincher sentence of each paragraph repeats or reflects two or three key words of the central fact of the picture.
3. Turn in your rough draft to your editor with the completed checklist attached.

Day 4

1. Write or type a final draft, making any corrections your editor asked you to make.
2. Paperclip the checklist, final draft, rough draft, and KWO together. Hand them in.

Look at the series of pictures. The first picture shows two scientists mixing chemicals in a science lab. You may give them names and tell the specific chemicals they are mixing. The second picture shows a a cloud of smoke. Are the scientists still there? The third picture shows one scientist beside a wisp of smoke. What happened to the other scientist? Did he run out of the room? Did he transform into something? Did he disappear? Was he incinerated? After you discuss the pictures, remind the students to use key words to write what they see in the picture on the central fact line. Students come up with ideas that describe the event in order to write the rest of the paragraph. Asking questions is key.

Source

Science Lab

I.

II.

III.

Sample

Key Word Outline

I. Central fact: _____ *2 scientists, lab, chemicals* _____

    1. _____ *randomly, tested, mixtures* _____

    2. _____ *desired, new, famous* _____

    3. _____ *++ mixtures, ++ failures, frustrated* _____

    4. _____ 💡, *b. soda + ammonia + acid* _____

    5. _____ *carefully, mixed, watched* _____

Clincher repeats or reflects 2–3 key words of central fact.

II. Central fact: _____ *lab, cloud, smoke* _____

    1. _____ *flask, hot, liquid* 🫧 _____

    2. _____ *smelled, rancid, burned* 👀 _____

    3. _____ *excited, made, discovery* _____

    4. _____ *paper, recorded, results* _____

    5. _____ *X breathe, X see, rm. rumbled* _____

Clincher repeats or reflects 2–3 key words of central fact.

III. Central fact: _____ *1 scientist, steam, lab* _____

    1. _____ *smoke, cleared,* ♂ *talked* _____

    2. _____ *shocked! where? X* 👀*, scared* _____

    3. _____ ♂ *"here,"* ♀ *touched, felt* ♂ _____

    4. _____ *excited, unbelievable, invisible* _____

    5. _____ ♂ + ♀ *screamed, "Worked! Famous"* _____

Clincher repeats or reflects 2–3 key words of central fact.

Title repeats 1–3 key words from final sentence.

?

who?

what?

when?

where?

why?

how?

doing?

thinking?

feeling?

saying?

before?

after?

outside?

Structure Practice

Topic Sentence

Use your KWO to guide you as you write your composition. Begin by looking at the words on the central fact line, the words that indicate what you see in the picture.

If you wrote *2 scientists, lab, chemicals* on the central fact line next to the first picture, your topic sentence could be

> Two **scientists** carefully mixed **chemicals** in the science **lab**.

Use the key words that you wrote on the KWO next to the first central fact (the topic line) to write a sentence that tells what you see in the picture. Remember to highlight or bold the key words.

Answers will vary.

Continue your composition by forming sentences from the key words placed on the KWO. When you reach the clincher line, write a sentence that repeats or reflects two or three key words of the central fact. The clincher for the sample above might be

> In the **lab** both **scientists** held their breath as the **chemicals** reacted.

Style Practice

#2 Prepositional Opener

Begin each sentence with a #2 prepositional opener. Follow the comma rule on page 113.

1. _____[2] In the lab_____ the scientists worked together.

2. _____[2] Out of the flask_____ a cloud of smoke rose.

#3 -ly Adverb Opener

Begin each sentence with a #3 -ly adverb opener. Follow the comma rule on page 133.

1. _____[3] Violently_____ the mixture exploded.

2. _____[3] Clearly,_____ someone was missing.

Look   at your KWO and consider openers to include in your composition.

www.asia Clause Dress-Up

Write a sentence with a *www.asia* clause that you could use in your composition. Remember to add the clause to a sentence that is already complete. Punctuate and mark correctly.

The flask became hot <u>when</u> the chemicals combined.

Because Clause Dress-Up

Write a sentence with a *because* clause that you could use in your composition. Remember to add the clause to a sentence that is already complete. Punctuate and mark correctly.

She screamed <u>because</u> they had successfully developed an invisibility potion.

Who/Which Clause Dress-Up

Write a sentence with a *who/which* clause that you could use in your composition. Punctuate and mark correctly.

The laboratory, <u>which</u> suddenly grew dark and cold, shook.

Quality Adjective Dress-Up

Next to each noun, write ideas for adjectives that create a strong image. Avoid banned adjectives.

1. the flask   *wide-bottomed, glass, hot, full*

2. the smoke   *colorful, thick, pungent, extensive*

Name and describe two additional things the scientists might see, hear, or feel.

bright, flashing light

sudden deafening explosion

Strong Verb Dress-Up and -ly Adverb Dress-Up

Look at your KWO and write ideas for each.

1. List strong verbs and -ly adverbs to include in your first paragraph.

   strong verbs _____ *tested, desired, mixed* _____

   -ly adverbs _____ *methodically, ardently, thoroughly* _____

2. List strong verbs and -ly adverbs to include in your second paragraph.

   strong verbs _____ *detected, burned, recorded* _____

   -ly adverbs _____ *gradually, instantly, accurately* _____

3. List strong verbs and -ly adverbs to include in your third paragraph.

   strong verbs _____ *cleared, touched, screamed* _____

   -ly adverbs _____ *eventually, cautiously, impulsively* _____

Vocabulary Practice

Listen   to someone read the vocabulary words for Lesson 15 aloud.

Speak   them aloud yourself.

Read   the definitions and sample sentences on the vocabulary cards.

Write   the words that match the definitions.

   _____ *methodically* _____   in a systematic and orderly way

   _____ *rancid* _____   having an offensive or unpleasant smell or taste

   _____ *ardently* _____   with intense emotion

   _____ *detect* _____   to discover the existence of

Think   about the words and their meanings so you can use them in your assignments.

Unit 5 Composition Checklist
Lesson 15: Science Lab

Writing
from
Pictures

Name: _____

IEW Institute for Excellence in Writing
Listen. Speak. Read. Write. Think!

STRUCTURE

☐ MLA format (see Appendix I) _____ 1 pt

☐ title centered and repeats 1–3 key words from **final sentence** _____ 2 pts

☐ clincher sentences repeat or reflect 2–3 key words of central fact (highlight or bold) _____ 5 pts

☐ checklist on top, final draft, rough draft, **key word outline** _____ 5 pts

STYLE

¶1 ¶2 ¶3 Dress-Ups (underline one of each) (2 pts each)

☐ ☐ ☐ -ly adverb _____ 6 pts

☐ ☐ ☐ *who/which* clause _____ 6 pts

☐ ☐ ☐ strong verb _____ 6 pts

☐ ☐ ☐ *because* clause _____ 6 pts

☐ ☐ ☐ quality adjective _____ 6 pts

☐ ☐ ☐ *www.asia* clause _____ 6 pts

Sentence Openers (number; one of each as possible) (2 pts each)

☐ ☐ ☐ [2] prepositional _____ 6 pts

☐ ☐ ☐ [3] -ly adverb _____ 6 pts

CHECK FOR BANNED WORDS (-1 pt for each use): think/thought, go/went, say/said, good, bad, big, small _____ pts

MECHANICS

☐ capitalization _____ 1 pt

☐ end marks and punctuation _____ 1 pt

☐ complete sentences _____ 1 pt

☐ correct spelling _____ 1 pt

VOCABULARY

☐ vocabulary words – label *(voc)* in left margin or after sentence

Total: _____ 65 pts

Custom Total: _____ pts

Checklist

Teachers are free to adjust a checklist by requiring only the stylistic techniques that have become easy, plus one new one. EZ+1

UNIT 5: WRITING FROM PICTURES

Intentionally blank so the checklist can be removed.

Lesson 16: Nikola Tesla

Structure:	Unit 6: Summarizing Multiple References source and fused outlines	
Style:	no new style	
Subject:	Nikola Tesla	

Teaching Writing: Structure and Style

Watch the sections for Unit 6: Summarizing Multiple References. At IEW.com/twss-help reference the TWSS Viewing Guides.

UNIT 6: SUMMARIZING MULTIPLE REFERENCES

Lesson 16: Nikola Tesla

Goals

- to learn the Unit 6 Summarizing Multiple References structural model
- to create source outlines from multiple references
- to create a fused outline
- to write a 1-paragraph report
- to review vocabulary words

Assignment Schedule

Day 1

1. Complete the Review.

2. Read New Structure—Summarizing Multiple References.

3. Read "Nikola Tesla" and take notes about Tesla's work regarding alternating current with Westinghouse by writing a source outline.

4. Read "Electrical Currents" and take additional notes about Tesla's work regarding alternating current with Westinghouse by writing another source outline. Note that the words on the topic line for this source outline are the same as the previous source outline because you are taking notes about the same topic. As you take notes, do not include facts that you already noted from the first source.

5. Using notes from both source outlines, write a fused outline.

Day 2

1. Review your fused outline.

2. Complete Style Practice.

3. Complete Vocabulary Practice. There are no new words for this lesson.

4. Using your fused outline as a guide, begin writing your rough draft.

5. Go over the checklist. Put a check in the box for each requirement you have completed.

Day 3

1. Review all vocabulary words learned thus far.

2. Finish writing your 1-paragraph report. Follow the topic-clincher rule.

3. Turn in your rough draft to your editor with the completed checklist attached.

Day 4

1. Write or type a final draft, making any corrections your editor asked you to make.

2. Paperclip the checklist, final draft, rough draft, and KWO together. Hand them in.

In this new unit the KWO is formed by taking key words from interesting and important facts, similar to Unit 4. In this unit students receive multiple sources related to each topic. For each topic students take 3–5 notes from each source to form a source outline. Using the source outlines, students combine the notes to form a fused outline. Help students limit which facts they choose.

Each paragraph is about a specific topic and should follow the topic-clincher rule.

Review

Review

The topic sentence and the clincher sentence MUST repeat or reflect two or three key words.

The subject is the thing you research.

A topic is a division or part of the subject.

There are numerous correct answers for number 3.

1. What is the topic-clincher rule?

2. What is the difference between a subject and a topic?

3. If weather is your subject, list four possible topics.

   clouds _____   *wind* _____

   air pressure _____   *forecast* _____

4. When you write your topic on the KWO, what pattern do you follow?

   subject _____ , *topic* _____ , *one more word about the topic*

Read this page to introduce the new structural unit, Unit 6: Summarizing Multiple References. Like Unit 4, students take notes from the source text to write a report. Because there are two source texts, students will take notes from both texts and then fuse them into one KWO. Students will write from the fused outline.

New Structure

Summarizing Multiple References

In Unit 6 you will again write reports. Remember when you write a report, your facts must be organized into paragraphs. Just like Unit 4 you will find the facts to support your topic in source texts, except this time you will use several sources from which to gather facts.

Each paragraph will begin with a topic sentence, contain facts, and end with a clincher sentence.

1 topic = 1 paragraph

Topic Sentence

The topic sentence tells what the paragraph is about. When you write the KWO, ask yourself, "What will the paragraph be about?" As you answer, write two or three key words on the Roman numeral line of the source outlines and the fused outline. The topic of the paragraph for this lesson will be given to you.

Facts

Gather facts by writing source outlines. Create one source outline for each source text. Once you have chosen your topic, read each of your sources and look for interesting or important facts that support the topic. Select three to five facts from each source and place them on the appropriate source outline using key words, symbols, numbers, and abbreviations.

Organize facts by writing a fused outline. Select five to seven facts from the source outlines and transfer them to the fused outline.

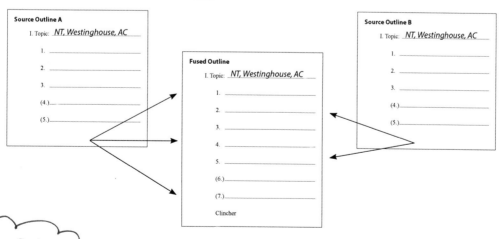

Clincher Sentence

The clincher sentence reminds the reader what the paragraph was about. Like Unit 4 the KWO ends with the word *clincher*. Do not place key words on the clincher line. Instead when you write your rough draft, repeat or reflect two or three key words from the topic line.

Source Text A

Nikola Tesla

In 1884 inventor Nikola Tesla moved from Europe to New York City to work with Thomas Edison. Tesla and Edison were experts in electricity. They worked together with direct current (DC) power, which is electricity that cannot change direction. A few years later Edison offered Tesla $50,000 to fix a DC generator. Tesla completed the work, but Edison refused to pay him, so Tesla quit his job. Eventually he went to work for George Westinghouse, Thomas Edison's rival. Westinghouse had learned about Tesla's accomplishments and bought many of his patents, which gave him the right to use his ideas. Together they worked on a plan to use alternating current (AC) power, which is electricity that can change direction, to bring electricity to the 1893 Chicago World's Fair. Edison also wanted to power the fair, but he preferred DC power. Since AC power would cost less, the contract was given to Westinghouse and Tesla. AC power was soon adopted by the nation and the world. Westinghouse also used Tesla's ideas to build the first hydroelectric dam at Niagara Falls. This was a dream come true for Nikola Tesla. As a boy he had seen a picture of the falls and imagined building a waterwheel under it. Now, many years later, these two men worked together to power Buffalo, New York, a city twenty miles away. This is something DC power would not be able to do in an affordable and safe manner. Tesla proved that AC power is safe and affordable. Additionally, he paved the way for many modern developments such as remote controls, fluorescent lights, x-rays, and robots.

Source Text B

Electrical Currents

When inventor Nikola Tesla was twenty-eight years old, he moved to New York City to work for Thomas Edison. Edison owned many factories that supported direct current (DC), a way to transfer electricity from one place to another. Tesla had recently discovered alternating current (AC). While working on the dynamos, machines that make power, Tesla tried to convince Edison to consider AC. Edison refused. Tesla left Edison and dug ditches for a time before starting his own company. He presented his patented ideas about AC to the American Institute of Electrical Engineers. When businessman and engineer George Westinghouse heard about his inventions, he hoped to use them to beat his rival, Thomas Edison. Westinghouse purchased the patents and permission to use Tesla's inventions. He then competed with Edison to see which company would be selected to power the 1893 Chicago World's Fair. Edison's DC technology would cost $554,000 to light up the event. Tesla's AC technology would cost $399,000. Even though Edison tried to convince the public that AC was not safe, Westinghouse and Tesla's bid was accepted. On May 1, President Grover Cleveland flipped the switch, and over 100,000 lights amazed the people who were at the fair. AC technology had won! Two years later, the world's first hydroelectric power plant was built with thirteen of Tesla's patents. Using AC technology, it powered Buffalo, New York, a city twenty miles away. Today, a statue of Nikola Tesla stands in Ontario, Canada, commemorating Tesla's greatest accomplishment.

Students must limit which facts they choose to note. Help them look only for the most interesting or most important facts that best explain Tesla's work regarding alternating current with Westinghouse.

Sample

Source Outlines

The assigned topic for this paragraph is AC. The titles of the source texts are on the Source line. The assigned topic is written in key words on the Roman numeral topic lines. Complete each source outline by looking at the appropriate source and noting three to five interesting or important facts about the topic.

1 paragraph = 1 topic

Topic: *Westinghouse*

Source A: *Nikola Tesla*

I. Topic: *NT, Westinghouse, alternating current*

1.   *T + Westinghouse, AC (⇆), 1893 Chicago World Fair*

2.   *AC --$, contract, T + W*

3.   *100,000 💡, AC, US + world*

(4.)   *AC, 1st, hydroelectric dam, Niagara Falls*

(5.)   *AC, safe, affordable*

Source B: *Electrical Currents*

I. Topic: *NT, Westinghouse, alternating current*

1.   *T, 28, moved, NY, discovered, AC*

2.   *1893, Chicago World's Fair, AC power*

3.   *DC cost ++ $$, AC -- $*

(4.)   *Pres. Grover Cleveland, 100,000 💡, AC, won*

(5.)   *AC, powered, Buffalo, NY 20 mi., away*

The topic on the source and fused outlines is identical. This is because students choose a topic to write about and then gather facts from both sources about the chosen topic. Only the fused outline has a clincher line because students write the paragraph using the fused outline.

Sample
Fused Outline

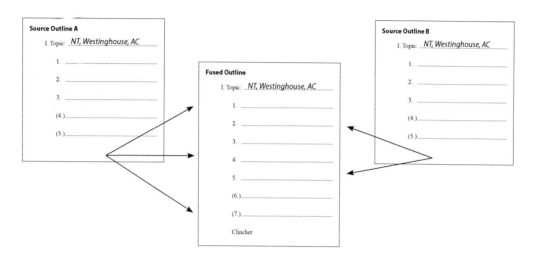

Select five to seven facts from the source outlines to transfer to the fused outline.

I. Topic: *NT, Westinghouse, alternating current*

1. _____ *T, 28, moved, NY, discovered, AC* _____

2. _____ *T + Westinghouse, AC, (⇆), 1893, Chicago World Fair* _____

3. _____ *AC -- $, contract, T + W* _____

4. _____ *Pres. Grover Cleveland, 100,000 💡 AC, won* _____

5. _____ *1st, hydroelectric dam, Niagara Falls* _____

(6.) _____ *powered, Buffalo, NY, 20 mi., away* _____

(7.) _____ *safe, affordable, US, world* _____

Clincher

Tell back the facts on the fused outline in complete sentences. Fix any notes you do not understand. For the clincher, repeat or reflect two or three key words from the topic line.

Reminder

The source outlines contain facts from the source texts. To create the fused outline, some facts are omitted. Other facts can be combined to create a fused outline that logically supports the topic.

Style Practice

#2 Prepositional Opener and #3 -ly Adverb Opener

Write sentences that can be used in your composition.

1. #2 prepositional opener _____

   [2] During the fair President Cleveland switched on 100,000 lights.

2. #3 -ly adverb opener _____

   [3] Obviously, AC power won because it cost less to power the fair.

Dress-Ups

Although this lesson does not contain specific practice exercises for the six dress-ups you have learned, you must include one of each in the paragraph you write. Look at your KWO and consider where you can include various clauses as well as strong verbs, quality adjectives, and -ly adverbs. When you write your paper, follow your checklist!

Vocabulary Practice

Think   about the words and their meanings.

   Which vocabulary words could you use in this assignment?

   desperately, ingenious, concluded, mesmerized

Unit 6 Composition Checklist
Lesson 16: Nikola Tesla

Summarizing
Multiple
References

Name: _____

IEW | Institute for Excellence in Writing

STRUCTURE

☐ MLA format (see Appendix I) _____ 2 pts

☐ title centered and repeats 1–3 key words from final sentence _____ 2 pts

☐ topic-clincher sentences repeat or reflect 2–3 key words (highlight or bold) _____ 6 pts

☐ checklist on top, final draft, rough draft, key word outline _____ 5 pts

STYLE

¶1 Dress-Ups (underline one of each)   (2 pts each)

☐ -ly adverb _____ 2 pts

☐ *who/which* clause _____ 2 pts

☐ strong verb _____ 2 pts

☐ *because* clause _____ 2 pts

☐ quality adjective _____ 2 pts

☐ *www.asia* clause _____ 2 pts

Sentence Openers (number; one of each as possible)   (2 pts each)

☐ [2] prepositional _____ 2 pts

☐ [3] -ly adverb _____ 2 pts

CHECK FOR BANNED WORDS (-1 pt for each use): think/thought, go/went, say/said, good, bad, big, small _____ pts

MECHANICS

☐ capitalization _____ 1 pt

☐ end marks and punctuation _____ 1 pt

☐ complete sentences _____ 1 pt

☐ correct spelling _____ 1 pt

VOCABULARY

☐ vocabulary words – label *(voc)* in left margin or after sentence

Total: _____ 35 pts

Custom Total: _____ pts

Checklist

Teachers are free to adjust a checklist by requiring only the stylistic techniques that have become easy, plus one new one. EZ+1

Intentionally blank so the checklist can be removed.

Lesson 17: Albert Einstein, Part 1

Structure:	Unit 6: Summarizing Multiple References
Style:	#6 vss opener
Subject:	physicist Albert Einstein

Lesson 17: Albert Einstein, Part 1

UNIT 6: SUMMARIZING MULTIPLE REFERENCES

Lesson 17: Albert Einstein, Part 1

Goals

- to practice the Unit 6 structural model
- to practice scanning multiple sources to determine topics for research
- to create source outlines from multiple references
- to create a fused outline
- to write the first paragraph of a 3-paragraph report
- to add a new sentence opener: #6 vss
- to use new vocabulary words: *accept, accomplish, inquisitively, technical*

Assignment Schedule

Day 1

1. Play No-Noose Hangman with phrases provided in the Teacher's Manual.

2. In Lessons 17–18 you will use more than one source of information to write a 3-paragraph report. This lesson contains three different source texts about Albert Einstein. You are going to use some of the information in these articles to write your report—one paragraph at a time.

3. Before you begin taking notes, you must determine what topics are available to write about. Scan the paragraphs in each source text, reading just enough of each paragraph to discern its topic. Write the topic of each paragraph in the margin.

4. Complete Structure Practice.

5. Choose the topic for your first paragraph about Einstein and write the topic on the topic line on page 166. Complete the source outlines.

6. Using notes from your source outlines, write a fused outline.

Day 2

1. Review your fused outline.

2. Learn a new sentence opener, the #6 vss opener. Read New Style and complete Style Practice.

3. Look at the vocabulary cards for Lesson 17. Complete Vocabulary Practice.

4. Using your fused outline as a guide, begin writing your rough draft.

5. Go over the checklist. Put a check in the box for each requirement you have completed.

In Lessons 17–18 students will follow the same process introduced in Lesson 16 to write a 3-paragraph report. The subject (Albert Einstein) is assigned, but students will need to choose their own three topics. Before students can choose topics to write about, they must scan the source texts and determine which topics are covered in the source material.

No-Noose Hangman

For this lesson use the following phrases and bonus questions:

CLEVER, ORIGINAL, AND INVENTIVE

Bonus: What is the vocabulary word? *ingenious*

FUSED OUTLINE

Bonus: What is the a fused outline? *An outline made by selecting facts from multiple source outlines. It is the outline used to write the paragraph.*

Exemplar

The Exemplars file contains a student's completed assignment for Lessons 17–18. The example is for the teacher and not intended to be used by the student.

See the blue page for download instructions.

Day 3

1. Review all vocabulary words learned thus far.

2. Finish writing your paragraph. Follow the topic-clincher rule.

3. Turn in your rough draft to your editor with the completed checklist attached.

Day 4

1. Write or type a final draft, making any corrections your editor asked you to make.

2. Paperclip the checklist, final draft, rough draft, and KWO together. Hand them in.

Study for Vocabulary Quiz 4. It will cover words from Lessons 1–17.

Help students find topics by reading each paragraph and asking, "What is this paragraph about?"

Source Text A

Albert Einstein

early life

Albert Einstein was born on March 14, 1879, in Ulm, Germany. He did not speak until he was four. When he did, he mumbled softly to himself and repeated the same phrase over and over. The family maid called him the dopey one. However, he loved math, and by age fourteen he understood calculus. Although he excelled at math, he failed the language and history portions of a college entrance exam when he was sixteen. The next year he passed the exam, and even though he was below the age required for admission, he became a student at Polytech in Zürich, Switzerland. He graduated in 1900 at age twenty-one, but he could not find a teaching job. Finally, he took a job at a patent office. The work was easy for him, so he spent time thinking, imagining, and writing papers.

career

In 1905 Einstein published four papers in a well-respected scientific journal. This was a turning point in his scientific career. After he received his Ph.D. in physics, he was offered a teaching position in Berlin. During this time he continued to imagine and work out math problems. In 1909 he began teaching theoretical physics at the University of Zurich. In 1916 he published "The Foundation of the General Theory of Relativity," a paper he considered his masterpiece. In this paper Einstein wrote that light bends when it is affected by gravity. During a 1919 solar eclipse, scientists found that Dr. Einstein was right. Almost overnight Einstein became famous. He visited the United States in 1921, and that same year he won a Nobel Prize in physics. He was celebrated as a hero.

later years

As he grew older, Einstein spent more time teaching, researching, and promoting peace. He learned he could think more clearly while playing the violin or sailing his boat. Because he did not care about public opinion, he was often seen with uncombed flyaway hair and in a baggy shirt and pants with no socks. This gave him a humorous appearance. Another oddity was that he did not drive a car. When Europe became increasingly influenced by the Nazi's hatred for Jews and intellectuals (Einstein was both), he moved to the United States. In 1933 he settled in Princeton, New Jersey. In 1939 Einstein and two friends wrote a letter to President Roosevelt, alerting him of their suspicions that Germany was creating an atomic bomb. The race was on to see who would develop the atomic bomb first. In 1943 the United States, using Einstein's discoveries, dropped two atomic bombs on Japan. Einstein was horrified to learn that the bombs were dropped on civilians. In 1955 he wrote a letter asking the world to renounce all atomic weapons. He died one week later on April 11, 1955. His ashes were scattered in a secret place, but his brain and eyes were preserved.

legacy

Einstein accomplished many things in his life, but he is most famous for the theory of relativity and his equation $E=mc^2$. He proved atoms exist. His ideas helped develop technology to build spaceships, computers, cell phones, lasers, global positioning systems (GPS), and solar power. He is considered the most intelligent man of the twentieth century.

Works Consulted (fictitious)

Doe, Jane. "Einstein." *World History*, The Institute for World History, 5 June 2023,
    IWH.edu/history.

Source Text B

Albert Einstein Genius

early life

Albert Einstein lived his early life in the European countries of Germany, Italy, and Switzerland. He was born in Germany in 1879. Thomas Edison had just invented the light bulb. He did well in math and science, but his language and history teachers were unhappy with his studies. His Greek teacher told him that he would never achieve anything. However, many years later when Einstein was a young man, he published several articles that made him famous for the equation $E=mc^2$.

career

The year 1905 was called the year of miracles for Einstein's scientific career. While he was working as a clerk in a patent office, Einstein published four articles in a physics scientific journal. The first paper explained that light was made of particles called photons. The second proved the existence of atoms. In the third paper, Einstein explained that the speed of light did not change. This is called special relativity. The fourth paper elaborated on energy and matter being related, which led to atomic energy. However, the paper that brought him the most honor was his 1917 paper "The Foundation of the General Theory of Relativity." In this paper Einstein showed that matter causes space to curve, and as a result, gravity causes light to bend. During the 1919 solar eclipse, scientists confirmed this. Einstein became famous, and many universities in Europe and the United States wanted to hire him.

In his later years, Einstein decided to leave Europe because Hitler and the Nazis were forcing Germany and other nations to turn against Jewish people like Einstein. When he first visited the United States in 1921, he was given a hero's welcome by twenty thousand fans in New York City. Since free speech was

allowed in the United States, he moved there. When Hitler came to power in 1933,

Einstein was a guest lecturer at Caltech in Pasadena, California. In the spring

later years of that year, Einstein visited Winston Churchill, the Prime Minister of England,

and asked him to help other Jewish scientists escape from Germany, which he

did. Einstein became a United States citizen in 1940 and settled in Princeton,

New Jersey. There he worked on his "Theory of Everything," played his violin,

and sailed his boat. He was an avid smoker and believed watching the smoke

dissipate helped him to think. In 1945 scientists used Einstein's findings to create

the atomic bomb, and two bombs were dropped on Japan. This ended World War

II, but Einstein was upset that so many civilians had been killed. He wrote about

preventing war until he died in 1955.

Einstein's many accomplishments are still well-known. In 1999 he was

named the Person of the Century by *Time Magazine*. Many schools and universities

have buildings named after the famous scientist. At Caltech there is a gargoyle of

Einstein with his violin, and at the University of Oregon, a wall sculpture shows

legacy Einstein with his tongue sticking out. Both honor Einstein, whose scientific

discoveries led to today's use of solar power, nuclear power plants, electronics,

computers, cell phones, bar code scanners, spaceships, and further study of black

holes. Although he could not remember names, dates, and phone numbers, Einstein

was a genius who made the world a better place.

Works Consulted (fictitious)

Smith, Andrew. "Einstein's Discoveries." *Famous Inventors*, Smart Publishers, 2020.

Source Text C

A Brilliant Thinker

The most famous scientist from the twentieth century, Albert Einstein, spent his early years thinking, imagining, and asking questions. His mother was a musician, who taught Albert to play the piano and violin. His father was an engineer, who wanted Albert to become a civil engineer. Young Einstein loved math, and he asked many questions at school. This led his teachers to call him disruptive. He also missed many classes at the university, so when he graduated and wanted to become a teacher, his professors did not recommend him. He took a job in a patent office. The work was easy for Einstein, giving him more time for imagining and thinking. While he was reviewing other people's patents, he invented a type of hearing aid. More importantly, he studied physics, a field of science that examines motion, matter, energy, and forces, and he completed his Ph.D.

early life

Einstein published many papers during his scientific career. In 1905 the same year he earned his doctorate in physics, he had four papers published in the *Annals of Physics*. His only tools were paper, pencils, and his imagination. He once said, "The true sign of intelligence is not knowledge but imagination." He received the Nobel Prize in 1921 for his discovery that light is made of particles called photons. That same year he visited the United States for the first time, and 20,000 people greeted him in New York City. He respected the American principle of free speech and their belief that hard work could help them get far. However, he found that some Americans were not well-respected, and later he would devote efforts to the Civil Rights movement.

career

later years

Einstein spent his later years in the United States. He wanted to be free from the Nazis who aimed their hate at Jews and intellectuals. In 1939 Einstein signed a letter addressed to President F.D. Roosevelt warning him that the Nazis were developing an atomic bomb. It is unclear whether this led to the United States using Einstein's discoveries to build a bomb a few years later. What is certain is that two bombs were dropped on Japan, ending World War II. Because of the destruction caused by the bombs, Einstein was deeply saddened and spent much of his time trying to prevent the use of these weapons in the future. Because he was Jewish and loved peace, he was asked to be the president of Israel. He politely declined. He spent his last years doing what he loved most: sailing his boat, playing the violin, following politics, and thinking about his theories. He died in 1955 in Princeton, New Jersey.

legacy

Even though Einstein could not remember names, dates, or keep his desk tidy, he accomplished much. He is most famous for his equation $E=mc^2$, which states that energy equals mass multiplied by the speed of light, then multiplied again. When atoms are fused, energy is released. This can result in light and power. This and other theories that Einstein described in his papers and lectures made possible the study of atoms and photons. It also led to the invention of nuclear energy, computers, cell phones, satellites, and global positioning system or GPS. Einstein accomplished so much that *Time Magazine* named him the Person of the Century in 1999.

Works Consulted (fictitious)

"Albert Einstein." *Anderson's Encyclopedia*, ABC Publishers, 2021.

Structure Practice

Identifying the Topic

Read the source text and then fill in these blanks.

1. The subject for this lesson is ___*Albert Einstein*___

2. Possible topics include

Source Text A	Source Text B	Source Text C
early life	*early life*	*early life*
career	*career*	*career*
later years	*later years*	*later years*
legacy	*legacy*	*legacy*

3. On the KWO indicate the topics on the topic lines following this pattern:
    subject, *topic*, one more word *about the topic*.

Students begin by choosing a topic from the list on the previous page and writing it after First Topic.

Guide students to write three words on the line after each Roman numeral. Because this becomes one paragraph, every topic line contains the same three words. The subject is *Albert Einstein* (abbreviated AE). The topic is the word written after First Topic. Now write one more word *about the topic*.

The term *early life* is a compound word and counts as one word on the KWO.

Sample
Source Outlines

The topic sentence tells what a paragraph is about.
Write the topic of your first paragraph on the line below.

1 paragraph = 1 topic

First Topic: ___*early life*___

Using key words, write the topic on the Roman numeral line of each source outline: *subject*, *topic*, one more word *about the topic*. Each topic line will have the same words. Look at the appropriate paragraphs of the source texts and note three to five interesting facts about the topic.

Source A: *Albert Einstein*

I. Topic: *AE, early life, education*

1.   *X speak, 4, mumbled, repeated*

2.   *♡ math, 14, calculus, X language*

3.   *↓ age, student, Polytech*

(4.)   *graduated, 21, X teaching, ✔ patent*

(5.)   *easy, thinking, writing*

Source B: *Albert Einstein Genius*

I. Topic: *AE, early life, education*

1.   *✔ math, science, X history*

2.   *Greek teacher, X achieve*

3.   *published, articles, formula E=mc²*

(4.)

(5.)

Sample

Source C: *A Brilliant Thinker*

I. Topic: _____ *AE, early life, education* _____

   1. _____ *thinking, imagining, asking ?* _____

   2. _____ *♡ math, asked ++?* _____

   3. _____ *missed, ++ classes → X recommend* _____

   (4.) _____ *studied, physics, Ph.D.* _____

   (5.) _____ *published, articles, formula E=mc²* _____

Fused Outline

Place the topic you are writing about on the topic line. Select five to seven facts from the source outlines to transfer to the fused outline.

I. Topic: _____ *AE, early life, education* _____

   1. _____ *X, speak, 4, mumbled, repeated* _____

   2. _____ *thinking, imagining, asking ?* _____

   3. _____ *♡ math, 14, calculus, X language* _____

   4. _____ *Greek teacher, X achieve* _____

   5. _____ *studied, physics, Ph.D.* _____

   (6.) _____ *published, articles, formula E=mc²* _____

   (7.) _____

Clincher

Tell back the facts on the fused outline in complete sentences. Fix any notes you do not understand. For the clincher, repeat or reflect two or three key words from the topic line.

New Style

#6 Vss Opener

#6 Vss Opener

The #6 vss opener must contain a written subject and verb.

Challenge advanced students to include a strong verb so that their very short sentences pack a punch.

In this lesson you will learn another sentence opener: the #6 very short sentence (vss).

This opener is simply a short sentence that contains two to five words. Remember that variety in sentence structure is important in good writing. In each paragraph you should have some sentences that are long, some that are of medium length, and some that are short.

Purposefully adding a very short sentence will help break up the pattern of sentences in a stylish way. It catches the reader's attention. As a result, it is best placed in a spot where you would like to emphasize something. Here is a portion of Source C, which contains a very short sentence.

> Because of the destruction caused by the bombs, Einstein was deeply saddened and spent much of his time trying to prevent the use of these weapons in the future. Because he was Jewish and loved peace, he was asked to be the President of the Israel nation. [6] He politely declined. He spent his last years doing what he loved most: sailing, playing the violin, following politics, and thinking about his theories.

Notice:

1. A very short sentence contains at least two but no more than five words. Each word counts as one.

    Albert Einstein studied motion and energy. (not a vss)

    Although *Albert Einstein* is one name, it counts as two words.

2. A very short sentence is a complete sentence. It is not a fragment.

    Einstein studied physics. (sentence)

    Success at last! (fragment)

3. To indicate a very short sentence, label it with a 6 in the left margin or place a [6] right before the sentence.

Practice

Write a sentence with a #6 vss opener. Label it with a [6].

[6] He passed the exam.

 From now on, each paragraph you write should include a #6 vss opener. Label it with a 6 in the margin or place a [6] before the sentence.

    Institute for Excellence in Writing

Style Practice

Sentence Openers

Write sentences that can be used in your composition.

1. #2 prepositional opener ___*[2] As a young boy Einstein did not speak.*___

2. #3 -ly adverb opener ___*[3] Regrettably, Einstein's teacher told him he would never accomplish anything.*___

3. #6 vss opener, 2–5 words ___*[6] Einstein proved his teacher wrong.*___

Dress-Ups

Strong Verb Dress-Up

As you write your composition, do not use the same words over and over. On the line below each sentence, write strong verbs that are synonyms of the italicized words. Use a thesaurus.

1. Einstein *thought* about how energy works.

    strong verbs ___*imagined, considered, reflected, visualized, conjured, pondered, reasoned, wondered, analyzed, evaluated*___

2. Einstein could not *find* a teaching job.

    strong verbs ___*gain, acquire, obtain*___

3. Einstein *loved* math and science.

    strong verbs ___*enjoyed, valued, delighted in*___

Look   at your KWO and consider dress-ups to include in your composition.

Vocabulary Practice

Listen   to someone read the vocabulary words for Lesson 17 aloud.

Speak   them aloud yourself.

Read   the definitions and sample sentences on the vocabulary cards.

Write   four sentences using one of this lesson's vocabulary words in each sentence.

accept   *Einstein accepted a job at a patent office.*

accomplish   *Some people did not believe that Einstein would accomplish anything.*

inquisitively   *Inquisitively he asked many questions at school.*

technical   *Einstein wrote four technical articles.*

Think   about the words and their meanings so you can use them in your assignments.

Unit 6 Composition Checklist
Lesson 17: Albert Einstein, Part 1

Summarizing
Multiple
References

Name: _____

IEW Institute for Excellence in Writing

Listen, Speak, Read, Write, Think!

STRUCTURE

☐ MLA format (see Appendix I) _____ 2 pts

☐ topic-clincher sentences repeat or reflect 2–3 key words (highlight or **bold**) _____ 2 pts

☐ checklist on top, final draft, rough draft, key word outline _____ 2 pts

STYLE

¶1 Dress-Ups (underline one of each) (2 pts each)

☐ -ly adverb _____ 2 pts

☐ *who/which* clause _____ 2 pts

☐ strong verb _____ 2 pts

☐ *because* clause _____ 2 pts

☐ quality adjective _____ 2 pts

☐ *www.asia* clause _____ 2 pts

Sentence Openers (number; one of each as possible) (2 pts each)

☐ [2] prepositional _____ 2 pts

☐ [3] -ly adverb _____ 2 pts

☐ [6] vss _____ 2 pts

CHECK FOR BANNED WORDS (-1 pt for each use): think/thought, go/went, say/said, good, bad, big, small _____ pts

MECHANICS

☐ capitalization _____ 1 pt

☐ end marks and punctuation _____ 2 pts

☐ complete sentences _____ 1 pt

☐ correct spelling _____ 2 pts

VOCABULARY

☐ vocabulary words – label *(voc)* in left margin or after sentence

Total: _____ 30 pts

Custom Total: _____ pts

Checklist

Teachers are free to adjust a checklist by requiring only the stylistic techniques that have become easy, plus one new one. EZ+1

UNIT 6: SUMMARIZING MULTIPLE REFERENCES

Intentionally blank so the checklist can be removed.

Lesson 18: Albert Einstein, Part 2

Structure:	Unit 6: Summarizing Multiple References works consulted
Style:	no new style
Subject:	physicist Albert Einstein

UNIT 6: SUMMARIZING MULTIPLE REFERENCES

Lesson 18: Albert Einstein, Part 2

Goals

- to practice the Unit 6 structural model
- to create source outlines from multiple references
- to create a fused outline
- to write the second and third paragraphs of a 3-paragraph report
- to add a works consulted page
- to take Vocabulary Quiz 4
- to use new vocabulary words: *grieved, instantly, plead, solve*

Assignment Schedule

Day 1

1. Play Around the World.

2. Take Vocabulary Quiz 4.

3. In this lesson you will complete the 3-paragraph report using the source texts provided in Lesson 17. Then you will add a works consulted page.

4. Choose the topic for your second paragraph about Einstein from the chart on page 165 and write the topic on the topic line on page 176. Complete the source outlines.

5. Using notes from your source outlines, write a fused outline.

Day 2

1. Choose the topic for your third paragraph about Einstein from the chart on page 165 and write the topic on the topic line on page 178. Complete the source outlines.

2. Using notes from your source outlines, write a fused outline.

3. Complete Style Practice.

4. Look at the vocabulary cards for Lesson 18. Complete Vocabulary Practice.

5. Using your fused outlines as a guide, begin writing your rough draft.

6. Go over the checklist. Put a check in the box for each requirement you have completed.

Day 3

1. Review all vocabulary words learned thus far.

2. Finish writing the second and third paragraphs of your 3-paragraph report.
   Follow the topic-clincher rule.

3. Read New Structure—Works Consulted. Create a works consulted page for your report.
   Begin by arranging the works consulted information at the bottom of each source text
   (pages 160, 162, and 164) in alphabetical order. The first source you list on your works
   consulted page will be "Albert Einstein." Copy the works consulted information from
   page 164. Finish your works consulted page by copying the works consulted information
   for the remaining entries.

4. Turn in your rough draft and works consulted page to your editor with the completed
   checklist attached.

Day 4

1. Write or type a final draft, making any corrections your editor asked you to make.
   Place the two paragraphs written in this lesson after the paragraph you wrote for
   Lesson 17 so that you have one 3-paragraph report. Include the works consulted page.

2. Paperclip the checklist, final draft, rough draft, and KWO together. Hand them in.

Note: The paragraphs you wrote in Lessons 17–18 will be used to compose a 5-paragraph essay
with an introduction and a conclusion in Lesson 24.

In Lesson 19 you will write a report about Maria Telkes. One source of information will be
provided for you. Find two additional sources either from the library or the Internet. Choose
fairly short, simple sources. History textbooks, encyclopedia articles, short children's books,
and Internet articles labeled "for kids" usually work well.

New Structure

Works Consulted

A works consulted list is a list of the sources that were used to write a research report. It is placed as the last page of the report. Follow these general guidelines to write a works consulted page:

Center the title (Works Consulted) at the top of the page.

Double-space the entire page.

List sources in alphabetical order. (Use the first word of each entry, but ignore *A, An, The*.)

Do not indent the first line but indent the following lines of the same entry ½ inch from left.

Books

Begin with the author's name. If a book has two authors, order the authors in the order they are presented in the book. If there are three or more authors, list only the first author followed by the phrase *et al*. Book titles are italicized. (If handwriting, underline.)

Last Name, First Name. "Chapter of Book." [in quotes] *Title of Book,*

[in italics] Publisher, Publication Date, p. #. [page number(s)]

Encyclopedia Articles

Cite encyclopedias like books. If the article has an author, begin with the name. Otherwise, begin with the title of the article.

Last Name, First Name. [if given] "Article Title." [in quotes] *Title of*

Encyclopedia, [in italics] Publisher, Publication Date, p. #. [page number(s)]

Websites

Often websites have a Cite icon, which can prove helpful. If the article has an author, begin with the name. Otherwise, begin with the title of the article followed by the title of the website, which is the logo at the top of the page (not the URL).

Last Name, First Name. [if given] "Title of Article." [in quotes] *Title of Website,*

[in italics] Publisher or sponsor, Day Month Year the article was posted,

[if available (If there is no publication date, use latest copyright date at the

bottom of the webpage.)] URL.

Students begin by choosing a topic from the list on page 165 and writing it after Second Topic.

Guide students to write three words on the line after each Roman numeral. Because this becomes one paragraph, every topic line contains the same three words. The subject is *Albert Einstein* (abbreviated AE). The topic is the word written after Second Topic. Now write one more word *about the topic*.

UNIT 6: SUMMARIZING MULTIPLE REFERENCES

Sample

Source Outlines

The topic sentence tells what a paragraph is about.
Write the topic of your second paragraph on the line below.   **1 paragraph = 1 topic**

Second Topic: ___*career*___

Using key words, write the topic on the Roman numeral line of each source outline: *subject*, *topic*, one more word *about the topic*. Each topic line will have the same words. Look at the appropriate paragraphs of the source texts and note three to five interesting facts about the topic.

Source A: *Albert Einstein*

II. Topic: ___*AE, career, successful*___

    1. ___*1905, 4 papers, scientific journal*___

    2. ___*teaching, imagine, math*___

    3. ___*1916, "The Foundation of the General Theory of Relativity," masterpiece*___

    (4.) ___*light, bends, gravity*___

    (5.) ___*famous, US, 1921, Nobel Prize, physics*___

Source B: *Albert Einstein Genius*

II. Topic: ___*AE, career, successful*___

    1. ___*3rd, speed, light, X change*___

    2. ___*4th, atomic energy*___

    3. ___*paper, gravity, bend,* 💡___

    (4.) ___*1919,* ☀ *eclipse, confirmed, famous*___

    (5.) _____

Sample

Source C: *A Brilliant Thinker*

II. Topic: *AE, career, successful*

1. *1905, 4 papers, Annals of Physics*

2. *tools = 📄, pencils, imagination*

3. *1921, Nobel Prize, light = photons*

(4.) *US, 20,000 people, greeted, NYC*

(5.) *free, speech, ++ work*

Fused Outline

Place the topic you are writing about on the topic line. Select five to seven facts from the source outlines to transfer to the fused outline.

II. Topic: *AE, career, successful*

1. *tools = 📄, pencils, imagination*

2. *1916, "The Foundation of the General Theory of Relativity," masterpiece*

3. *gravity, light, bend*

4. *1919, ☀ eclipse, confirmed, famous*

5. *1921, Nobel Prize, physics*

(6.) *US, 20,000 people, greeted, NYC*

(7.) _____

Clincher

Tell back the facts on the fused outline in complete sentences. Fix any notes you do not understand. For the clincher, repeat or reflect two or three key words from the topic line.

Students begin by choosing a topic from the list on page 165 and writing it after Third Topic.

Guide students to write three words on the line after each Roman numeral. Because this becomes one paragraph, every topic line contains the same three words. The subject is *Albert Einstein* (abbreviated AE). The topic is the word written after Third Topic. Now write one more word *about the topic*.

Sample

Source Outlines

The topic sentence tells what a paragraph is about.
Write the topic of your third paragraph on the line below.

1 paragraph = 1 topic

Third Topic: *later years*

Using key words, write the topic on the Roman numeral line of each source outline: *subject*, *topic*, one more word *about the topic*. Each topic line will have the same words. Look at the appropriate paragraphs of the source texts and note three to five interesting facts about the topic.

Source A: *Albert Einstein*

III. Topic: *AE, later years, eventful*

1. *teaching, researching, peace*

2. *thinking, violin, sailing*

3. *Jew, intellectual, Nazi* ☹

(4.) *1933, moved, US, Princeton, NJ*

(5.) *1943, US, E discoveries, 2 bombs, Japan*

Source B: *Albert Einstein Genius*

III. Topic: *AE, later years, eventful*

1. *left, Eu, Nazi, X Jews*

2. *? Winston Churchill, J, scientists, escape*

3. *1945, findings, atomic bomb*

(4.) *wrote, prevent, war*

(5.)

Institute for Excellence in Writing

Sample

Source C: *A Brilliant Thinker*

III. Topic: ___*AE, later years, eventful*___

   1. _____*1939, letter, Pres. Roosevelt, warning*_____

   2. _____*2 bombs, Japan, ended, WWII*_____

   3. _____*E, ☹, prevent, weapons, future*_____

 (4.) _____*Jewish, ♡ peace*_____

 (5.) _____*sail, violin, politics*_____

Fused Outline

Place the topic you are writing about on the topic line. Select five to seven facts from the source outlines to transfer to the fused outline.

III. Topic: ___*AE, later years, eventful*___

   1. _____*teaching, researching, peace*_____

   2. _____*Jew, intellectual, Nazi ☹*_____

   3. _____*1933, moved, US, Princeton, NJ*_____

   4. _____*? Winston Churchill, J, scientists, escape*_____

   5. _____*1943, US, E discoveries, 2 bombs, Japan*_____

 (6.) _____*E, ☹, prevent, weapons, war*_____

 (7.) _____*sail, violin, politics*_____

Clincher

Tell back the facts on the fused outline in complete sentences. Fix any notes you do not understand. For the clincher, repeat or reflect two or three key words from the topic line.

Style Practice

Sentence Openers

Write sentences that can be used in your composition.

1. #2 prepositional opener _____ *[2] In 1921 Einstein received the Nobel Prize in Physics.* _____

2. #3 -ly adverb opener _____ *[3] Diligently Einstein studied matter, motion, and energy.* _____

3. #6 vss opener, 2–5 words _____ *[6] He instantly became famous.* _____

Dress-Ups

Look at your KWO and consider where you can include various clauses as well as strong verbs, quality adjectives, and -ly adverbs.

Vocabulary Practice

Listen   to someone read the vocabulary words for Lesson 18 aloud.

Speak   them aloud yourself.

Read   the definitions and sample sentences on the vocabulary cards.

Write   the words that match the definitions.

_____ *solve* _____   to find the correct answer or explanation

_____ *instantly* _____   immediately

_____ *grieved* _____   with a feeling of sorrow

_____ *plead* _____   to ask for something in a serious and emotional way

Think   about the words and their meanings so you can use them in your assignments.

Unit 6 Composition Checklist
Lesson 18: Albert Einstein, Part 2

Summarizing
Multiple
References

Name: _____

IEW Institute for Excellence in Writing

STRUCTURE

- ☐ MLA format (see Appendix I) _____ 2 pts
- ☐ title centered and repeats 1–3 key words from final sentence _____ 2 pts
- ☐ topic-clincher sentences repeat or reflect 2–3 key words (highlight or bold) _____ 2 pts
- ☐ works consulted entries in proper format _____ 5 pts
- ☐ checklist on top, final draft, rough draft, key word outline _____ 2 pts

STYLE

¶2 ¶3 Dress-Ups (underline one of each)   (1 pt each)

- ☐ ☐ -ly adverb _____ 2 pts
- ☐ ☐ *who/which* clause _____ 2 pts
- ☐ ☐ strong verb _____ 2 pts
- ☐ ☐ *because* clause _____ 2 pts
- ☐ ☐ quality adjective _____ 2 pts
- ☐ ☐ *www.asia* clause _____ 2 pts

Sentence Openers (number; one of each as possible)   (1 pt each)

- ☐ ☐ [2] prepositional _____ 2 pts
- ☐ ☐ [3] -ly adverb _____ 2 pts
- ☐ ☐ [6] vss _____ 2 pts

CHECK FOR BANNED WORDS (-1 pt for each use): think/thought, go/went, say/said, good, bad, big, small _____ pts

MECHANICS

- ☐ capitalization _____ 1 pt
- ☐ end marks and punctuation _____ 1 pt
- ☐ complete sentences _____ 1 pt
- ☐ correct spelling _____ 1 pt

VOCABULARY

- ☐ vocabulary words – label *(voc)* in left margin or after sentence

Total: _____ 35 pts
Custom Total: _____ pts

Checklist

The checklist indicates ¶2 and ¶3 because this checklist is for the second and third paragraphs of the 3-paragraph composition. ¶1 was written in the last lesson.

Teachers are free to adjust a checklist by requiring only the stylistic techniques that have become easy, plus one new one. EZ+1

UNIT 6: SUMMARIZING MULTIPLE REFERENCES

Intentionally blank so the checklist can be removed.

Lesson 19: Maria Telkes

Structure:	Unit 6: Summarizing Multiple References
Style:	no new style
Subject:	inventor Maria Telkes
	additional sources required

UNIT 6: SUMMARIZING MULTIPLE REFERENCES

Lesson 19: Maria Telkes

Goals

- to practice the Unit 6 structural model
- to create source outlines from multiple references
- to create a fused outline
- to write a 2-paragraph report
- to use new vocabulary words: *devise, immigrate, industriously, potable*

Assignment Schedule

Day 1

1. Play Tic-Tac-Toe with questions provided in the Teacher's Manual.

2. In this lesson you will write a 2-paragraph report about Maria Telkes using a source text provided in this lesson as well as two additional sources that you found at the library or from the Internet. Then you will add a works consulted page.

3. Before you begin taking notes, you must determine what topics are available to write about. The subject is Telkes. Scan each source text to discern possible topics. You will find information about Telkes's early life, her inventions, her work with solar power, and her legacy. There will be many topics on this subject.

4. Read Structure—Refining the Topic.

5. For your first paragraph, choose a topic that is covered in at least two sources. It is possible that the topic you choose may not be covered in the source text provided in this lesson. Write the topic on the topic line on page 188. Follow the pattern: *subject, topic, one more word about the topic.* Complete the source outlines using the sources that contain information about your topic.

6. Using notes from your source outlines, write a fused outline.

Day 2

1. For the second paragraph, choose another topic that is covered in at least two sources. Write the topic on the topic line on page 190. Again, follow the pattern: *subject, topic, one more word about the topic.* Complete the source outlines using the sources that contain information about your topic.

2. Using notes from your source outlines, write a fused outline.

3. Complete Style Practice.

4. Look at the vocabulary cards for Lesson 19. Complete Vocabulary Practice.

5. Using your fused outlines as a guide, begin writing your rough draft.

6. Go over the checklist. Put a check in the box for each requirement you have completed.

In Lessons 17–18 the report subject was assigned and students found their own topics using provided simplified source texts.

In this lesson the report subject is assigned and students will find their own topics. This time only one source text is provided. Students must find two additional sources outside of this book. Encourage students to look for books in the juvenile section of the library or Internet articles labeled "for kids." It will be easier to identify topics in these types of sources than it will be in longer, more mature sources.

Tic-Tac-Toe

Questions for Tic-Tac-Toe are on the next page.

Day 3

1. Review all vocabulary words learned thus far.

2. Finish writing your 2-paragraph report. Follow the topic-clincher rule.

3. Write a works consulted page that includes all three sources you used. Follow the format on page 175.

4. Turn in your rough draft and works consulted page to your editor with the completed checklist attached.

Day 4

1. Write or type a final draft, making any corrections your editor asked you to make.

2. Paperclip the checklist, final draft, rough draft, and KWO together. Hand them in.

Tic-Tac-Toe

1. What is a fused outline? *(An outline made by selecting facts from multiple source outlines. It is the outline from which the paragraph will be written.)*

2. Once you know your subject and have chosen your topics for a report from multiple sources, will your first set of outlines be all from the same source or all for the same topic? *(topic)*

3. When writing source outlines, what should you write on the line next to the Roman numeral? *(the topic of the paragraph you are working on)*

4. What is a works consulted page, and where is it placed? *(a list of sources used, placed after the report as a separate page)*

5. In what order should you list your sources on a works consulted page? *(alphabetical)*

6. Do you indent the first line of each entry on a works consulted page? *(no)*

7. If a works consulted entry (one of your sources) requires more than one line, what must you do to the second line? *(indent 1/2 inch)*

8. What should a works consulted entry begin with, if known? *(author's last name, first name)*

9. On a works consulted page, what must you do to titles of websites? *(italicize)*

10. On a works consulted page, what must you do to titles of articles within a website? *(quotation marks)*

Use vocabulary definitions if more questions are needed. Students answer by telling the vocabulary word.

Although students can complete this writing assignment without using this source text, it is advantageous to begin with this source text simply to practice the skill of finding possible topics to write about.

Source Text A

The Sun Queen

early life

Maria Telkes was born in Budapest, Hungary, in 1900. When she was in high school, she became interested in learning how to use energy from the sun for heat. She attended the University of Budapest, where she received her Ph.D. in physical chemistry. She moved to the United States in 1925 and worked with a clinic in Cleveland, Ohio. There she worked to create a photoelectric device that could use light to record brainwaves.

inventions

In 1937 Telkes was hired by Westinghouse Electric, where she worked to find a way to convert heat energy into electric energy. In 1940 she joined the Massachusetts Institute of Technology's Solar Energy Conservation Project. While working on this project, she invented new ways to capture and use solar energy. She also found a way to use solar power to remove salt from ocean water. This method is called desalinization. Her desalinization plant could be small enough and portable enough to allow soldiers in World War II to drink sea water when they were on a life raft. It could be large enough to provide drinking water to the U.S. Virgin Islands. Additionally, she invented a stove that could be used anywhere in the world to cook food using heat from the sun. In the 1970s Telkes developed an air conditioner that stored cool nighttime air so that it could be used the next day to lower the temperature of the home.

In 1950 Telkes worked with two other women to build the Dover Sun House in Massachusetts, a livable home that could store heat from the sun. The home's second story had huge windows that collected energy to heat Glauber's salt. This *solar power*

allowed heat to be stored for two days with no sunshine. Unfortunately, the system failed after three years. However, Telkes did not give up. She helped to build another solar-powered home in 1980 in Carlisle, Massachusetts. This home was not only heated with energy from the sun, but also Telkes found a way to covert heat into electricity by using photovoltaic cells.

legacy

Telkes was nicknamed the Sun Queen because of her work harnessing the sun to create heat and electricity. She was determined and eager to find solutions even though technology was not ready. Throughout her career she continued to find ways to use solar energy and received several patents for her work. In 1952 Telkes became the first person to receive the Society of Women Engineers Achievement Award. In 1977 she received a lifetime achievement award from the National Academy of Sciences Building Research Advisory Board for her contributions to solar-energy technology. Maria Telkes stated, "Sunlight will be used as a source of energy sooner or later. Why wait?" Today's scientists continue to think about ways to use solar energy to replace fossil fuels and to make it more affordable. More and more homes, businesses, and cities are powered by solar radiation from the sun due to the work of Maria Telkes.

Structure

Refining the Topic

The topic sentence tells what the paragraph is about. When you write your KWO, you begin by placing key words on the topic line. When writing multi-paragraph compositions, it helps to follow the pattern: *subject*, *topic*, one more word *about the topic*.

Subject

The subject of a report is the entire thing being written about. For this assignment the subject is *Telkes*. The first word you place on the KWO topic line is *Telkes*.

Topic

The topics are the divisions—the things within the subject. Because the assignment is to write two paragraphs, you must scan the source texts and find two topics about the subject.

if 1 topic = 1 paragraph
then 2 topics = 2 paragraphs

The second item you place on the KWO will indicate your chosen topic. If you choose to write about early life, write *early life*. If you write about inventions, write *inventions*. You may choose to write one paragraph just about solar power. If you do, write *solar power*. Many possibilities exist.

About the Topic

A well-written paragraph will be focused. You do not want it to sound like a list of items. To further narrow the topic, choose one specific thing to focus on by asking *what about the topic?*

When you chose your topic, if you chose inventions, you will now ask *what about inventions?* Your answer becomes the third word on KWO topic line.

> If you choose to describe Telkes's inventions as useful, your KWO topic line may look like this: Topic: I. *Telkes, inventions, useful*

> If you choose to describe Telkes's inventions as ingenious, your KWO topic line may look like this: Topic: I. *Telkes, inventions, ingenious*

The three key words you place on the topic line determine the facts that you search for during the research process.

Subjects and Topics

When students fail to refine their topics, they often write paragraphs that contain an odd collection of facts about a subject. It can sound like a grocery list.

Guide students to choose the third word for the topic line by asking questions. If the topic is *inventions*, ask, "What about the inventions?"

By refining a topic, students are forced to limit the type of information they choose to insert on the KWO and ultimately in the paragraph. This results in a more focused paragraph with facts that support, prove, and illustrate the topic.

The subject is *Maria Telkes* (abbreviated MT).

Sample

Source Outlines

Write the name of the first topic you will research on the line below.

First Topic: ___*inventions*_____

Choose your first source. Write the title on the Source line. Using key words, write the topic on the Roman numeral line. Complete the source outline by noting three to five interesting facts about the topic. Repeat the process with the second source and, if applicable, with the third.

Source A: ___*The Sun Queen*_____

I. Topic: ___*MT, inventions, useful*_____

   1. ___*1937, heat → electric energy*_____

   2. ___*capture + use, ☼ energy*_____

   3. ___*☼ power, remove, salt, 〜〜 H_2O*_____

 (4.) ___*soldiers, WWII, drink, raft*_____

 (5.) ___*stove, cook, heat ☼*_____

Source B: _____

I. Topic: ___*MT, inventions, useful*_____

   1. _____

   2. _____

   3. _____

 (4.) _____

 (5.) _____

Source C: _____

I. Topic: ___*MT, inventions, useful*_____

   1. _____

   2. _____

   3. _____

 (4.) _____

 (5.) _____

Institute for Excellence in Writing

The topic indicates what the paragraph will be about. Require students to follow the established pattern: *subject, topic*, one more word *about the topic*. The words on the topic lines of the source and fused outlines are identical. Only the fused outline has a clincher line because students write the paragraph using the fused outline.

Sample

Fused Outline

Source Outline A

I. Topic: _____

1. _____
2. _____
3. _____
(4.) _____
(5.) _____

Source Outline B

I. Topic: _____

1. _____
2. _____
3. _____
(4.) _____
(5.) _____

Source Outline C

I. Topic: _____

1. _____
2. _____
3. _____
(4.) _____
(5.) _____

Fused Outline

I. Topic: _____

1. _____
2. _____
3. _____
4. _____
5. _____
(6.) _____
(7.) _____

Clincher

Place the topic you are writing about on the topic line. Select five to seven facts from the source outlines to transfer to the fused outline.

I. Topic: *MT, inventions, useful* _____

  1. *The fused outline will depend upon each student's choice of topic and additional sources.*

  2. _____

  3. _____

  4. _____

  5. _____

(6.) _____

(7.) _____

Clincher

Tell back the facts on the fused outline in complete sentences. Fix any notes you do not understand. For the clincher, repeat or reflect two or three key words from the topic line.

Sample

Source Outlines

Write the name of the second topic you will research on the line below.

Second Topic: ___*solar power*___

Choose your first source. Write the title on the Source line. Using key words, write the topic on the Roman numeral line. Complete the source outline by noting three to five interesting facts about the topic. Repeat the process with the second source and, if applicable, with the third.

Source A: ___*The Sun Queen*___

II. Topic: ___*MT, solar power, beneficial*___

   1. ___*1950, home, store, heat* ☼___

   2. ___*WINDOWS, energy, heat, 2 d., X* ☼___

   3. ___*failed, 3 yrs, X give up*___

  (4.) ___*1980, another* ☼ *powered* 🏠___

  (5.) ___*heat →, electricity, photovoltaic*___

Source B: _____

II. Topic: ___*MT, solar power, beneficial*___

   1. _____

   2. _____

   3. _____

  (4.) _____

  (5.) _____

Source C: _____

II. Topic: ___*MT, solar power, beneficial*___

   1. _____

   2. _____

   3. _____

  (4.) _____

  (5.) _____

Sample

Fused Outline

Place the topic you are writing about on the topic line. Select five to seven facts from the source outlines to transfer to the fused outline.

II. Topic: *MT, solar power, beneficial*

1. *The fused outline will depend upon each student's choice of topic and additional sources.*

2. _____

3. _____

4. _____

5. _____

(6.) _____

(7.) _____

Clincher

Tell back the facts on the fused outline in complete sentences. Fix any notes you do not understand. For the clincher, repeat or reflect two or three key words from the topic line.

Style Practice

Sentence Openers

Write sentences that can be used in your composition.

1. #2 prepositional opener _____ *[2] With two other women Telkes built a solar-powered home.*

2. #3 -ly adverb opener _____ *[3] Successfully Telkes converted solar power into energy.*

3. #6 vss opener, 2–5 words _____ *[6] She did not give up.*

Dress-Ups

Look at your KWO and consider where you can include various clauses as well as strong verbs, quality adjectives, and -ly adverbs.

Vocabulary Practice

Listen   to someone read the vocabulary words for Lesson 19 aloud.

Speak   them aloud yourself.

Read   the definitions and sample sentences on the vocabulary cards.

Write   the correct words in the blanks.

Maria Telkes _____ *immigrate (d)* _____ from Hungary to the United States.

Telkes worked _____ *industriously* _____ to advance solar power technology.

Removing salt from ocean water makes the water _____ *potable* _____ .

Telkes _____ *devise (d)* _____ a stove that cooks food using heat from the sun.

Think   about the words and their meanings so you can use them in your assignments.

Unit 6 Composition Checklist
Lesson 19: Maria Telkes

Summarizing
Multiple
References

Name: _____

Institute for **Excellence** in **Writing**
IEW
Listen. Speak. Read. Write. Think!

STRUCTURE

☐ MLA format (see Appendix I)	_____	1 pt
☐ title centered and repeats 1–3 key words from final sentence	_____	3 pts
☐ topic-clincher sentences repeat or reflect 2–3 key words (highlight **or** bold)	_____	5 pts
☐ works consulted entries in proper format	_____	5 pts
☐ checklist on top, final draft, rough draft, key word outline	_____	1 pt

STYLE

¶1 ¶2 Dress-Ups (underline one of each)   (2 pts each)

☐ ☐ -ly adverb		_____	4 pts
☐ ☐ *who/which* clause		_____	4 pts
☐ ☐ strong verb		_____	4 pts
☐ ☐ *because* clause		_____	4 pts
☐ ☐ quality adjective		_____	4 pts
☐ ☐ *www.asia* clause		_____	4 pts

Sentence Openers (number; one of each as possible)   (2 pts each)

☐ ☐ [2] prepositional		_____	4 pts
☐ ☐ [3] -ly adverb		_____	4 pts
☐ ☐ [6] vss		_____	4 pts

CHECK FOR BANNED WORDS (-1 pt for each use): think/thought, go/went, say/said, good, bad, big, small   _____   pts

MECHANICS

☐ capitalization	_____	1 pt
☐ end marks and punctuation	_____	1 pt
☐ complete sentences	_____	1 pt
☐ correct spelling	_____	1 pt

VOCABULARY

☐ vocabulary words – label *(voc)* in left margin or after sentence

Total:	_____	55 pts
Custom Total:	_____	pts

Checklist

Teachers are free to adjust a checklist by requiring only the stylistic techniques that have become easy, plus one new one. EZ+1

Intentionally blank so the checklist can be removed.

Lesson 20: Favorite Invention, Part 1

Structure: Unit 7: Inventive Writing
            body paragraphs

Style: #5 clausal opener, *www.asia.b* clause

Subject: a specific invention

Teaching Writing: Structure and Style

Watch the sections for Unit 7: Inventive Writing. At <u>IEW.com/twss-help</u> reference the TWSS Viewing Guides.

Lesson 20: Favorite Invention, Part 1

UNIT 7: INVENTIVE WRITING

Lesson 20: Favorite Invention, Part 1

Goals

- to learn the Unit 7 Inventive Writing structural model
- to create a KWO from a writing prompt
- to write the body paragraphs of a 4-paragraph composition
- to add a new sentence opener: #5 clausal opener
- to use new vocabulary words: *alter, innovative, persistently, unique*

Assignment Schedule

Day 1

1. Play Around the World or Vocabulary Lightning.
2. Read New Structure—Inventive Writing: Body Paragraphs and the prompt.
3. Read Notes from the Brain and follow the instructions to write a 2-paragraph KWO.

Day 2

1. Read New Style and complete Style Practice.
2. Look at the vocabulary cards for Lesson 20. Complete Vocabulary Practice.
3. Using your KWO as a guide, begin writing your 2-paragraph rough draft.
4. Go over the checklist. Put a check in the box for each requirement you have completed.

Day 3

1. Review all vocabulary words learned thus far.
2. Finish writing your 2-paragraph composition. Follow the topic-clincher rule.
3. Turn in your rough draft to your editor with the completed checklist attached.

Day 4

1. Write or type a final draft, making any corrections your editor asked you to make.
2. Paperclip the checklist, final draft, rough draft, and KWO together. Hand them in.

Note: In Lesson 21 you will write an introduction and a conclusion to add to the paragraphs written for this lesson.

Study for Vocabulary Quiz 5. It will cover words from Lessons 1–20.

In this new unit students do not have a source text or even pictures to look at. The KWO is formed by asking good questions. Key words for the outline are found in the answers to the questions. Be patient with yourself and your student. This is a practicable skill that will take time to perfect.

New Structure

Inventive Writing: Body Paragraphs

In Unit 7 you will write compositions that begin with an introduction and end with a conclusion. Look at the 5-paragraph model below: three body paragraphs plus an introduction and a conclusion. The model can be adapted by simply changing the number of body paragraphs.

Reminder

Notice that the first body paragraph begins with Roman numeral II. The first paragraph of the composition will be written in Lesson 21.

	I.	Introduction	*attention getter, background, state topics*
Body	II.	Topic A	*topic, 5–7 details, clincher*
Paragraphs	III.	Topic B	*topic, 5–7 details, clincher*
	IV.	Topic C	*topic, 5–7 details, clincher*
	V.	Conclusion	*restate topics, most significant/why, last sentence ➜ title*

Your entire composition should be about one subject. Once you know what the subject of the composition is, you determine how many body paragraphs to write. Once you know the number of body paragraphs, you determine the topics. Each body paragraph equals one topic. When you follow this model, write from the inside out beginning with the body paragraphs.

Sometimes you are given a prompt and asked to write a response. Where do you find the information for your paper? When learning to write from the "blank page," one technique to help develop content is to ask yourself questions. In Unit 5 when you wrote from a series of pictures, you began with brain-helping questions. You will again use those same questions in Unit 7. The ability to ask questions and develop answers is the core skill required for all inventive writing.

Analyze the prompt below and then ask yourself questions.

Prompt

People have been inventing things since the beginning of time. Significant inventions include the wheel, the microscope, and the automobile. Choose one invention to write about. It could be something that already exists, or it could be something that you would like to invent. Describe two uses for this invention.

Notes from the Brain

When learning to write from the blank page, one technique to help come up with content is to ask yourself questions about the prompt.

1. Based on the prompt, the subject for this lesson is ___ *a chosen invention, e.g., wheel.*

2. Possible topics include ___ *Answers will vary.*

3. How many body paragraphs do you need to write to complete the assignment? _2_

The topic sentence of each paragraph will state a specific use for the invention.
On the KWO indicate the topics on the topic lines. Follow this pattern:

subject, topic, one more word *about the topic.*

if 1 topic = 1 paragraph
then 2 topics = 2 paragraphs

On the lines under the first Roman numeral, describe the first topic by asking yourself questions. Brain-helping questions are listed on the KWO. These helpful questions include:

How do you use this invention?

When do you use it?

Who else uses it?

Where do you use it?

Why do you use it like this?

How does it make you think? feel?

What has changed because of this invention?

What are some potential problems/solutions?

In what ways does this **affect** the future?

The answers to your questions become the details for the outline. As you answer a question, place two or three key words on the KWO. Use symbols, numbers, and abbreviations when possible. You do not have to answer every question, nor do you need to ask in the order they are written. Keep your answers brief. You can add more details when you write your composition.

Repeat this process for the second topic.

Help students ask questions to discover possible topics. Uses for an invention can be something that is common or unusual. Begin by having students choose a specific invention. Discuss different ways this invention can be used.

Once students have chosen two topics to write about, ask additional questions to refine the topic.

If a student writes about a toothbrush, ask what are some different uses for the toothbrush. If the student decides one way to use a toothbrush is to clean, have the student choose one item to clean. The topic line might be this: *toothbrush, clean, shoes.*

If a student writes about a microscope, uses might be to observe small items. The topic line might be this: *microscope, observe, -- items.*

In this lesson students write two body paragraphs. Once the composition is completed, these paragraphs will be the second and third paragraphs of the paper. Thus, the first body paragraph is marked with Roman numeral II and the second with III.

The key to the process is asking questions. Here are the questions asked that resulted in the sample KWO.

Topic A

What is the subject? (*toothbrush*)

What is your specific topic for this paragraph? (*clean*)

What about the topic? (*shoes*)

1. Why do you clean shoes?
2. Why do you need a toothbrush?
3. How do you use the toothbrush?
4. What else is required?
5. What are some potential problems/solutions?
6. How do you feel?

Topic B

What is the subject? (*toothbrush*)

What is your specific topic for this paragraph? (*art*)

What about the topic? (*texturize*)

1. What type of medium?
2. How do you use the toothbrush (notes 2–3)?
4. What other type of medium?
5. How does the brush enhance your sculpture (notes 5–6)?

UNIT 7: INVENTIVE WRITING

Sample

Key Word Outline

II. Topic A: _____ toothbrush, clean, shoes _____

  1. _____ remove, mud, tread _____

  2. _____ tiny, bristles, fit, sm. places _____

  3. _____ dip, H_2O, scrub, spaces _____

  4. _____ time + effort, success _____

  5. _____ X dissolve, mud, soap _____

  (6.) _____ ☺, satisfied, 👀, new _____

  (7.) _____

  Clincher

III. Topic B: _____ toothbrush, art, texturize _____

  1. _____ painting, add, dimension _____

  2. _____ dry, bristles, 3-D, designs _____

  3. _____ wet, bristles, waves, ◎ _____

  4. _____ sculptures, clay, sand _____

  5. _____ + depth, engrave, patterns _____

  (6.) _____ brush, intricate, designs _____

  (7.) _____

  Clincher

?

who?

what?

when?

where?

why?

how?

how feel?

problems?

solutions?

best thing?

worst thing?

value?

significance?

meaning?

examples?

description?

198

Institute for Excellence in Writing

New Style

#5 Clausal Opener

In this lesson you will learn another sentence opener: the #5 clausal opener.

The clausal opener is an adverb clause placed at the beginning of a sentence. The clausal opener begins with one of these words: *when, while, where, as, since, if, although, because.*

This should look familiar. The *because* clause dress-up and the *www.asia* clause dress-up will now be combined into one dress-up called the *www.asia.b* clause dress-up.

> [5] When my invention worked, I celebrated.
>
> I celebrated <u>when</u> my invention worked.

Notice:

1. A *www.asia.b* clause that begins a sentence is called a clausal opener. Label it with a 5 in the left margin or place a [5] right before the sentence.

2. A *www.asia.b* clause placed in the middle or end of the sentence is called a *www.asia.b* dress-up. Mark it by underlining the first word of the clause.

3. A *www.asia.b* clause contains a subject and a verb.

   > When my *invention worked*, I celebrated.
   >
   > I celebrated <u>when</u> my *invention worked.*

4. A *www.asia.b* clause is added to a sentence that is already complete.

   > [5] When my invention worked, *I celebrated.*
   >
   > *I celebrated* <u>when</u> my invention worked.

❟ If the *www.asia.b* clause is at the beginning of the sentence, follow the entire clause with a comma. We do not usually put a comma before a *www.asia.b* clause.

www.asia.b

when

while

where

as

since

if

although

because

#5 Clausal Opener

The #5 clausal opener and the *www.asia.b* dress-up are formed exactly the same way. The only difference is the position in the sentence. Openers begin sentences; dress-ups do not.

Teach students these two comma rules.

adverb clause comma main clause (AC, MC)

main clause no comma adverb clause (MC AC)

Practice

Write a sentence with a #5 clausal opener. Remember to insert a comma. Label it with a [5].

[5] If I had not persevered, I would not have succeeded.

✎ From now on, include two *www.asia.b* clauses—a clausal opener and a *www.asia.b* dress-up—in each paragraph you write. Label the opener with a 5 in the margin or place a [5] before the sentence. Underline the dress-up. There are now five, not six, dress-ups on the checklist.

Style Practice

Sentence Openers

Write sentences that can be used in your body paragraphs.

1. #2 prepositional opener ———————— *[2] With soapy water I scrubbed vigorously.* ————

2. #3 -ly adverb opener ———————— *[3] Finally, my shoes were clean.* ————————

3. #5 clausal opener – *www.asia.b* — *[5] As I scrubbed, the dirt fell away.* ————————

4. #6 vss opener, 2–5 words ———— *[6] My shoes looked new.* ————————————

Dress-Ups

Look at your KWO and consider dress-ups to include in your body paragraphs.

Vocabulary Practice

Listen   to someone read the vocabulary words for Lesson 20 aloud.

Write   the words that match the definitions.

———— *persistently* ———— continuing in spite of opposition or obstacles

———— *unique* ———— unusual

———— *innovative* ———— new, original, and advanced

———— *alter* ———— to change or modify

Think   about the words and their meanings so you can use them in your assignments.

Unit 7 Composition Checklist
Lesson 20: Favorite Invention, Part 1 body paragraphs

Inventive Writing

Institute for **Excellence** in **Writing**
Listen. Speak. Read. Write. Think!

Name: _____

STRUCTURE

☐ MLA format (see Appendix I)   _____   2 pts

☐ checklist on top, final draft, rough draft, key word outline   _____   2 pts

Body

☐ topic-clincher sentences repeat or reflect 2–3 key words (highlight or bold)   _____   5 pts

☐ facts stay on topic   _____   5 pts

STYLE

¶2 ¶3 Dress-Ups (underline one of each)   (2 pts each)

☐ ☐ -ly adverb   _____   4 pts

☐ ☐ *who/which* clause   _____   4 pts

☐ ☐ strong verb   _____   4 pts

☐ ☐ quality adjective   _____   4 pts

☐ ☐ *www.asia.b* clause   _____   4 pts

Sentence Openers (number; one of each as possible)   (2 pts each)

☐ ☐ [2] prepositional   _____   4 pts

☐ ☐ [3] -ly adverb   _____   4 pts

☐ ☐ [5] clausal – *www.asia.b*   _____   4 pts

☐ ☐ [6] vss   _____   4 pts

CHECK FOR BANNED WORDS (-1 pt for each use): think/thought, go/went, say/said,   _____   pts
good, bad, big, small

MECHANICS

☐ spelling, grammar, and punctuation (-1 pt per error)   _____   pts

VOCABULARY

☐ vocabulary words – label *(voc)* in left margin or after sentence

Total: _____   50 pts

Custom Total: _____   pts

Checklist

Teachers are free to adjust a checklist by requiring only the stylistic techniques that have become easy, plus one new one. EZ+1

Intentionally blank so the checklist can be removed.

Institute for Excellence in Writing

Lesson 21: Favorite Invention, Part 2

Structure: Unit 7: Inventive Writing
                                 introduction and conclusion

Style: no new style

Subject: a specific invention

Lesson 21: Favorite Invention, Part 2

UNIT 7: INVENTIVE WRITING

Lesson 21: Favorite Invention, Part 2

Goals

- to practice the Unit 7 structural model
- to create KWOs for an introduction and a conclusion paragraph
- to write an introduction and a conclusion paragraph
- to complete a 4-paragraph composition
- to take Vocabulary Quiz 5
- to use new vocabulary words: *certainly, consequently, furthermore, similarly*

Assignment Schedule

Day 1

1. Take Vocabulary Quiz 5.
2. Play Find the *www.asia* Clause Starters.
3. Read New Structure—Inventive Writing: Introduction and Conclusion. Both paragraphs have their own unique structure. Take time to memorize the components.
4. Write a KWO for a conclusion and then write a KWO for an introduction.

Day 2

1. Review both KWOs from Day 1.
2. Complete Style Practice.
3. Look at the vocabulary cards for Lesson 21. Complete Vocabulary Practice.
4. Using your conclusion KWO as a guide, write your conclusion. Highlight or bold the topic key words.
5. Go over the checklist. Put a check in the box for each requirement you have completed.

Day 3

1. Review all vocabulary words learned thus far.
2. Using your introduction KWO as a guide, write your introduction. Highlight or bold the topic key words.
3. Turn in your rough draft to your editor with the completed checklist attached.

Day 4

1. Write or type a final draft, making any corrections your editor asked you to make. Add the introduction and the conclusion to the final draft body paragraphs written in Lesson 20.
2. Paperclip the checklist, final draft, rough drafts, and KWOs together. Hand them in.

Wonders of Science Writing Lessons: Student Book

203

In this lesson students add an introduction paragraph and a conclusion paragraph to the body paragraphs written in Lesson 20. Help students understand that these paragraphs are not about specific topics. Therefore, neither contains topic or clincher sentences. Both paragraphs follow their own unique structure.

Encourage students to memorize the components of the introduction and of the conclusion.

New Structure

Inventive Writing: Introduction and Conclusion

Now that you have completed the body paragraphs, you are ready to add the introduction and conclusion. Look at the model below and notice the components that make up the introduction and conclusion. These two paragraphs are not about specific topics. Therefore, neither contains topic or clincher sentences. Both paragraphs follow their own unique structure.

I.   Introduction   *attention getter, background, state topics*

       Body Paragraphs

IV.   Conclusion   *restate topics, most significant/why, last sentence* ➜ *title*

Read Sample Paragraphs on page 208. The introduction must get the readers' attention by enticing readers to keep reading. It also introduces the readers to the subject of the paper and states the topics. The conclusion reminds the readers of the topics and then indicates what is most important about the subject and why. The conclusion also brings finality to the paper.

It is important that the conclusion flows smoothly from the final body paragraph. Since you have just written the body paragraphs and the details are fresh on your mind, you will outline and write the conclusion before you outline and write the introduction.

Key Word Outline—Conclusion

 **Restate the Topics**

Write a sentence or two about each topic. Try to convey the main idea of each body paragraph; in other words, reword the topic sentences. Highlight or bold the topic key words.

 **Most Significant and Why**

What is the most important, most interesting, or most significant thing to remember about all that you wrote and why? You may choose one of your topics and tell why it is the most significant, or you may choose something that tells the importance of the entire subject.

 **Final Sentence**

End with a sentence from which you can create a title. Be sure that your paper sounds complete.

Sample

Key Word Outline for Conclusion

IV.   Topic A: _____ *toothbrush, clean, shoes* _____

Topic B: _____ *toothbrush, art, texturize* _____

Most significant _____ *benefit, reach, sm. spaces* _____

Why? _____ *handle, leverage* _____

_____ *bristles, precision* _____

_____ *unique, method, X dirt* _____

Title repeats 1–3 key words from final sentence.

Highlight or bold the topic key words in your paragraph.

Key Word Outline—Introduction

Attention Getter

Start your introduction with a sentence that encourages your reader to continue reading. Create three different attention getters. When you are done, choose the one you like the best.

1. Ask your reader a question.

    Example: *What item do you use every day?*

    Write a question that you might use to begin your introduction.

    Answers will vary.

2. Write a very short sentence (#6 vss).

    Example: *Inventions improve quality of life.*

    Write a very short sentence that you might use to begin your introduction.

3. State a famous quote or fact. (If you do not know one, search the Internet for a quote about your specific invention.)

    Example: *"Necessity is the mother of invention" (Plato).*

    Write a quote or fact that you might use to begin your introduction.

Background

Tell your reader what the subject of the composition is about but <u>do not say anything</u> <u>similar to</u> "*This composition is about* . . . ." Simply make a general statement about the subject. Then provide background information you think would be interesting or important. The background information should flow into the introduction of the topics.

Topics

End your introduction by listing the topics you wrote about in your body paragraphs. You can write a sentence about each topic or simply list the topics in one sentence. Highlight or bold the topic key words.

Sample

Key Word Outline for Introduction

I.   Attention getter   *What item do you use every day?*

      Background   *daily, toothbrush, teeth*

                                ++, other, uses, cleaning

                                appliances, grout, jewelry

      Topic A: *toothbrush, clean, shoes*

      Topic B: *toothbrush, art, texturize*

Highlight or bold the topic key words in your paragraph.

Sample Paragraphs

Introduction

[Attention getter] What item do you use every day? [Background] [3] Daily, people use a toothbrush to keep their teeth clean and <u>healthy</u>. A toothbrush can be useful in several other ways. [5] If appliances, grout, or jewelry need to be scrubbed, a toothbrush is a handy tool for the job. [6] It is inexpensive and effective. A toothbrush can be used to clean small spaces <u>because</u> its bristles are thin and short. [Topics] I have <u>successfully</u> used a toothbrush to **clean** the soles of my shoes, <u>which</u> are often caked with mud. [2] With a toothbrush I can also <u>texturize</u> my **art** projects.

Conclusion

[Restate the topics] I <u>rely</u> on my trusty toothbrush to **clean** my shoes <u>when</u> other methods do not work. [2] Without a toothbrush I would not be able to create special **texture** on my art projects. Toothbrushes are handy tools. Most significantly, a toothbrush is the perfect tool to reach small spaces <u>which</u> need to be cleaned <u>thoroughly</u>. (voc) The long handle provides the right amount of leverage. [6] The thin bristles are <u>flexible</u>. [3] Consequently, I can clean with precision. (voc) [5] When I need a unique method to remove dirt, I always reach for a toothbrush. (voc)

Ideas will depend upon chosen topics. The suggested answers work with the sample KWO.

Style Practice

Sentence Openers

Write sentences that can be used in your introduction and conclusion.

1. #2 prepositional opener _____ *[2] With a toothbrush I can also texturize my art projects.*

2. #3 -ly adverb opener _____ *[3] Daily most people use a toothbrush to keep their teeth clean and healthy.*

3. #5 clausal opener – *www.asia.b* _____ *[5] If appliances, grout, or jewelry need to be scrubbed, a toothbrush is a handy tool for the job.*

4. #6 vss opener, 2–5 words (This can be your attention getter.) _____

   [6] Toothbrushes are handy tools.

Dress-Ups

Write ideas for various dress-up you could use in your introduction and conclusion.
Use a thesaurus or your vocabulary words.

1. strong verbs _____ *scrub, texturize, caked, scrape, create, rely, reach, provide*

2. -ly adverbs _____ *successfully, thoroughly, significantly, easily, conveniently*

3. quality adjectives _____ *healthy, flexible, thin, useful, handy, inexpensive, special, unique*

   Look   at your KWOs and consider dress-ups to include in your introduction and conclusion.

Ideas will depend upon chosen topics. The suggested answers work with the sample KWO.

UNIT 7: INVENTIVE WRITING

Vocabulary Practice

Listen   to someone read the vocabulary words for Lesson 21 aloud.

Speak   them aloud yourself.

Read   the definitions and sample sentences on the vocabulary cards.

Write   the part of speech and the definition beside each word.

certainly   _adverb; without doubt_

consequently   _adverb; therefore; as a result_

furthermore   _adverb; in addition; use to introduce a statement that adds to_

the previous statement

similarly   _adverb; in almost the same way_

Think   about the words and their meanings so you can use them in your assignments.

Unit 7 Composition Checklist
Lesson 21: Favorite Invention, Part 2 introduction and conclusion

Inventive Writing

Name: _____

IEW Institute for Excellence in Writing
[Listen Speak Read Write Think]

STRUCTURE

- ☐ MLA format (see Appendix I) _____ 2 pts
- ☐ title centered _____ 2 pts
- ☐ checklist on top, final draft, rough draft, key word outline _____ 1 pt

Introduction

- ☐ introduction includes attention getter, background information, and states topics (bold or highlight) _____ 10 pts

Body

- ☐ insert body paragraphs _____ 2 pts

Conclusion

- ☐ conclusion restates topics (bold or highlight) and indicates most significant/why _____ 10 pts
- ☐ final sentence repeats 1–3 key words for the title _____ 2 pts

STYLE

¶1 ¶4 Dress-Ups (underline one of each)   (2 pts each)

- ☐ ☐ -ly adverb _____ 4 pts
- ☐ ☐ *who/which* clause _____ 4 pts
- ☐ ☐ strong verb _____ 4 pts
- ☐ ☐ quality adjective _____ 4 pts
- ☐ ☐ *www.asia.b* clause _____ 4 pts

Sentence Openers (number; one of each as possible)   (2 pts each)

- ☐ ☐ [2] prepositional _____ 4 pts
- ☐ ☐ [3] -ly adverb _____ 4 pts
- ☐ ☐ [5] clausal – *www.asia.b* _____ 4 pts
- ☐ ☐ [6] vss _____ 4 pts

CHECK FOR BANNED WORDS (-1 pt for each use): think/thought, go/went, say/said, good, bad, big, small _____ pts

MECHANICS

- ☐ spelling, grammar, and punctuation (-1 pt per error) _____ pts

VOCABULARY

- ☐ vocabulary words – label *(voc)* in left margin or after sentence

Total: _____ 65 pts

Custom Total: _____ pts

Checklist

Teachers are free to adjust a checklist by requiring only the stylistic techniques that have become easy, plus one new one. EZ+1

Intentionally blank so the checklist can be removed.

Lesson 22: Exploring a Place Outdoors, Part 1

Structure: Unit 7: Inventive Writing
                            body paragraphs

Style: no new style

Subject: a specific place outdoors

Lesson 22: Exploring a Place Outdoors, Part 1

UNIT 7: INVENTIVE WRITING

Lesson 22: Exploring a Place Outdoors, Part 1

Goals

- to practice the Unit 7 structural model
- to create a KWO from a writing prompt
- to write the body paragraphs of a 5-paragraph composition
- to use new vocabulary words: *explore, investigate, meander, scrutinize*

Assignment Schedule

Day 1

1. Play No-Noose Hangman.
2. Read Structure—Notes from the Brain. Follow instructions to write a 3-paragraph KWO.

Day 2

1. Review your KWO from Day 1.
2. Complete Style Practice.
3. Look at the vocabulary cards for Lesson 22. Complete Vocabulary Practice.
4. Using your KWO as a guide, begin writing your 3-paragraph rough draft.
5. Go over the checklist. Put a check in the box for each requirement you have completed.

Day 3

1. Review all vocabulary words learned thus far.
2. Finish writing your 3-paragraph composition. Follow the topic-clincher rule.
3. Turn in your rough draft to your editor with the completed checklist attached.

Day 4

1. Write or type a final draft, making any corrections your editor asked you to make.
2. Paperclip the checklist, final draft, rough draft, and KWO together. Hand them in.

Note: In Lesson 23 you will write an introduction and a conclusion to add to the paragraphs written for this lesson.

No-Noose Hangman

For this lesson use the following phrases and bonus questions.

TOPICS, MOST SIGNIFICANT, WHY

Bonus: What will these words help you write? *a conclusion paragraph*

What are the components of an introduction paragraph? *attention getter, background, state the topics*

ASK YOURSELF QUESTIONS

Bonus: Why do you ask yourself questions? *To get ideas for details in your paragraphs.* What are some question starter words? *Starter words are listed on page 198.*

Exemplar

The Exemplars file contains a student's completed assignment for Lessons 22–23. The example is for the teacher and not intended to be used by the student.

See the blue page for download instructions.

Prompt

Science involves exploration. Write about a place outdoors that you have explored. This could be a place you have explored often, such as your backyard or a park near your home. It could also be a place you visited on vacation. Write about three unique aspects of this place.

Structure

Notes from the Brain

When learning to write from the "blank page," one technique to help come up with content is to ask yourself questions about the prompt.

1. Based on the prompt, the subject for this lesson is _____ *a specific place outdoors.*

2. Possible topics include _____ *Answer will vary.*

3. How many body paragraphs do you need to write to complete the assignment? _____ *3*

The topic sentence of each paragraph will state a specific aspect about a place that you have explored. On the KWO indicate the topics on the topic lines. Follow this pattern:

subject, topic, one more word *about the topic.*

if 1 topic = 1 paragraph
then 3 topics = 3 paragraphs

On the lines under the first Roman numeral, describe the first topic by asking yourself questions. Brain-helping questions are listed on the KWO. These helpful questions include:

Where is this place?

Why do I like it?

What have I done there?

When do I visit this place?

What does it look like?

Who have I gone with?

How do I feel when I go there?

What do I say and do when I go there?

The answers to your questions become the details for the outline. As you answer a question, place two or three key words on the KWO. Use symbols, numbers, and abbreviations when possible. You do not have to answer every question or ask in the order they are written. Keep your answers brief. You can add more details when you write your composition.

Repeat this process for the second and third topics.

The key to the process is asking questions. Here are the questions asked that resulted in the sample KWO for two of the topics.

Sample Lesson 22: Exploring a Place Outdoors, Part 1

Key Word Outline

II. Topic A: _backyard, treehouse, unique_
1. _5yo, dad, kids, built_
2. _enter, boards, ↑, trunk_
3. _8ft, ↑, 6x6, railing, walls_
4. _slide, swing, zipline_
5. _hammock, carpet, cushions_
(6.) _games, 📖, overlook, property_
(7.) _sisters, tea parties_
Clincher

III. Topic B: _backyard, chickens, characteristics_
1. _4 brown, 1 black, 1 white_
2. _ea., lay, 1 egg/day_
3. _brown, 🐔🐔, bully, others_
4. _devour, all, food_
5. _peck, bugs, leaves_
(6.) _fence, coop, safe_
(7.) _friendly, pet, carry_
Clincher

IV. Topic C: _backyard, creek, entertaining_
1. _shallow, wade, rocky_
2. _splash, collect, rocks_
3. _bridge, dangle, 👣, mesmerizing_
4. _hear, water, rippling_
5. _skip, smooth, rocks_
(6.) _____
(7.) _____
Clincher

?

who?
what?
when?
where?
why?
how?
how feel?
problems?
solutions?
best thing?
worst thing?
value?
significance?
meaning?
examples?
description?

Topic A

What is the subject? (backyard)

What is your specific topic for this paragraph? (treehouse)

What about the topic? (unique)

1. Who built treehouse? When?
2. How do you enter the treehouse?
3. What is its size?
4. How do you exit?
5. What is in it?
6. What do you do inside? (notes 6–7)

Topic B

What is the subject? (backyard)

What is your specific topic for this paragraph? (chickens)

What about the topic? (characteristics)

1. How many chickens are there?
2. What do they do? (notes 2–3)
4. How do they bully?
5. What else do they do?
6. Where are they?
7. What are they like?

Ideas will depend upon chosen topics. The suggested answers work with the sample KWO.

UNIT 7: INVENTIVE WRITING

Style Practice

Sentence Openers

Write sentences that can be used in your body paragraphs.

1. #2 prepositional opener _____ *[2] In the morning the hens lay eggs.* _____

2. #3 -ly adverb opener _____ *[3] Selfishly the brown hens devour all the food.* _____

3. #5 clausal opener – *www.asia.b* __ *[5] When they are outside the coop, they peck bugs and leaves.*

4. #6 vss opener, 2–5 words _____ *[6] The fence protects them.* _____

Dress-Ups

Strong Verb Dress-Up and -ly Adverb Dress-Up

Look at your KWO and write ideas for each.

1. List strong verbs and -ly adverbs to include in your first paragraph.

   strong verbs __ *built, constructed, ascend, descend, relax* __

   -ly adverbs __ *creatively, precisely, collectively, effortlessly, conveniently, frequently* __

2. List strong verbs and -ly adverbs to include in your second paragraph.

   strong verbs __ *reside, occupy, devour, bully, peck, shields* __

   -ly adverbs __ *constantly, greedily, selfishly, cruelly, meticulously, effectively* __

3. List strong verbs and -ly adverbs to include in your third paragraph.

   strong verbs __ *wade, splash, dangle, skip, observe* __

   -ly adverbs __ *gingerly, delightfully, leisurely, skillfully, routinely* __

www.asia.b Clause Dress-Up

Write two sentences with a *www.asia.b* clause that you could use in your body paragraphs. Remember to add the clause to a sentence that is already complete. Punctuate and mark correctly.

I stare at the water <u>as</u> I dangle my feet.

I play games <u>although</u> my sisters have tea parties.

Who/Which Clause Dress-Up

Write two sentences with a *who/which* clause that you could use in your body paragraphs. Punctuate and mark correctly.

The brown hens, <u>which</u> bully the others, devour all the food.

I dangle my feet from the bridge, <u>which</u> spans the creek.

Quality Adjective Dress-Up

Look at your KWO and list three different nouns that you could use in your body paragraphs. Next to each noun, write ideas for adjectives that create a strong image or feeling. Avoid banned adjectives.

1. *treehouse*   *wooden, unique, charming, pleasurable*

2. *hens*   *curious, selfish, friendly, plump*

3. *creek*   *glistening, mesmerizing, refreshing, cool*

Vocabulary Practice

Listen   to someone read the vocabulary words for Lesson 22 aloud.

Speak   them aloud yourself.

Read   the definitions and sample sentences on the vocabulary cards.

Write   four sentences using one of this lesson's vocabulary words in each sentence.

explore   *I explore my backyard.*

investigate   *I investigate the life within the water.*

meander   *The creek meanders along the edge of the property.*

scrutinize   *The hens scrutinize the bugs and leaves.*

Think   about the words and their meanings so you can use them in your assignments.

Unit 7 Composition Checklist
Lesson 22: Exploring a Place Outdoors, Part 1 body paragraphs

Inventive Writing

Name: _____

IEW Institute for Excellence in Writing
Listen. Speak. Read. Write. Think!

STRUCTURE

☐ MLA format (see Appendix I) _____ 3 pts

☐ checklist on top, final draft, rough draft, key word outline _____ 3 pts

Body

☐ topic-clincher sentences repeat or reflect 2–3 key words (highlight or **bold**) _____ 5 pts

☐ facts stay on topic _____ 5 pts

STYLE

¶2 ¶3 ¶4 Dress-Ups (underline one of each) (2 pts each)

☐ ☐ ☐ -ly adverb _____ 6 pts

☐ ☐ ☐ *who/which* clause _____ 6 pts

☐ ☐ ☐ strong verb _____ 6 pts

☐ ☐ ☐ quality adjective _____ 6 pts

☐ ☐ ☐ *www.asia.b* clause _____ 6 pts

Sentence Openers (number; one of each as possible) (2 pts each)

☐ ☐ ☐ [2] prepositional _____ 6 pts

☐ ☐ ☐ [3] -ly adverb _____ 6 pts

☐ ☐ ☐ [5] clausal – *www.asia.b* _____ 6 pts

☐ ☐ ☐ [6] vss _____ 6 pts

CHECK FOR BANNED WORDS (-1 pt for each use): think/thought, go/went, say/said, good, bad, big, small _____ pts

MECHANICS

☐ spelling, grammar, and punctuation (-1 pt per error) _____ pts

VOCABULARY

☐ vocabulary words – label *(voc)* in left margin or after sentence

Total: _____ 70 pts

Custom Total: _____ pts

Checklist

Teachers are free to adjust a checklist by requiring only the stylistic techniques that have become easy, plus one new one. EZ+1

UNIT 7: INVENTIVE WRITING

Intentionally blank so the checklist can be removed.

Lesson 23: Exploring a Place Outdoors, Part 2

Structure: Unit 7: Inventive Writing
                                     introduction and conclusion

Style: no new style

Subject: a specific place

UNIT 7: INVENTIVE WRITING

Lesson 23: Exploring a Place Outdoors, Part 2

Goals

- to practice the Unit 7 structural model
- to create KWOs for an introduction and a conclusion paragraph
- to write an introduction and a conclusion paragraph
- to complete a 5-paragraph composition
- to review vocabulary words

Assignment Schedule

Day 1

1. Play Vocabulary Pictionary.
2. Write a KWO for a conclusion and then a KWO for an introduction.

Day 2

1. Review both KWOs from Day 1.
2. Complete Style Practice.
3. Complete Vocabulary Practice. There are no new words for this lesson.
4. Using your conclusion KWO as a guide, write your conclusion. Highlight or bold the topic key words.
5. Go over the checklist. Put a check in the box for each requirement you have completed.

Day 3

1. Review all vocabulary words learned thus far.
2. Using your introduction KWO as a guide, write your introduction. Highlight or bold the topic key words.
3. Turn in your rough draft to your editor with the completed checklist attached.

Day 4

1. Write or type a final draft, making any corrections your editor asked you to make. Add the introduction and the conclusion to the final draft body paragraphs written in Lesson 22.
2. Paperclip the checklist, final draft, rough drafts, and KWOs together. Hand them in.

Key Word Outline—Conclusion

Restate the Topics

> Write a sentence or two about each topic. Try to convey the main idea of each body paragraph. Highlight or bold the topic key words.

Most Significant and Why

> What is the most important, most interesting, or most significant thing to remember about all that you wrote and why? You may choose one of your topics and tell why it is the most significant, or you may choose something that tells the importance of the entire subject.

Final Sentence

> End with a sentence from which you can create a title. Be sure that your paper sounds complete.

Sample

Key Word Outline for Conclusion

V.   Topic A: _____ *backyard, treehouse, unique* _____

Topic B: _____ *backyard, chickens, characteristics* _____

Topic C: _____ *backyard, creek, entertaining* _____

Most significant _____ *relaxing, creek, afternoon* _____

Why? _____ *daydream, play, explore* _____

_____ *X worries, X work, pleasant* _____

_____ *backyard, favorite, place* _____

Title repeats 1–3 key words from final sentence.

Highlight or bold the topic key words in your paragraph.

Key Word Outline—Introduction

Attention Getter

Start your introduction with a sentence that encourages your reader to continue reading. Create three different attention getters. When you are done, choose the one you like the best.

1. Ask your reader a question.

    Example: *Where shall we explore tomorrow?*

    Write a question that you might use to begin your introduction.

    _____*Answers will vary.*_____

2. Write a very short sentence (#6 vss).

    Example: *I never stop exploring.*

    Write a very short sentence that you might use to begin your introduction.

    _____

3. State a famous quote or fact. (If you do not know one, search the Internet for a quote about a specific place.)

    Example: *"In wisdom gathered over time I have found that every experience is a form of exploration" (Ansel Adams).*

    Write a quote or fact that you might use to begin your introduction.

    _____

Background

Make a general statement about the subject. Then, provide background information you think would be interesting or important. The background information should help you flow into introducing your topics.

Topics

End your introduction by listing the topics you wrote about in your body paragraphs. You can write a sentence about each topic or simply list the topics in one sentence. Highlight or bold the topic key words.

Sample

Key Word Outline for Introduction

I.   Attention getter   *I, X stop, exploring*

Background   *daily, visit, 5 acres*

++ activities, behind, house

alone, friends, family

Topic A: *backyard, treehouse, unique*

Topic B: *backyard, chickens, characteristics*

Topic C: *backyard, creek, entertaining*

Highlight or bold the topic key words in your paragraph.

Ideas will depend upon chosen topics. The suggested answers work with the sample KWO.

Style Practice

Sentence Openers

Write sentences that can be used in your introduction or conclusion.

1. #2 prepositional opener *[2] Throughout the day I love to explore the great outdoors.*

2. #3 -ly adverb opener *[3] Undoubtedly, my favorite outdoor space is right in my backyard.*

3. #5 clausal opener – *www.asia.b* *[5] When I wander around the yard, I climb into my treehouse, observe the chickens, or visit the creek.*

4. #6 vss opener, 2–5 words (This can be your attention getter.) *[6] I wander throughout.*

Dress-Ups

Write ideas for various dress-up you could use in your introduction and conclusion.
Use a thesaurus or your vocabulary words.

1. strong verbs *explore, visit, climb, observe, visit, wander*

2. -ly adverbs *frequently, commonly, eagerly, actively, similarily*

3. quality adjectives *unique, pleasant, favorite, entertaining, beloved*

Look at your KWOs and consider dress-ups to include in your introduction and conclusion.

Vocabulary Practice

Think   about the words and their meanings.
Which vocabulary words could you use in this assignment?

intently, vital, wondrous, glide, significant, mesmerized, cautiously, detect, unique,

certainly, similarily

Unit 7 Composition Checklist

Inventive Writing

Lesson 23: Exploring a Place Outdoors, Part 2 introduction and conclusion

Name: _____

Institute for **Excellence** in **Writing**
Listen. Speak. Read. Write. Think.

STRUCTURE

☐ MLA format (see Appendix I) .... _____ 2 pts

☐ title centered .... _____ 2 pts

☐ checklist on top, final draft, rough draft, key word outline .... _____ 1 pt

Introduction

☐ introduction includes attention getter, background information, and states topics (bold or highlight) .... _____ 10 pts

Body

☐ insert body paragraphs .... _____ 2 pts

Conclusion

☐ conclusion restates topics (bold or highlight) and indicates most significant/why .... _____ 10 pts

☐ final sentence repeats 1–3 key words for the title .... _____ 2 pts

STYLE

¶1 ¶5 **Dress-Ups** (underline one of each)   (2 pts each)

☐ ☐ -ly adverb .... _____ 4 pts

☐ ☐ *who/which* clause .... _____ 4 pts

☐ ☐ strong verb .... _____ 4 pts

☐ ☐ quality adjective .... _____ 4 pts

☐ ☐ *www.asia.b* clause .... _____ 4 pts

Sentence Openers (number; one of each as possible)   (2 pts each)

☐ ☐ [2] prepositional .... _____ 4 pts

☐ ☐ [3] -ly adverb .... _____ 4 pts

☐ ☐ [5] clausal – *www.asia.b* .... _____ 4 pts

☐ ☐ [6] vss .... _____ 4 pts

CHECK FOR BANNED WORDS (-1 pt for each use): think/thought, go/went, say/said, good, bad, big, small .... _____ pts

MECHANICS

☐ spelling, grammar, and punctuation (-1 pt per error) .... _____ pts

VOCABULARY

☐ vocabulary words – label *(voc)* in left margin or after sentence

Total: _____ 65 pts

Custom Total: _____ pts

Checklist ____

Teachers are free to adjust a checklist by requiring only the stylistic techniques that have become easy, plus one new one. EZ+1

Intentionally blank so the checklist can be removed.

Institute for Excellence in Writing

Lesson 24: Albert Einstein, Part 3

Structure:	Unit 8: Formal Essay Models introduction and conclusion	
Style:	#1 subject opener, #4 -ing opener	
Subject:	physicist Albert Einstein	

Teaching Writing: Structure and Style

Watch the sections for Unit 8: Formal Essay Models. At IEW.com/twss-help reference the TWSS Viewing Guides.

Lesson 24: Albert Einstein, Part 3

UNIT 8: FORMAL ESSAY MODELS

Lesson 24: Albert Einstein, Part 3

Goals

- to learn the Unit 8 Formal Essay structural model
- to review the components of an introduction and a conclusion paragraph
- to create KWOs for an introduction and a conclusion paragraph
- to write an introduction and a conclusion paragraph
- to complete a 5-paragraph essay with a works consulted page
- to add a new sentence opener: #4 -ing opener
- to understand the #1 subject sentence opener
- to use new vocabulary words: *achievement, advantage, benefit, contribution*

Assignment Schedule

Day 1

1. Play Two Strikes and You're Out.

2. Using the three paragraphs you wrote in Unit 6 as your body paragraphs, you will write an introduction and a conclusion to form a 5-paragraph essay about Albert Einstein. Read New Structure—Basic Essay Model: Introduction and Conclusion.

3. Read the three paragraphs you wrote in Lessons 17–18 to refresh your memory of the topics.

4. Write a KWO for a conclusion and then write a KWO for an introduction.

Day 2

1. Read New Style and complete Style Practice.

2. Revise the body paragraphs that you wrote in Lessons 17–18 by adding sentence openers #1 subject, #4 -ing, and #5 clausal.

   Note: For an abbreviated assignment option, add body paragraphs without revision to the introduction and conclusion paragraphs. If you choose this option, use the alternative checklist on page 240.

3. Look at the vocabulary cards for Lesson 24. Complete Vocabulary Practice.

Students craft an essay about Albert Einstein by adding an introduction and conclusion to the body paragraphs written in Lessons 17–18. Remind students that both the introduction and conclusion paragraphs follow their own unique structure.

Exemplar

The Exemplars file contains a student's completed assignment for Lesson 24. The example is for the teacher and not intended to be used by the student.

See the blue page for download instructions.

Day 3

1. Review both KWOs from Day 1.

2. Using your conclusion KWO as a guide, write your conclusion. Highlight or bold the topic key words.

3. Using your introduction KWO as a guide, write your introduction. Highlight or bold the topic key words.

4. Add the introduction and the conclusion to the body paragraphs revised on Day 2.

5. Go over the checklist. Put a check in the box for each requirement you have completed.

6. Turn in your rough draft to your editor with the completed checklist attached.

Day 4

1. Review all vocabulary words learned thus far.

2. Write or type a final draft, making any corrections your editor asked you to make. Include the works consulted page written in Lesson 18 as the final page.

3. Paperclip the checklist, final draft, rough drafts, and KWOs together. Hand them in.

In Lessons 25–26 you will write a report about a prominent scientist. In preparation for Lesson 25, find three fairly short, simple sources either from the library or the Internet. There is a list of possible subjects on page 243.

New Structure

Basic Essay Model: Introduction and Conclusion

Unit 8 Formal Essay Models teaches various types of essays. Essays begin with an introduction and end with a conclusion. The essays you will write in this book follow the basic essay model, which looks like the following.

I.   Introduction   *attention getter, background, state topics*

      Body Paragraphs

V.   Conclusion   *restate topics, most significant/why, last sentence ➜ title*

The model can be adapted by simply changing the number of body paragraphs. You have already used this structure to write compositions in Unit 7. In this lesson you will use the same structure to complete the Unit 6 report you wrote about Albert Einstein in Lessons 17–18. To complete your essay, you will simply add an introduction and a conclusion to the three body paragraphs that you have already written. This will allow you to understand the structure of the basic essay model as you continue to practice writing introductory and concluding paragraphs.

Review the information in the three body paragraphs you wrote in Lessons 17 and 18 so that the details are fresh on your mind. Even though the conclusion will be placed last, you will outline and write it before the introduction.

Key Word Outline—Conclusion

Restate the Topics

> Write a sentence or two about each topic. Try to convey the main idea of each body paragraph. Highlight or bold the topic key words.

Most Significant and Why

> What is the most important, most interesting, or most significant thing to remember about all that you wrote and why? You may choose one of your topics and tell why it is the most significant, or you may choose something that tells the importance of the entire subject.

> If you are struggling, consider what Einstein's most significant contribution or achievement was and why. Alternatively, consider the most significant advantage or benefit of Einstein's discoveries.

Final sentence

> End with a sentence from which you can create a title. Be sure that your paper sounds complete.

Sample

Key Word Outline for Conclusion

V.   Topic A: _____ *AE, early life, education* _____

Topic B: _____ *AE, career, successful* _____

Topic C: _____ *AE, later years, eventful* _____

Most significant _____ *discoveries, changed, world* _____

Why? _____ *perseverance, intelligence, ++ work* _____

improve, energy, technology _____

better, convenient, safe _____

Title repeats 1–3 key words from final sentence.

Highlight or bold the topic key words in your paragraph.

Key Word Outline—Introduction

Attention Getter

Start your introduction with a sentence that encourages your reader to continue reading. Create three different attention getters. When you are done, choose the one you like the best.

1. Ask your reader a question.

    Example*: Who is considered the most intelligent man of the twentieth century?*

    Write a question that you might use to begin your introduction.

    Answers will vary.

2. Write a very short sentence (#6 vss).

    Example*: Discoveries require diligent work.*

    Write a very short sentence that you might use to begin your introduction.

3. State a famous quote or fact. (If you do not know one, search the Internet for a quote or fact about Einstein.)

    Example*: "Strive not to be a success, but rather to be of value" (Albert Einstein).*

    Write a quote or fact that you might use to begin your introduction.

Background

Tell your reader what the subject of the composition is about but do not say anything similar to "*This composition is about . . . .*" Simply make a general statement about the subject. Then provide background information you think would be interesting or important. The background information should flow into the introduction of the topics.

Topics

End your introduction by listing the topics you wrote about in your body paragraphs. You can write a sentence about each topic or simply list the topics in one sentence. Highlight or bold the topic key words.

Sample

Key Word Outline for Introduction

I.   Attention getter   *"Strive not to be a success, but rather to be of value."*

      Background   *genius, ++ intelligent, 20th century*

                                 b. 1879, Germany → Italy, Switzerland, d. 1955

                                   technology, spaceships, computers, GPS

      Topic A: *AE, early life, education*

      Topic B: *AE, career, successful*

      Topic C: *AE, later years, eventful*

Institute for Excellence in Writing

New Style

#4 -ing Opener

In this lesson you will learn another sentence opener: the #4 -ing opener.

The -ing opener is a participial phrase placed at the beginning of a sentence.
It follows the pattern: -ing word/phrase + comma + subject of sentence.

> [4] Solving mathematical equations, Einstein made many discoveries.

Notice:

1. The sentence must begin with an action word that ends in -ing. This is called a participle.

   [4] *Solving* mathematical equations, Einstein made many discoveries.

2. The -ing word/phrase and comma must be followed by a complete sentence.

   [4] Solving mathematical equations, *Einstein made many discoveries.*

3. The thing (subject of sentence) after the comma must be the thing doing the inging.

   [4] Solving mathematical equations, *Einstein* made many discoveries.

   Who was solving? *Einstein.* The subject *Einstein* follows the comma.

4. To indicate that a sentence begins with an -ing opener, label it with a 4 in the left margin or place a [4] right before the sentence.

The thing after the comma must be the thing doing the inging.

Warning:

1. Beware of the illegal #4, which is grammatically incorrect. If the thing after the comma is not the thing doing the inging, the sentence does not make sense. This is known as a *dangling modifier.*

   [4] Asking questions, the teachers called him disruptive.

   Who was asking questions? *The teachers.* This is incorrect because *the teachers* were not asking questions.

2. Beware of two impostor #4s, which begin with an -ing word but do not follow the pattern.

   [1] Asking questions helped him learn.

   This is a #1 subject opener. There is neither a comma nor a subject doing the inging.

   [2] During his time as a teacher, Einstein solved math problems.

   This is a #2 prepositional opener. *Einstein* (the subject) is not doing the *during.*
   Prepositions ending in -ing include *concerning, according to, regarding, during.*

#1 Subject Opener

The sixth and final opener is the subject opener.

The subject opener is simply a sentence that begins with its subject. This is the kind of sentence you most naturally write if you do not purposely try to use one of the other sentence openers.

> [1] Light is made of particles called photons.

> [1] The first paper explained that light is made of photons.

Notice:

1. A subject opener begins with the subject of the sentence.

   In the second example there are adjectives (the first) in front of the subject (paper), but that does not change the sentence structure. It is still a #1 subject opener.

2. To indicate that a sentence begins with a subject opener, label it with a 1 in the left margin or place a [1] right before the sentence.

Practice

Write a sentence with a #4 -ing opener: -ing word/phrase + comma + subject of sentence. Label it with a [4].

[4] Working in the patent office, Einstein invented a type of hearing aid.

Write a sentence with a #1 subject opener. Label it with a [1].

[1] Einstein's discoveries enabled him to win the Nobel Prize in Physics.

Congratulations! You have learned all the different sentence openers! Your literary toolbox is filling up. To continue practicing and using them appropriately, here is a new rule for you to follow.

> ## "Each sentence opener should be in every paragraph as possible. No more than two of the same in a row. "

 From now on, label each sentence in every paragraph, using no more than two of the same sentence opener in a row. If you are unsure what a particular sentence is, mark it as a #1 subject opener.

Style Practice

Sentence Openers

Write sentences that can be used in your introduction and conclusion.

1. #1 subject opener _____ *[1] Einstein was named the Person of the Century.*

2. #2 prepositional opener _____ *[2] Throughout his life he continually asked questions.*

3. #3 -ly adverb opener _____ *[3] Evidently, mathematical formulas occupied his thoughts*
   at all times.

4. #4 -ing opener _____ *[4] Working tirelessly, he developed theories that*
   advanced science and technology.

5. #5 clausal opener – *www.asia.b* _____ *[5] Although he performed poorly in language and*
   history, his excellence in math and science led to many famous discoveries.

6. #6 vss opener, 2–5 words _____ *[6] Einstein studied physics.*

Dress-Ups

Look at your KWO and consider where you can include various clauses as well as strong verbs, quality adjectives, -ly adverbs, and sentence openers.

These words can assist students writing the conclusion. As students define each word, challenge them to consider what Einstein's most significant achievement or contribution was and why. Discuss the most significant advantage or benefit of Einstein's discoveries and why.

UNIT 8: FORMAL ESSAY MODELS

Vocabulary Practice

Listen   to someone read the vocabulary words for Lesson 24 aloud.

Speak   them aloud yourself.

Read   the definitions and sample sentences on the vocabulary cards.

Write   the part of speech and the definition beside each word.
When writing sentences, you may use other forms of the vocabulary words including achieve, advantageous, beneficial, and contribute.

achievement   _noun; something accomplished by special ability, effort, or courage_

advantage   _noun; something that helps make someone or something better_

benefit   _noun; something that is good or helpful_

contribution   _noun; something given for a charitable purpose_

Think   about the words and their meanings so you can use them in your assignments.

Unit 8 Composition Checklist
Lesson 24: Albert Einstein, Part 3

Formal
Essay
Models

Name: _____

Institute for Excellence in Writing

STRUCTURE

☐ MLA format (see Appendix I) _____ 2 pts

☐ title centered _____ 2 pts

☐ works consulted entries in proper format _____ 1 pt

☐ checklist on top, final draft, rough draft, key word outline _____ 1 pt

Introduction

☐ introduction includes attention getter, background information, and states topics (bold or highlight) _____ 10 pts

Body

☐ insert body paragraphs _____ 2 pts

Conclusion

☐ conclusion restates topics (**bold** or highlight) and indicates most significant/why _____ 10 pts

☐ final sentence repeats 1–3 key words for the title _____ 2 pts

STYLE

¶1 ¶2 ¶3 ¶4 ¶5 Dress-Ups (underline one of each) (1 pt each)

☐ ☐ ☐ ☐ ☐ -ly adverb _____ 5 pts

☐ ☐ ☐ ☐ ☐ *who/which* clause _____ 5 pts

☐ ☐ ☐ ☐ ☐ strong verb _____ 5 pts

☐ ☐ ☐ ☐ ☐ quality adjective _____ 5 pts

☐ ☐ ☐ ☐ ☐ *www.asia.b* clause _____ 5 pts

Sentence Openers (number; one of each as possible) (1 pt each)

☐ ☐ ☐ ☐ ☐ [1] subject _____ 5 pts

☐ ☐ ☐ ☐ ☐ [2] prepositional _____ 5 pts

☐ ☐ ☐ ☐ ☐ [3] -ly adverb _____ 5 pts

☐ ☐ ☐ ☐ ☐ [4] -ing _____ 5 pts

☐ ☐ ☐ ☐ ☐ [5] clausal – *www.asia.b* _____ 5 pts

☐ ☐ ☐ ☐ ☐ [6] vss _____ 5 pts

CHECK FOR BANNED WORDS (-1 pt for each use): think/thought, go/went, say/said, good, bad, big, small _____ pts

MECHANICS

☐ spelling, grammar, and punctuation (-1 pt per error) _____ pts

VOCABULARY

☐ vocabulary words – label *(voc)* in left margin or after sentence

Total: _____ 85 pts

Custom Total: _____ pts

Checklist

Teachers are free to adjust a checklist by requiring only the stylistic techniques that have become easy, plus one new one. EZ+1

Unit 8 Composition Checklist *for Abbreviated Assignment Option*
Lesson 24: Albert Einstein, Part 3 introduction and conclusion

Formal Essay Models

IEW Institute for Excellence in Writing
Listen, Speak, Read, Write, Think!

Name: _____

STRUCTURE

☐ MLA format (see Appendix I) _____ 2 pts

☐ title centered _____ 2 pts

☐ works consulted entries in proper format _____ 2 pts

☐ checklist on top, final draft, rough draft, key word outline _____ 1 pt

Introduction

☐ introduction includes attention getter, background information, and states topics (bold or highlight) _____ 10 pts

Body

☐ insert body paragraphs _____ 2 pts

Conclusion

☐ conclusion restates topics (**bold** or highlight) and indicates most significant/why _____ 10 pts

☐ final sentence repeats 1–3 key words for the title _____ 2 pts

STYLE

¶1 ¶5 Dress-Ups (underline one of each) (2 pts each)

☐ ☐ -ly adverb _____ 4 pts

☐ ☐ *who/which* clause _____ 4 pts

☐ ☐ strong verb _____ 4 pts

☐ ☐ quality adjective _____ 4 pts

☐ ☐ *www.asia.b* clause _____ 4 pts

Sentence Openers (number; one of each as possible) (2 pts each)

☐ ☐ [1] subject _____ 4 pts

☐ ☐ [2] prepositional _____ 4 pts

☐ ☐ [3] -ly adverb _____ 4 pts

☐ ☐ [4] -ing _____ 4 pts

☐ ☐ [5] clausal – *www.asia.b* _____ 4 pts

☐ ☐ [6] vss _____ 4 pts

CHECK FOR BANNED WORDS (-1 pt for each use): think/thought, go/went, say/said, good, bad, big, small _____ pts

MECHANICS

☐ spelling, grammar, and punctuation (-1 pt per error) _____ pts

VOCABULARY

☐ vocabulary words – label *(voc)* in left margin or after sentence

Total: _____ 75 pts

Custom Total: _____ pts

Lesson 25: A Prominent Scientist, Part 1

Structure:	Unit 8: Formal Essay Models
	body paragraphs
Style:	no new style
Subject:	a prominent scientist
	additional sources required

UNIT 8: FORMAL ESSAY MODELS

Lesson 25: A Prominent Scientist, Part 1

Goals

- to practice the Unit 8 structural model
- to practice scanning multiple sources to determine three topics for an essay
- to create source outlines from multiple sources
- to create three fused outlines about three different topics
- to write the body paragraphs of a 5-paragraph essay
- to review vocabulary words

Assignment Schedule

Day 1

1. Play Vocabulary Pictionary.

2. In Lessons 25–26 you will use more than one source of information to write an essay about a prominent scientist. You will write the body paragraphs in this lesson.

3. Read New Structure—Basic Essay Model: Body Paragraphs.

4. After you choose an individual to write about (the subject of your essay), find sources and choose three topics.

5. For your first body paragraph, choose a topic that is covered in two or three sources. Write the topic on the topic line on page 244. Complete the source outlines. Using notes from your source outlines, write a fused outline.

6. For your second body paragraph, choose another topic that is covered in two or three sources. Write the topic on the topic line on page 246. Complete the source outlines. Using notes from your source outlines, write a fused outline.

Day 2

1. For your third body paragraph, choose a third topic that is covered in two or three sources. Write the topic on the topic line on page 248. Complete the source outlines. Using notes from your source outlines, write a fused outline.

2. Complete Style Practice.

3. Complete Vocabulary Practice. There are no new words for this lesson.

4. Using your fused outline as a guide, begin writing your rough draft.

5. Go over the checklist. Put a check in the box for each requirement you have completed.

Day 3

1. Review all vocabulary words learned thus far.

2. Finish writing your three body paragraphs. Follow the topic-clincher rule.

3. Turn in your rough draft to your editor with the completed checklist attached.

Day 4

1. Write or type a final draft, making any corrections your editor asked you to make.

2. Paperclip the checklist, final draft, rough draft, and KWO together. Hand them in.

New Structure

Basic Essay Model: Body Paragraphs

In Lessons 25–26 you will write a 5-paragraph essay. Consider again the Basic Essay Model.

	I.	Introduction	*attention getter, background, state topics*
Body	II.	Topic A	*topic, 5–7 details, clincher*
	III.	Topic B	*topic, 5–7 details, clincher*
Paragraphs	IV.	Topic C	*topic, 5–7 details, clincher*
	V.	Conclusion	*restate topics, most significant/why, last sentence* ➜ *title*

An essay is a multiple-paragraph composition written about one subject. Once you know what the subject of the composition is, you determine how many body paragraphs to write. Once you know the number of body paragraphs, you determine the topics. Each body paragraph equals one topic. Remember, the model can be adapted by simply changing the number of body paragraphs. When you follow this model, write from the inside out beginning with the body paragraphs.

This should sound familiar. You followed this same structure to write your Unit 7 compositions. In Unit 7 you asked yourself questions to create your KWO. Because this essay requires research, look at your sources to determine the topics of your body paragraphs. For each topic that you choose, you will take notes using source outlines and fuse those notes using a fused outline approach.

Prompt

Write a 5-paragraph research essay about a prominent scientist. Below is a short list of possible subjects.

Choose a Subject

Hippocrates	Aristotle	Archimedes
Ptolemy	Isaac Newton	Galileo Galilei
Robert Boyle	Michael Faraday	Louis Pasteur
Marie Curie	Thomas Edison	Antonie van Leeuwenhoek
Edwin Hubble	Stephen Hawking	Matthew Fontaine Maury
Barbara McClintock	James Clerk Maxwell	

Find Sources

Once you determine the subject you will research, find at least three sources of information about it. History textbooks, Internet articles (especially those labeled "for kids"), encyclopedia articles, and short children's books make the best sources. Choose short, easy sources.

Choose Topics

Identify various topics that you might write about by skimming your sources. Look at the table of contents, chapter titles, and headings. For a 5-paragraph paper, you must choose three topics.

if 1 paragraph = 1 topic
then 3 paragraphs = 3 topics

When writing about famous people, your three topics may include early life, what work or idea made the person famous, and later years. If you are writing about an individual who is famous for a variety of accomplishments, consider writing about three different accomplishments.

After you have chosen three topics to write about, you are ready to research each topic in more detail using source outlines. Remember to follow this pattern for the topic lines of your KWO: *subject, topic,* one more word *about the topic.*

Source Outlines

Write the name of the first topic you will research on the line below.

First Topic: _____ *Write the topic of the first paragraph here.* _____

Choose your first source. Write the title on the Source line. Using key words, write the topic on the Roman numeral line. Complete the source outline by noting three to five interesting facts about the topic. Repeat the process with the second source and, if applicable, with the third.

Source A: _____ *Write the title of one of the sources from the library or the Internet.* _____

II. Topic: _____ *subject, topic, one more word about the topic* _____

1. _____ *The topic lines of the source outlines and the fused outline must be the same.*

2. _____

3. _____

(4.) _____

(5.) _____

Source B: _____ *Write the title of one of the sources from the library or the Internet.* _____

II. Topic: _____

1. _____

2. _____

3. _____

(4.) _____

(5.) _____

Source C: _____ *Write the title of one of the sources from the library or the Internet.* _____

II. Topic: _____

1. _____

2. _____

3. _____

(4.) _____

(5.) _____

Fused Outline

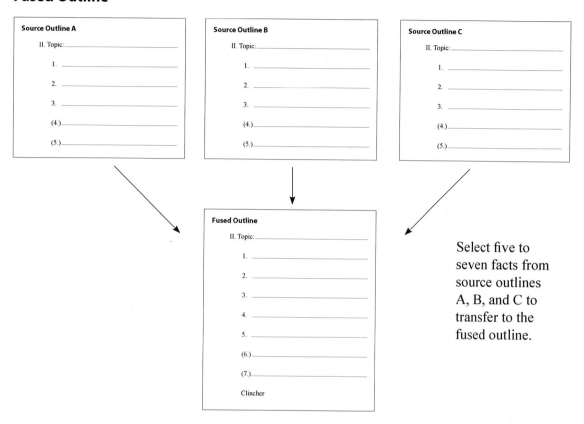

Select five to seven facts from source outlines A, B, and C to transfer to the fused outline.

Using key words, write the topic on the Roman numeral line. This should be the same topic that you placed on the source outlines.

II. Topic: _____

    1. _____

    2. _____

    3. _____

    4. _____

    5. _____

   (6.) _____

   (7.) _____

Clincher

Source Outlines

Write the name of the second topic you will research on the line below.

Second Topic: *Write the topic of the second paragraph here.*

Choose your first source. Write the title on the Source line. Using key words, write the topic on the Roman numeral line. Complete the source outline by noting three to five interesting facts about the topic. Repeat the process with the second source and, if applicable, with the third.

Source A: *Write the title of one of the sources from the library or the Internet.*

III. Topic: *subject, topic, one more word about the topic*

    1.   *The topic lines of the source outlines and the fused outline must be the same.*

    2.   _____

    3.   _____

    (4.)   _____

    (5.)   _____

Source B: *Write the title of one of the sources from the library or the Internet.*

III. Topic: _____

    1.   _____

    2.   _____

    3.   _____

    (4.)   _____

    (5.)   _____

Source C: *Write the title of one of the sources from the library or the Internet.*

III. Topic: _____

    1.   _____

    2.   _____

    3.   _____

    (4.)   _____

    (5.)   _____

Fused Outline

Using key words, write the topic on the Roman numeral line. This should be the same topic that you placed on the source outlines. Select five to seven facts from the source outlines to transfer to the fused outline.

III. Topic: _____

    1. _____

    2. _____

    3. _____

    4. _____

    5. _____

(6.) _____

(7.) _____

Clincher

Source Outlines

Write the name of the third topic you will research on the line below.

Third Topic: _____ *Write the topic of the third paragraph here.* _____

Choose your first source. Write the title on the Source line. Using key words, write the topic on the Roman numeral line. Complete the source outline by noting three to five interesting facts about the topic. Repeat the process with the second source and, if applicable, with the third.

Source A: _____ *Write the title of one of the sources from the library or the Internet.* _____

IV. Topic: _____ *subject, topic, one more word about the topic* _____

   1. _____ *The topic lines of the source outlines and the fused outline must be the same.*

   2. _____

   3. _____

  (4.) _____

  (5.) _____

Source B: _____ *Write the title of one of the sources from the library or the Internet.* _____

IV. Topic: _____

   1. _____

   2. _____

   3. _____

  (4.) _____

  (5.) _____

Source C: _____ *Write the title of one of the sources from the library or the Internet.* _____

IV. Topic: _____

   1. _____

   2. _____

   3. _____

  (4.) _____

  (5.) _____

Fused Outline

Using key words, write the topic on the Roman numeral line. This should be the same topic that you placed on the source outlines. Select five to seven facts from the source outlines to transfer to the fused outline.

IV. Topic: _____

    1. _____

    2. _____

    3. _____

    4. _____

    5. _____

    (6.) _____

    (7.) _____

Clincher

Style Practice

Dress-Ups

Write ideas for various dress-ups you could use in your body paragraphs.
Use a thesaurus or your vocabulary words.

1. strong verbs _____ *Encourage the student to look at the fused outline and*

_____ *consider words to include in the composition.*

2. -ly adverbs _____

_____

3. quality adjectives _____

_____

Sentence Openers

Look at your KWO and consider sentence openers to include in your body paragraphs.

Vocabulary Practice

Think   about the words and their meanings.
Which vocabulary words could you use in this assignment?

_____ *Ideas will depend upon student's chosen subject.*

_____

Unit 8 Composition Checklist
Lesson 25: A Prominent Scientist, Part 1 body paragraphs

Formal
Essay
Models

Name: _____

Institute for **Excellence** in **Writing**

STRUCTURE

☐ MLA format (see Appendix I) _____ 2 pts

☐ checklist on top, final draft, rough draft, key word outline _____ 2 pts

Body

☐ topic-clincher sentences repeat or reflect 2–3 key words (highlight or **bold**) _____ 4 pts

☐ facts stay on topic _____ 4 pts

STYLE

¶2 ¶3 ¶4 Dress-Ups (underline one of each)   (1 pt each)

☐ ☐ ☐ -ly adverb _____ 3 pts

☐ ☐ ☐ *who/which* clause _____ 3 pts

☐ ☐ ☐ strong verb _____ 3 pts

☐ ☐ ☐ quality adjective _____ 3 pts

☐ ☐ ☐ *www.asia.b* clause _____ 3 pts

Sentence Openers (number; one of each as possible)   (1 pt each)

☐ ☐ ☐ [1] subject _____ 3 pts

☐ ☐ ☐ [2] prepositional _____ 3 pts

☐ ☐ ☐ [3] -ly adverb _____ 3 pts

☐ ☐ ☐ [4] -ing _____ 3 pts

☐ ☐ ☐ [5] clausal – *www.asia.b* _____ 3 pts

☐ ☐ ☐ [6] vss _____ 3 pts

CHECK FOR BANNED WORDS (-1 pt for each use): think/thought, go/went, say/said, good, bad, big, small _____ pts

MECHANICS

☐ spelling, grammar, and punctuation (-1 pt per error) _____ pts

VOCABULARY

☐ vocabulary words – label *(voc)* in left margin or after sentence

Total: _____ 45 pts

Custom Total: _____ pts

> *Checklist*
>
> Teachers are free to adjust a checklist by requiring only the stylistic techniques that have become easy, plus one new one. EZ+1

Intentionally blank so the checklist can be removed.

Lesson 26: A Prominent Scientist, Part 2

Structure: Unit 8: Formal Essay Models
                      introduction and conclusion

Style: no new style

Subject: a prominent scientist

UNIT 8: FORMAL ESSAY MODELS

Lesson 26: A Prominent Scientist, Part 2

Goals

- to practice the Unit 8 structural model
- to create KWOs for an introduction and a conclusion paragraph
- to write an introduction and a conclusion paragraph
- to complete a 5-paragraph essay with a works consulted page
- to review vocabulary words

Assignment Schedule

Day 1

1. Play the Question Game.
2. Write a KWO for a conclusion and then write a KWO for an introduction.

Day 2

1. Review your KWOs from Day 1.
2. Complete Style Practice.
3. Complete Vocabulary Practice. There are no new words for this lesson.
4. Using your conclusion KWO as a guide, write your conclusion. Highlight or bold the topic key words.
5. Go over the checklist. Put a check in the box for each requirement you have completed.

Day 3

1. Review all vocabulary words learned thus far.
2. Using your introduction KWO as a guide, write your introduction. Highlight or bold the topic key words.
3. Write a works consulted page that includes all the sources you used. Follow the format on page 175.
4. Turn in your rough draft to your editor with the completed checklist attached.

Day 4

1. Write or type a final draft, making any corrections your editor asked you to make. Add the introduction and conclusion to the final draft body paragraphs written in Lesson 25. Include the works consulted page.
2. Paperclip the checklist, final draft, rough drafts, and KWOs together. Hand them in.

Key Word Outline—Conclusion

Restate the Topics

> Write a sentence or two about each topic you wrote about in Lesson 25. Highlight or bold the topic key words.

Most Significant and Why

> Why is the person you researched remembered and studied in history? How did he or she influence or impact others? What admirable character traits does he or she possess?

> Do not use the word "I" when stating what is most important or significant. When you use "I," it limits the impact your statement has on your reader. Consider these two statements:

>> I think Matthew Fontaine Maury's most significant achievement was his data about the oceans' currents, winds, and weather, enabling him to write shipping charts that allowed ships to shorten their voyages.

>> Matthew Fontaine Maury's most significant achievement was his data about the oceans' currents, winds, and weather, enabling him to write shipping charts that allowed ships to shorten their voyages.

> The second is clearly stronger and more persuasive.

Final Sentence

> End with a sentence from which you can create a title. Be sure that your paper sounds complete.

Key Word Outline for Conclusion

V.   Topic A: _____*Each student's outline will be different.*_____

      Topic B: _____

      Topic C: _____

      Most significant _____

      Why? _____

      _____

      Title repeats 1–3 key words from final sentence.

Highlight or bold the topic key words in your paragraph.

Key Word Outline—Introduction

Attention Getter

Start your introduction with a sentence that encourages your reader to continue reading. Begin with a question, a very short sentence, or a famous quote or fact.

Background

Tell your reader what the subject of the composition is about by making a general statement about the subject. Then provide background information you think would be interesting or important. The background information should flow into the introduction of the topics.

Topics

End your introduction by listing the topics you wrote about in your body paragraphs. Highlight or bold the topic key words.

Key Word Outline for Introduction

I.   Attention getter   _Each student's outline will be different._

Background   _____

_____

_____

Topic A: _____

Topic B: _____

Topic C: _____

Highlight or bold the topic key words in your paragraph.

Ideas will depend upon the student's chosen subject. The sample ideas are general enough to be used with any chosen subject of a prominent scientist.

UNIT 8: FORMAL ESSAY MODELS

Style Practice

Sentence Openers

Write sentences that can be used in your introduction or conclusion.

1. #1 subject opener _____

    _____ *[1] Scientists use their curiousity to make discoveries.* _____

2. #2 prepositional opener _____

    _____ *[2] Throughout history great scientists have arisen.* _____

3. #3 -ly adverb opener _____

    _____ *[3] Certainly, some scientists are controversial.* _____

4. #4 -ing opener _____

    _____ *[4] Striving to understand the universe, scientists research and experiment.* _____

5. #5 clausal opener – *www.asia.b* _____

    _____ *[5] When scientists fail, they try again.* _____

6. #6 vss opener, 2–5 words (This can be your attention getter.) _____

    _____ *[6] Scientists perservere.* _____

Dress-Ups

Look at your KWOs and consider dress-ups to include in your introduction and conclusion.

Vocabulary Practice

Think   about the words and their meanings.
Which vocabulary words could you use in this assignment?

    Ideas will depend upon student's chosen subject.

    _____

Unit 8 Composition Checklist

Formal Essay Models

Lesson 26: A Prominent Scientist, Part 2 introduction and conclusion

Name: _____

Institute for Excellence in Writing

STRUCTURE

- ☐ MLA format (see Appendix I) _____ 1 pt
- ☐ works consulted entries in proper format _____ 2 pts
- ☐ checklist on top, final draft, rough draft, key word outline _____ 1 pt

Introduction

- ☐ introduction includes attention getter, background information, and states topics (bold or highlight) _____ 10 pts

Body

- ☐ insert body paragraphs _____ 2 pts

Conclusion

- ☐ conclusion restates topics (**bold** or highlight) and indicates most significant/why _____ 10 pts
- ☐ final sentence repeats 1–3 key words for the title _____ 2 pts

STYLE

¶1 ¶5 Dress-Ups (underline one of each)   (1 pt each)

- ☐ ☐ -ly adverb _____ 2 pts
- ☐ ☐ *who/which* clause _____ 2 pts
- ☐ ☐ strong verb _____ 2 pts
- ☐ ☐ quality adjective _____ 2 pts
- ☐ ☐ *www.asia.b* clause _____ 2 pts

Sentence Openers (number; one of each as possible)   (1 pt each)

- ☐ ☐ [1] subject _____ 2 pts
- ☐ ☐ [2] prepositional _____ 2 pts
- ☐ ☐ [3] -ly adverb _____ 2 pts
- ☐ ☐ [4] -ing _____ 2 pts
- ☐ ☐ [5] clausal – *www.asia.b* _____ 2 pts
- ☐ ☐ [6] vss _____ 2 pts

CHECK FOR BANNED WORDS (-1 pt for each use): think/thought, go/went, say/said, good, bad, big, small _____ pts

MECHANICS

- ☐ spelling, grammar, and punctuation (-1 pt per error) _____ pts

VOCABULARY

- ☐ vocabulary words – label *(voc)* in left margin or after sentence

Total: _____ 50 pts

Custom Total: _____ pts

Checklist

Teachers are free to adjust a checklist by requiring only the stylistic techniques that have become easy, plus one new one. EZ+1

Intentionally blank so the checklist can be removed.

Lesson 27: George Washington Carver, Part 1

Structure:	Unit 9: Formal Critique body paragraphs
Style:	no new style
Subject:	critique of "The Plant Doctor"

Teaching Writing: Structure and Style

Watch the sections for Unit 9: Formal Critique. At IEW.com/twss-help reference the TWSS Viewing Guides.

Lesson 27: George Washington Carver, Part 1

UNIT 9: FORMAL CRITIQUE AND RESPONSE TO LITERATURE

Lesson 27: George Washington Carver, Part 1

Goals

- to learn the Unit 9 Formal Critique structural model
- to create a KWO
- to write the body paragraphs of a short story critique
- to learn and practice critique vocabulary
- to use new vocabulary words: *antagonist, climax, protagonist, theme*

Assignment Schedule

Day 1

1. Play a vocabulary game such as Vocabulary Lightning.
2. Read New Structure—Formal Critique Model: Body Paragraphs.
3. Read "The Plant Doctor."
4. Write a KWO by answering the Story Sequence Chart questions.

Day 2

1. Review your KWO from Day 1.
2. Complete Style Practice.
3. Look at the vocabulary cards for Lesson 27. Complete Vocabulary Practice.
4. Using your KWO as a guide, begin writing a rough draft.
5. Go over the checklist. Put a check in the box for each requirement you have completed.

Day 3

1. Review all vocabulary words learned thus far.
2. Finish writing your three body paragraphs.
3. Turn in your rough draft to your editor with the completed checklist attached.

Day 4

1. Write or type a final draft, making any corrections your editor asked you to make.
2. Paperclip the checklist, final draft, rough draft, and KWO together. Hand them in.

Mechanics

Titles of short stories are placed in quotation marks. Commas and periods always go inside closing quotation marks.

In Lessons 27–28 students write a 5-paragraph formal critique. They begin by forming the body paragraphs based on the Story Sequence Chart. Help students focus on writing about the story rather than simply telling the story. Using words from the Critique Thesaurus in Appendix III will help.

Remind students that these paragraphs do not contain topic or clincher sentences.

Exemplar

The Exemplars file contains a student's completed assignment for Lessons 27–28. The example is for the teacher and not intended to be used by the student.

See the blue page for download instructions.

New Structure

Formal Critique Model: Body Paragraphs

In Unit 9 you will write critiques of literature. Do this by combining your knowledge of how to retell narrative stories (Unit 3) with how to write introduction and conclusion paragraphs (Units 7 and 8). You may follow this model to critique short stories, movies, novels, plays, and television shows.

The model contains an introduction, three body paragraphs, and a conclusion. The body paragraphs follow the Story Sequence Chart. The elements required in the introduction and conclusion are specific to critiques. Notice the paragraphs in this model do not contain topic or clincher sentences.

	I.	Introduction	*attention getter, background*
Story	II.	Characters and Setting	
Sequence	III.	Conflict or Problem	
Chart	IV.	Climax and Resolution	
	V.	Conclusion	*your opinion/why, message/moral, last sentence ➜ title*

Like other 5-paragraph compositions, write from the inside out beginning with the body paragraphs. When you write a critique, it is not necessary to tell about every character or detail of the story. Instead, provide a brief summary of different parts of the story in order to give your opinion about those specific parts. To do this, use the Story Sequence Chart.

Although Unit 9 does not contain topic or clincher sentences, each body paragraph may begin with the focus of the paragraph. For example, the first body paragraph may begin "The Plant Doctor" *is set in* ___. In this paragraph you will explain the setting and indicate the characters of the story.

The second body paragraph may begin *The problem is* ___. In this paragraph indicate the primary conflict or problem of the story and how the characters attempt to solve the problem.

The third body paragraph may begin *The climax occurs* ___. After indicating the climax of the story, the rest of the paragraph explains how the author brought the story to an end. When applicable, this paragraph may tell the message or moral of the story.

Critique Thesaurus

Use the words on the Critique Thesaurus in Appendix III to enhance your critique. In the body paragraphs, use words that describe the *setting*, *characters*, *conflict*, *climax*, and *resolution*.

Source Text

The Plant Doctor

Growing up on a rural farm near Diamond, Missouri, in the aftermath of the U.S. Civil War, George Washington Carver understood firsthand the difficulties farmers face. As a child of slaves whose father died before he was born and mother was kidnapped by lawless bushwhackers when he was just one, young George was raised by his mother's former owners Susan and Moses Carver, whom he called Aunt and Uncle and whose last name he chose as his own. Despite being hardworking and resourceful, the Carvers grew barely enough food for the family. George was fascinated with plants and spent hours traipsing through the forests and fields surrounding the farm, collecting every specimen he could find to transplant in his flourishing garden. He created paint from plants and other natural resources because he was too poor to purchase paint. People from town regularly brought their diseased plants to George for him to diagnose and make healthy again. Soon he was known as the Little Plant Doctor. Whether the plant was yellowing from malnourishment or covered with fungus or bugs, George examined and experimented until he could give a diagnosis and a solution to the problem.

George craved more knowledge than he could learn at home. Unfortunately, the only school near him was exclusively for white people, so George left the farm at the age of eleven and set off on his own to Neosho, Missouri, to enroll in a school for black children. George's thirst for knowledge drove him for seventeen

Mechanics _____

Separate a city and state with a comma. When a city and state are placed in the middle of a sentence, place a comma on both sides of the state.

difficult years. He traveled from town to town and job to job, supporting himself and attending school when he could. Eventually, he enrolled in college to study plants, reasoning "I could help poor black farmers work their farms more efficiently if I studied horticulture." Scientists were learning that some crops deplete the nutrients of soils while others replenish them. His teacher Dr. Wallace taught him "Nations last only as long as their topsoil." Plentiful crops and successful farms depended on good soil, so George studied how to create healthy soil.

Booker T. Washington approached Carver to establish an agriculture department at his Tuskegee Normal and Industrial Institute in Macon County, Alabama, an all-Black college Washington had established to help ex-slaves learn a trade to be able to make a living. At the time, 85% of all southern Blacks were farmers barely able to make ends meet. George Washington Carver found his chance to help Black farmers succeed. At the time, farmers in the South planted only cotton. Cotton plants severely depleted the soil of necessary nutrients, especially nitrogen, needed to grow healthy crops. When weather or unhealthy soil destroyed the crop or the market prices declined, farmers could not afford to replant their fields or feed their families. He had to find a way to convince the farmers to diversify their crops to replenish the topsoil and provide food for their families. "Plant legumes like peanuts and sweet potatoes to replenish the nitrogen, and the soil will stay healthy and produce good crops," he implored them. "You will also have food to feed your families and surplus to sell." He wanted them to dream about being more than tenant farmers.

Because peanuts and sweet potatoes were South American crops the farmers were unfamiliar with, he had a difficult time convincing them. He produced a pamphlet with 125 recipes for the legumes, even pointing out that the skins and shells provided excellent nourishment for their cattle and pigs.

To gain their trust, he established The Farmer's Institute. He and his students loaded up wagons with informational bulletins and jars of food products made from peanuts and sweet potatoes for the wives to sample. They dispersed across the state and visited farm after farm offering a free soil analysis and solutions for improving the farm's yield. The farmers listened, but most went right back to farming cotton because that was what they knew how to do.

In February 1904 George Washington Carver opened an official notice from the Department of Agriculture that read, "The boll weevil is moving north at a steady rate. It knows no political boundaries, and it has crossed from Mexico into Texas. At this state we can see no reason why it will not proceed into your region." Boll weevils lay their eggs in the boll of the cotton plant, where the fiber is formed. When the eggs hatch, the baby beetles eat the cotton fiber inside the boll and destroy the crop. George Washington Carver warned the farmers of the coming calamity and once again explained the folly of relying on a single crop. Would they take his advice?

The many farmers who planted sweet potatoes and peanuts were unaffected by the beetle. They grew enough to feed their families and livestock as well as extra to sell. They harvested an abundance of peanuts. On the other hand, those who had sown cotton were devastated as the boll weevil ate its way into Alabama.

"What are we going to do with all these peanuts?" the farmers who took Carver's advice asked. "We can't eat them all!" Carver locked himself in his science lab with three bushels of peanuts. He separated the peanut into its individual elements—sugar, starch, fat, oil, gum, pectin, and amino acids. By the time he emerged from his lab three days later, he had over three hundred uses for the peanut, including cleaning agents, skin and hair products, fabric dyes, and plastic.

Using the techniques Carver taught them, farmers averaged 266 bushels of peanuts and $75 profit per acre. Soon peanut farms covered over ten million acres. By 1920 peanuts brought almost $80 million a year to the South.

Because he received national attention after the boll weevil crisis, the government called on him during the Great Depression to teach families how to grow gardens and raise chickens to survive the difficult time. George Washington Carver used science to help poor Southern farmers be more than tenant farmers.

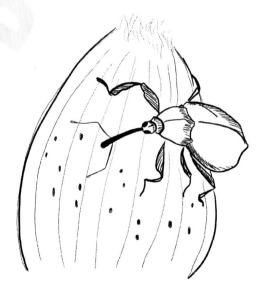

Sample

Key Word Outline—Story Sequence Chart

Identify the Story Sequence Chart elements. Use words such as *setting, characters, conflict, climax, resolution,* and their synonyms found on the Critique Thesaurus in Appendix III.

Characters and Setting

> When and where does the story occur? This is the *setting.*
>
> Name and describe each main *character.*

II. ___setting, S U.S., factual, < details___

  1. ___m character, resourceful, George W. Carver___

  2. ___> Civil War, struggles, farmers___

  3. ___studies, horticulture, help, ♡___

  4. ___☁ deplete, soil, nitrogen___

  (5.) ___crop rotation, benefit, GWC admirable___

Conflict or Problem

> What does the main character want or need? This is the *conflict.*
>
> Tell what the main characters do, say, and think in order to solve the problem.
>
> Tell how they feel as they try to solve the problem.

III. ___problem, GWC, "plant, legumes" SP + P___

  1. ___X ☁, R. sympathize, GWC___

  2. ___pamphlet, 125 recipes SP + P___

  3. ___marvel, innovative 💡___

  4. ___GWC, Farmer's Institute, farmers, ed, soil___

  (5.) ___X 🌀, plant ☁, R. frustrated!___

Climax and Resolution

> What event in the story reveals how the conflict will work out (whether the problem will be solved or not)? This is the *climax.*
>
> What is the outcome for the main characters at the end of the story? This is the *resolution.*

IV. ___climax, boll weevil, destroy___

  1. ___⬭⬭, babies, eat, ☁, R. fear!___

  2. ___resolution, GWC, encourages SP + P___

  3. ___F 🌀, Do?, X eat, all___

  4. ___GWC, lab, 3 bushels P, parts___

  (5.) ___300 uses, avg. 266 bushels, $75 acre___

These paragraphs do not contain topic-clincher sentences.

II. Characters and Setting

The story is set in the South during the time immediately following the United States Civil War. The main character that students must mention is George Washington Carver. Students should focus on Carver's interest in and study of plants.

III. Conflict or Problem

In this paragraph students critique the main problem: George Washington Carver needs to convince poor Southern farmers to plant crops other than cotton to replenish topsoil and provide food for their families.

IV. Climax and Resolution

The climax occurs when a boll weevil infestation threatens the cotton crop. Farmers must listen to Carver and plant sweet potatoes and peanuts for their farms and families to survive. Those who follow Carver's advice have an abundance of crop to eat and to sell.

Style Practice

Dress-Ups and Sentence Openers

Look at your KWO and consider where you can include various clauses as well as strong verbs, quality adjectives, -ly adverbs, and sentence openers.

Vocabulary Practice

Listen   to someone read the vocabulary words for Lesson 27 aloud.

Speak   them aloud yourself.

Read   the definitions and sample sentences on the vocabulary cards.

Write   four sentences using one of this lesson's vocabulary words in each sentence.

antagonist   *The farmers who George Washington Carver must convince to plant*

sweet potatoes and peanuts are the antagonists in the story.

climax   *The invasion of the boll weevil into Alabama is the climax of the story.*

protagonist   *George Washington Carver is the protagonist.*

theme   *Carver's resourcefulness in helping the farmers succeed is the theme*

of this story.

Think   about the words on the critique vocabulary chart in Appendix III.
Try to use words from this chart in sentences or phrases that could be in your critique.

Unit 9 Composition Checklist
Lesson 27: George Washington Carver, Part 1 body paragraphs

Formal Critique

Name: _____

Institute for Excellence in Writing
Listen. Speak. Read. Write. Think!

STRUCTURE

☐ MLA format (see Appendix I) _____ 1 pt

☐ checklist on top, final draft, rough draft, key word outline _____ 1 pt

Body

☐ Unit 9: 3 paragraphs follow Story Sequence Chart (Unit 3) and include words from the Critique Thesaurus page in each paragraph _____ 15 pts

STYLE

¶2 ¶3 ¶4 Dress-Ups (underline one of each)   (1 pt each)

☐ ☐ ☐ -ly adverb _____ 3 pts

☐ ☐ ☐ *who/which* clause _____ 3 pts

☐ ☐ ☐ strong verb _____ 3 pts

☐ ☐ ☐ quality adjective _____ 3 pts

☐ ☐ ☐ *www.asia.b* clause _____ 3 pts

Sentence Openers (number; one of each as possible)   (1 pt each)

☐ ☐ ☐ [1] subject _____ 3 pts

☐ ☐ ☐ [2] prepositional _____ 3 pts

☐ ☐ ☐ [3] -ly adverb _____ 3 pts

☐ ☐ ☐ [4] -ing _____ 3 pts

☐ ☐ ☐ [5] clausal – *www.asia.b* _____ 3 pts

☐ ☐ ☐ [6] vss _____ 3 pts

CHECK FOR BANNED WORDS (-1 pt for each use): think/thought, go/went, say/said, good, bad, big, small _____ pts

MECHANICS

☐ spelling, grammar, and punctuation (-1 pt per error) _____ pts

VOCABULARY

☐ vocabulary words – label *(voc)* in left margin or after sentence

Total: _____ 50 pts

Custom Total: _____ pts

Checklist

Teachers are free to adjust a checklist by requiring only the stylistic techniques that have become easy, plus one new one. EZ+1

Reminder

Titles of short stories are placed in quotation marks. Commas and periods always go inside closing quotation marks.

Intentionally blank so the checklist can be removed.

Lesson 28: George Washington Carver, Part 2

Structure:	Unit 9: Formal Critique introduction and conclusion
Style:	no new style
Subject:	critique of "The Plant Doctor"

UNIT 9: FORMAL CRITIQUE AND RESPONSE TO LITERATURE

Lesson 28: George Washington Carver, Part 2

Goals

- to practice the Unit 9 structural model
- to create KWOs for an introduction and a conclusion paragraph
- to add an introduction and a conclusion paragraph to the short story critique
- to review vocabulary words

Assignment Schedule

Day 1

1. Complete the Review.
2. Read New Structure—Formal Critique Model: Introduction and Conclusion.
3. Write a KWO for a conclusion and then write a KWO for an introduction.

Day 2

1. Complete Style Practice.
2. Complete Vocabulary Practice. There are no new words for this lesson.
3. Using your conclusion KWO as a guide, write your conclusion.
4. Go over the checklist. Put a check in the box for each requirement you have completed.

Day 3

1. Review all vocabulary words learned thus far.
2. Using your introduction KWO as a guide, write your introduction.
3. Turn in your rough draft to your editor with the completed checklist attached.

Day 4

1. Write or type a final draft, making any corrections your editor asked you to make. Add the introduction and the conclusion to the final draft body paragraphs written in Lesson 27.
2. Paperclip the checklist, final draft, rough drafts, and KWOs together. Hand them in.

> Study for the Final Vocabulary Quiz. It will cover words from Lessons 1–27.

Students complete the formal critique begun in the last lesson by adding an introduction and a conclusion. The structures of the introduction and conclusion paragraphs are unique to this unit. Help students recognize and incorporate each important element.

Review

Explain the structure of a basic 5-paragraph critique by writing the purpose of each paragraph.

I. *Introduction (attention getter, background)*

II. *Characters and Setting*

III. *Conflict or Problem*

IV. *Climax and Resolution*

V. *Conclusion (your opinion/why, message/moral, last sentence)*

New Structure

Formal Critique Model: Introduction and Conclusion

Now that you have completed the body paragraphs, you are ready to add the introduction and conclusion. Look at the model below and notice the components that make up the introduction and conclusion. In the critique model, these two paragraphs follow their own unique structure.

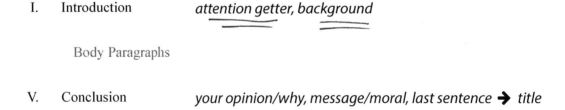

I. Introduction   *attention getter, background*

    Body Paragraphs

V. Conclusion   *your opinion/why, message/moral, last sentence* ➜ *title*

The introduction must get the reader's attention by enticing the reader to keep reading. This paragraph must also introduce the story to the reader. This is where you write the title of the story, tell when it was written, and provide details about the author and/or publisher.

The conclusion is where you tell if you like or do not like the story and why. This paragraph must indicate your opinion of the story, which is the purpose of a critique. For this reason, the conclusion is the most important paragraph of the critique and often the longest. Because the conclusion must flow smoothly from the final body paragraph, you will outline and write the conclusion before you outline and write the introduction.

Institute for Excellence in Writing

Key Word Outline—Conclusion

In the conclusion do not use *I*, *my*, *we*, *us*, or *you*. Consider these statements:

> In my opinion, this story is about being resourceful when tackling a problem.
>
> This story is about being resourceful when tackling a problem.

The second is clearly stronger and more persuasive.

Your Opinion

> Begin the conclusion with your overall impression of the story. Do not use vague adjectives like *good*, *bad*, *interesting*, or *wonderful*. Use specific adjectives like *predictable, engrossing, boring, tragic, classic, thought-provoking, delightful.*
>
> > The inspiring story of George Washington Carver's life displays how one man used his resourcefulness to change a nation's farming practices.

Why

> Support your opinion by telling a few things you like or do not like about the story. You may mention the style of writing, the best or worst aspect of the story, how realistic the characters appear, how much action the story contains, what makes the conflict exciting or boring, what makes the climax suspenseful or predictable, and if the story ends well.

Message/Moral

> Indicate if there is a message or moral found within the story and what that message's overall effect has upon the reader.

Final Sentence

> Make sure your final sentence makes the paper sound complete and contains words you can use to create a title.

Sample

Key Word Outline for Conclusion

V.   Your opinion   resourcefulness, tackle, problems

    Why?   young, plants, paint

                             rotate, 125 recipes, uses

                             F.I., visits, analysis

    Message/moral   GWC, answer, problems, persistent

                             opposition, → work, contributions

Title repeats 1–3 key words from final sentence.

Never use *I*, *my*, *we*, *us*, *you*.

Key Word Outline—Introduction

Attention Getter

Begin with something intriguing that will make your reader want to read more. Consider using a quote about the author or from the story.

Background

In this section of the introduction, provide basic information specific to the author and the story including the title, type of story, and publisher. In addition to mentioning where the story is found, you could mention the historical time of the story and any events that parallel the story. You could also indicate some information about the story's author including when he or she lived, the names of some contemporaries, and awards received for authoring this short story.

Sample

Key Word Outline for Introduction

I.   Attention getter ___quote, final sentence___

Background ___biography, L 27, WOS___

___X author, publisher, IEW, 4 pgs___

___insects, destroy, crops, AL___

___historical, crop rotation___

___statistics, $ peanuts, early 1900s___

Style Practice

Dress-Ups and Sentence Openers

Look at your KWOs and consider where you can include various clauses as well as strong verbs, quality adjectives, -ly adverbs, and sentence openers.

Vocabulary Practice

Think   about the words on the critique vocabulary chart in Appendix III. Try to use words from this chart in sentences or phrases that could be in your critique. Write at least two ideas below.

___narrative, rural, crisis, lesson___

Lesson 28: George Washington Carver, Part 2

Unit 9 Composition Checklist

Formal Critique

Lesson 28: George Washington Carver, Part 2 introduction and conclusion

Name: _____

Institute for Excellence in Writing

STRUCTURE

☐ MLA format (see Appendix I) _____ 1 pt

☐ checklist on top, final draft, rough draft, key word outline _____ 1 pt

Introduction

☐ Unit 9: introduction includes attention getter, background information (title, author, publisher, type of story, awards) _____ 10 pts

Body

☐ insert body paragraphs _____ 2 pts

Conclusion

☐ Unit 9: your opinion of the story: well written or not, like/dislike and why, may also discuss character development, conflict, message, effect of story on reader _____ 10 pts

☐ no *I, my, we, us, you* _____ 3 pts

☐ final sentence repeats 1–3 key words for the title _____ 1 pt

STYLE

¶1 ¶5 Dress-Ups (underline one of each)   (1 pt each)

☐ ☐ -ly adverb _____ 2 pts

☐ ☐ *who/which* clause _____ 2 pts

☐ ☐ strong verb _____ 2 pts

☐ ☐ quality adjective _____ 2 pts

☐ ☐ *www.asia.b* clause _____ 2 pts

Sentence Openers (number; one of each as possible)   (1 pt each)

☐ ☐ [1] subject _____ 2 pts

☐ ☐ [2] prepositional _____ 2 pts

☐ ☐ [3] -ly adverb _____ 2 pts

☐ ☐ [4] -ing _____ 2 pts

☐ ☐ [5] clausal – *www.asia.b* _____ 2 pts

☐ ☐ [6] vss _____ 2 pts

CHECK FOR BANNED WORDS (-1 pt for each use): think/thought, go/went, say/said, good, bad, big, small _____ pts

MECHANICS

☐ spelling, grammar, and punctuation (-1 pt per error) _____ pts

VOCABULARY

☐ vocabulary words – label *(voc)* in left margin or after sentence

Total: _____ 50 pts

Custom Total: _____ pts

Checklist

Teachers are free to adjust a checklist by requiring only the stylistic techniques that have become easy, plus one new one. EZ+1

Intentionally blank so the checklist can be removed.

Lesson 29: Nathaniel Bowditch, Part 1

Structure: Unit 9: Formal Critique and Response to Literature
body paragraphs

Style: no new style

Subject: character analysis of "The Great Navigator"

UNIT 9: FORMAL CRITIQUE AND RESPONSE TO LITERATURE

Lesson 29: Nathaniel Bowditch, Part 1

Goals

- to learn a variation of the Unit 9 structural model: Response to Literature
- to write the body paragraphs of a character analysis essay
- to learn the TRIAC technique for developing a paragraph supporting an opinion
- to take Final Vocabulary Quiz

Assignment Schedule

Day 1

1. Play a vocabulary game such as Around the World.
2. Take Final Vocabulary Quiz.
3. Read New Structure—Character Analysis: Body Paragraphs.
4. Read "The Great Navigator."
5. Follow the Story Sequence Chart to outline and write paragraph II. This paragraph does not have a topic or clincher sentence.
6. Go over the checklist. Put a check in the box for each requirement you have completed.

Day 2

1. Complete Style Practice and Vocabulary Practice.
2. Follow the TRIAC model to outline paragraph III.

Day 3

1. Review your KWO from Day 2.
2. Using your KWO as a guide, write paragraph III. This paragraph does have a topic and clincher sentence.
3. Go over the checklist. Put a check in the box for each requirement you have completed.
4. Turn in your rough draft to your editor with the completed checklist attached.

Day 4

1. Write or type a final draft, making any corrections your editor asked you to make.
2. Paperclip the checklist, final draft, rough draft, and KWO together. Hand them in.

Lessons 29–30 can be combined into one lesson. To simplify, do not require students to complete the conclusion paragraph in Lesson 30.

In Lessons 29–30 instead of writing a critique on the entire story, students analyze a particular aspect of the literature. The first body paragraph, a summary of the entire story, is formed by following a modified version of the critique model. The second body paragraph, an analysis paragraph, is formed by using the TRIAC model.

Exemplar

The Exemplars file contains a student's completed assignment for Lessons 29–30. The example is for the teacher and not intended to be used by the student.

See the blue page for download instructions.

New Structure

Character Analysis: Body Paragraphs

In Lessons 29–30 you will use a variation of Unit 9 to analyze a particular aspect of literature. Rather than write a critique on the entire story, you will critique one aspect of one character. Notice that the first body paragraph contains all the elements of the Story Sequence Chart, and the second body paragraph follows the TRIAC model.

	I.	Introduction	*attention getter, background, state topic*
Write Body	II.	Story Summary	*characters and setting, conflict or problem, climax and resolution*
Paragraphs	III.	Character Analysis	*topic, restriction, illustration, analysis, clincher*
	IV.	Conclusion	*restate topic, personal feelings/significance, most significant/why, last sentence* ➜ *title*

Critique Thesaurus

Use the words on the Critique Thesaurus in Appendix III to enhance your critique.

Sample Paragraph

This example analyzes a character from "The Plant Doctor."

Character Analysis

[Topic] [1] George Washington Carver <u>displays</u> <u>dogged</u> **resourcefulness** [Restrict] <u>because</u> he knows he must convince the farmers to plant sweet potatoes and peanuts for their **farms** to **survive**. [Illustration] [2] In order to persuade farmers to diversify crops and replenish nutrients in their soil, "he produced a pamphlet with 125 recipes for legumes, even pointing out that the skins and shells provided excellent nourishment for their cattle and pigs." [3] Additionally, he prepares samples from the recipes and <u>tirelessly</u> travels from farm to farm to educate the farmers about these new crops, <u>which</u> replenish nitrogen in the soil. [4] Analyzing soil on each farm, he tells the farmer how planting only cotton depletes the soil of nitrogen. [Analysis] [5] Because he becomes friends with farmers, they trust him. [2] As a result, the farmers listen and plant peanuts when an insect threatens their farms. [6] The crops thrive. [Clincher] [1] George Washington Carver's **clever thinking saves** the **farms** in the South during the boll weevil infestation and creates a new cash crop.

Short Story

The Great Navigator

On December 25, 1802, the merchant ship *The Putnam* headed to its home port of Salem, Massachusetts, during an intense blizzard. Ice and snow weighed down the sails, covered the decks, and soaked the sailors. Howling winds blew, and fierce waves swamped the ship. The driving snowstorm hid the ship's surroundings.

Twenty-nine-year-old Nathaniel Bowditch captained *The Putnam*. It was his first voyage at the helm. He had a reputation as a brilliant, self-taught mathe-matician and navigator. As a young sailor working his way through the officer ranks, he had discovered a new mathematical formula to use lunar measurements to calculate a ship's location. Publishers working on a new edition of John Hamilton Moore's *The Practical Navigato*r, which was the primary reference sailors used to plot a ship's course, asked Bowditch to check the charts and data. The reference was filled with navigational charts and maps, data on wind speed and ocean currents, and mathematical formulas. Bowditch found over eight thousand errors and missing data that had caused countless ships to sail off course or wreck.

In 1802 publishers printed *The New American Practical Navigator* with Nathaniel Bowditch's name as the author. Every chart in the book was filled with data Bowditch himself had calculated and checked. In publishing his book, he had set himself as an authority on navigation. *The Putnam's* officers looked to

Mechanics _____

When a date includes the month, day, and year, place a comma between the day and year. If the date is placed in the middle of a sentence, place a comma on both sides of the year.

Titles of books are italicized. If a report is handwritten, underline the title of a book.

Bowditch for direction. Certainly, he would not choose to sail into port using only his charts during a blinding snowstorm!

Captain Bowditch knew from the last sighted measurements taken two days earlier that their ship was off Nantucket close to the harbor of Salem. He wondered, *Who would trust the charts of an uneducated sailor over those written by the First Lord Admiralty of the Royal British Navy? This is my chance to prove that my charts are correct.* Although he knew that crashing his ship on the rocks would mean he would lose not only his ship, his cargo, and possibly his crew but also his reputation, Bowditch set a course for the port.

He guided the ship into the dangerous waters with nothing but his charts to guide the way. One false move would crash the ship on the rocks. As night fell and darkness engulfed the ship, the crew grew uneasy.

"Our old man goes ahead as if it were noonday!" said one crew member.

Onward they crept. Bowditch steered the ship past rocks and shallow ridges and even Bowditch Ledge, named after his great grandfather, who had wrecked there. Bowditch pushed forward. He knew where he was. Many hidden obstacles remained in their path. The crew's anxiety eased as one by one they cleared Marblehead shore, Peach's Point, and three dangerous shoals.

"The lighthouse at Baker's Island!" shouted a member of the crew. The small glimpse of light gave the crew hope. Finally the vessel entered the port and

Mechanics _____

Punctuate thoughts like quotations. Place thoughts in quotation marks when handwriting. Place thoughts in italics when typing.

docked. The simple entry in Bowditch's logbook after the treacherous journey read, "Arrived at Salem Dec. 25, in the evening."

Nathaniel Bowditch's skillful sailing that night cemented his reputation as one of the most respected navigators in history. *The New American Practical Navigator* became known as the seaman's bible and is still used today.

Key Word Outline—Story Summary

Follow the Story Sequence Chart to outline and write paragraph II. Use the elements listed in the chart to provide a brief overview of the entire story in one paragraph. To be successful, you must limit the details, giving only key elements the reader must have to understand the main points of the story.

Key Word Outline for Story Summary

II.   Characters and Setting

12/25/1802, NB + crew, The Putnam, blizzard

headed, port, Salem, MA

Conflict or Problem

NB, prove, charts, correct

guide, dangerous H$_2$O, sail

Climax and Resolution

B, navigate, → port, blizzard

sailors, ʻ👀ʼ, lighthouse, shore

This paragraph does not contain a topic or clincher sentence.

Characters and Setting

On Christmas day, 1802, Nathaniel Bowditch, a trusted navigator and brilliant mathematician, and his crew are on board the merchant ship *The Putman* during a blizzard. They are headed for their home port of Salem, Massachusetts.

Conflict or Problem

The conflict begins when Bowditch wants to prove his charts are correct.

Climax and Resolution

The climax occurs when Bowditch guides the ship into the dangerous waters to sail for port in Salem. The ship arrives safely at port that same evening. Bowditch's confidence in his charts proved accurate.

Key Word Outline—Character Analysis

Follow the TRIAC model to outline and write paragraph III. This differs from the formal critique because in this assignment you focus on one aspect of one character. This is the most important paragraph of this composition because it is where you give your personal critique.

Because the illustration should include at least one quotation from the source text, it is often easier to build your paragraph around a quote by or about a character than to awkwardly fit a quote into something you have already written.

For example, this quote is found when Bowditch is trying to decide whether to blindly continue sailing for port in the dangerous waters: "Who would trust the charts of an uneducated sailor over those written by the First Lord Admiralty of the Royal British Navy? This is my chance to prove that my charts are correct."

Topic

> State the topic. Choose one character in the story and make a statement about a quality, motive, effect, change, or something the character learned.
>
> If you decided to use the quote above, the topic will highlight Bowditch's confidence in his updated charts. The key words in the topic line may be *Bowditch, confidence, ability*. Using those words, the topic sentence might be *Nathaniel Bowditch's confidence in his charts and navigational skills saved his ship and crew during a dangerous blizzard.*

Restriction

> Make a statement or claim about the topic, focusing the paragraph.

Illustration

> Give an example illustrating the statement or claim. This must be a quotation from the source text story.

Analysis

> Explain the illustration.

Clincher

> Repeat or reflect two or three key words from the topic sentence.

TRIAC

The key word outline guides the students in the process. For additional information on the TRIAC model, see pages 162–164 of *Teaching Writing: Structure and Style Seminar Workbook.*

Key Word Outline for Character Analysis

III.   Topic   _NB, confidence, precision, charts_

      Restriction   _sails, → port, snowstorm_

      Illustration   _continue, "Chance, prove . . . "_

                      TNAPN, new, resource, sailors

      Analysis   _B, lose, everything?_

                      sailors, wait, X storm

      Clincher   _NB, confidence, precision, charts_

Highlight or bold 2–3 key words that repeat or reflect in the topic and clincher sentences.

Style Practice

Dress-Ups and Sentence Openers

Look at your KWO and consider where you can include various clauses as well as strong verbs, quality adjectives, -ly adverbs, and sentence openers.

Vocabulary Practice

Think   about the words on the critique vocabulary chart in Appendix III.
       Try to use words from this chart in sentences or phrases that could be in your critique.
       Write at least two ideas below.

                      Ideas will depend upon student's chosen topic.

Unit 9 Composition Checklist
Lesson 29: Nathaniel Bowditch, Part 1 body paragraphs

Formal
Critique

Name: _____

Institute for
Excellence in
Writing

STRUCTURE

☐ MLA format (see Appendix I) _____ 1 pt

☐ checklist on top, final draft, rough draft, key word outline _____ 1 pt

Body

☐ body ¶1 follows Story Sequence Chart (Unit 3) _____ 7 pts

☐ body ¶2 follows TRIAC Model _____ 7 pts

STYLE

¶2 ¶3 Dress-Ups (underline one of each)   (2 pts each)

☐ ☐ -ly adverb _____ 4 pts

☐ ☐ *who/which* clause _____ 4 pts

☐ ☐ strong verb _____ 4 pts

☐ ☐ quality adjective _____ 4 pts

☐ ☐ *www.asia.b* clause _____ 4 pts

Sentence Openers (number; one of each as possible)   (2 pts each)

☐ ☐ [1] subject _____ 4 pts

☐ ☐ [2] prepositional _____ 4 pts

☐ ☐ [3] -ly adverb _____ 4 pts

☐ ☐ [4] -ing _____ 4 pts

☐ ☐ [5] clausal – *www.asia.b* _____ 4 pts

☐ ☐ [6] vss _____ 4 pts

CHECK FOR BANNED WORDS (-1 pt for each use): think/thought, go/went, say/said, _____ pts
good, bad, big, small

MECHANICS

☐ spelling, grammar, and punctuation (-1 pt per error) _____ pts

VOCABULARY

☐ vocabulary words – label *(voc)* in left margin or after sentence

Total: _____ 60 pts

Custom Total: _____ pts

Checklist

Teachers are
free to adjust
a checklist by
requiring only
the stylistic
techniques
that have
become easy,
plus one new
one. EZ+1

Intentionally blank so the checklist can be removed.

Lesson 30: Nathaniel Bowditch, Part 2

Structure: Unit 9: Formal Critique and Response to Literature
introduction and conclusion

Style: no new style

Subject: character analysis of "The Great Navigator"

Lesson 30: Nathaniel Bowditch, Part 2

UNIT 9: FORMAL CRITIQUE AND RESPONSE TO LITERATURE

Lesson 30: Nathaniel Bowditch, Part 2

Goals

- to learn a variation of the Unit 9 structural model: Response to Literature
- to create KWOs for an introduction and a conclusion paragraph
- to add an introduction and a conclusion paragraph to the character analysis essay
- to review vocabulary words

Assignment Schedule

Day 1

1. Play Vocabulary Pictionary.

2. Read New Structure—Character Analysis: Introduction and Conclusion

3. Write a KWO for a conclusion and then write a KWO for an introduction.

Day 2

1. Using your conclusion KWO as a guide, write your conclusion.

2. Go over the checklist. Put a check in the box for each requirement you have completed.

Day 3

1. Review all vocabulary words.

2. Using your introduction KWO as a guide, write your introduction.

3. Turn in your rough draft to your editor with the completed checklist attached.

Day 4

1. Write or type a final draft, making any corrections your editor asked you to make. Add the introduction and the conclusion to the final draft body paragraphs written in Lesson 29.

2. Paperclip the checklist, final draft, rough draft, and KWO together. Hand them in.

Students complete the critique begun in the last lesson by adding an introduction and conclusion. The structures of the introduction and conclusion paragraphs are unique to this unit. Help students recognize and incorporate each important element.

New Structure

Character Analysis: Introduction and Conclusion

Now that you have completed the body paragraphs, you are ready to add the introduction and conclusion. The elements required in the introduction and conclusion are specific to this type of critique.

I.	Introduction	*attention getter, background, state topic*
	Body Paragraphs	
IV.	Conclusion	*restate topic, personal feelings/significance, most significant/why, last sentence ➜ title*

Critique Thesaurus

Use the words on the Critique Thesaurus in Appendix III to enhance your critique.

Sample Paragraph

This conclusion is from a character analysis critique of "The Plant Doctor."

Conclusion

[Topic] [1] This narrative from George Washington Carver's life story is about how he <u>displays</u> **resourcefulness** to tackle his problems. [Personal feelings] [4] Beginning at an early age when he learns how to make paint from plants <u>because</u> he is too poor to purchase it or when he leaves home at the age of eleven to find a school for black children, his life teaches that those <u>who</u> put their mind to it can find solutions. [3] Diligently he works to convince the farmers to rotate their cotton crops with sweet potatoes and peanuts to replenish the nitrogen in the <u>depleted</u> soil so that their farms will survive. [2] At every turn, he discovers ways for farmers to use these unfamiliar crops and travel to their farms offering free soil analysis. [6] The farmers <u>finally</u> listen. [Most significant] [1] The most important lesson for people to learn from George Washington Carver's actions is that people find answers to their problems when they put their minds to seeking a solution. [Why?] [5] When the farmers do not listen, George Washington Carver locks himself in a room, considers what he has to work with, and does not leave until he has a plan. His ideas help Southern farmers thrive.

Key Word Outline—Conclusion

The Response to Literature conclusion is structured differently than the other conclusions.

Restate Topic

> The character analysis topic in paragraph III is the main focus of the composition. Begin the conclusion by stating the topic and explaining its importance.

Personal Feelings/Significance

> Your opinion regarding the topic is very important. For that reason, include a sentence with the phrase *This story demonstrates . . . or teaches . . .* or *This story reminds one of . . .* or *This story changes the reader . . .* or *causes the audience to think . . . .* Use this as a way to make a personal connection with the story.

Most Significant and Why

> Similar to other conclusions you have written, tell what is most significant, moving, or important about this narrative. Then explain why.

Final Sentence

> End with a sentence from which you can create a title. Be sure that your paper sounds complete.

Sample

Key Word Outline for Conclusion

IV.	Restate topic	*NB, confidence, precision, charts*
	Personal feelings/ significance	*trusts, X arrogant, safe*
		ship, 🪨, obstacles, calculations, ✔
	Most significant	*confidently, trust, abilities*
	Why?	*B, saved, lives*
		continue, use, "seaman's bible"

Title repeats 1–3 key words from final sentence.

Highlight or bold the topic in your paragraph.

Never use *I, me, we, us, you.*

Key Word Outline—Introduction

The structure for the Response to Literature introduction should look familiar. It begins just like the formal critique introduction. The only difference is that this introduction has an additional element.

Attention Getter

> Begin with something intriguing that will make your reader want to read more. Consider using a quote about the author or from the story.

Background

> In this section of the introduction, provide basic information specific to the author and the story including the title, type of story, and publisher. In addition to mentioning where the story is found, you could mention the historical time of the story. You could also indicate some information about the story's author, including when he or she lived.

State Topic

> The character analysis topic in paragraph III is the main focus of the composition. Introduce that topic by ending the introductory paragraph with a sentence that reflects the topic sentence of paragraph III.

Sample

Key Word Outline for Introduction

I.   Attention getter _____ *"Old 𝑋, ahead, noonday!"*

     Background _____ *blizzard, correct, decision?*

     _____ *"TGN", 3-page, NB, published, IEW*

     _____ *NB, ++ respected, navigators, history*

     _____ *well-researched, suspenseful, event*

     State topic _____ *story, teaches, confidence*

Highlight or bold the topic in your paragraph.

Unit 9 Composition Checklist

Lesson 30: Nathaniel Bowditch, Part 2 introduction and conclusion

Formal Critique

Name: _____

Institute for Excellence in Writing

STRUCTURE

☐ MLA format (see Appendix I) _____ 1 pt

☐ checklist on top, final draft, rough draft, key word outline _____ 1 pt

Introduction

☐ attention getter, background, states topic (bold or highlight) _____ 5 pts

Body

☐ insert body paragraphs _____ 5 pts

Conclusion

☐ conclusion restates topic (bold or highlight) and indicates most significant/why _____ 5 pts

☐ no *I, my, we, us, you* _____ 2 pts

☐ final sentence repeats 1–3 key words for the title _____ 2 pts

STYLE

¶1 ¶4 Dress-Ups (underline one of each)   (2 pts each)

☐ ☐ -ly adverb _____ 4 pts

☐ ☐ *who/which* clause _____ 4 pts

☐ ☐ strong verb _____ 4 pts

☐ ☐ quality adjective _____ 4 pts

☐ ☐ *www.asia.b* clause _____ 4 pts

Sentence Openers (number; one of each as possible)   (2 pts each)

☐ ☐ [1] subject _____ 4 pts

☐ ☐ [2] prepositional _____ 4 pts

☐ ☐ [3] -ly adverb _____ 4 pts

☐ ☐ [4] -ing _____ 4 pts

☐ ☐ [5] clausal – *www.asia.b* _____ 4 pts

☐ ☐ [6] vss _____ 4 pts

CHECK FOR BANNED WORDS (-1 pt for each use): think/thought, go/went, say/said, good, bad, big, small _____ pts

MECHANICS

☐ spelling, grammar, and punctuation (-1 pt per error) _____ pts

VOCABULARY

☐ vocabulary words – label *(voc)* in left margin or after sentence

Total: _____ 65 pts

Custom Total: _____ pts

Checklist

Teachers are free to adjust a checklist by requiring only the stylistic techniques that have become easy, plus one new one. EZ+1

Intentionally blank so the checklist can be removed.

Contents

Appendices

APPENDICES

If your students are handwriting their assignments, disregard the MLA requirement on the checklist.

Appendix I: Modified MLA Format

Format your paper in the following manner:

1. Double-space the entire composition, including the heading and title. Set 1-inch margins all the way around.

2. Only the first page should have the heading in the upper left corner with your name, lesson number, and the date.

3. If your paper is more than one page, every page (including the first) must have a header in the top right corner with your last name and page number. Look at the example below.

4. The text should be left justified. Use 12 pt Times New Roman or similar serif font. Paragraphs should be indented half an inch. There should only be one space after end punctuation to separate sentences.

Your essay should use the format shown below at 3/4 scale.

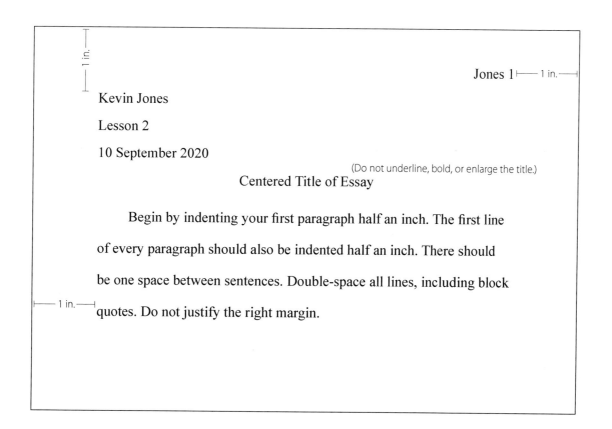

Jones 1 ⊢— 1 in. —⊣

1 in.

Kevin Jones

Lesson 2

10 September 2020

(Do not underline, bold, or enlarge the title.)

Centered Title of Essay

Begin by indenting your first paragraph half an inch. The first line

of every paragraph should also be indented half an inch. There should

be one space between sentences. Double-space all lines, including block

⊢— 1 in. —⊣ quotes. Do not justify the right margin.

APPENDICES

Appendix II: Mechanics

Well-written compositions are not only written with structure and style, but they also contain correctly spelled words and proper punctuation. This list represents all of the directions that address correct mechanics or writing which are included within various lessons.

Numbers

Occasionally you will incorporate numbers into your writing. Here are rules to keep in mind:

1. Spell out numbers that can be expressed in one or two words.

    twenty, fifty-three, three hundred

2. Use numerals for numbers that are three or more words.

    123, 204

3. Spell out ordinal numbers.

    the fifth flower, the first circle

4. Use numerals with dates. Do not include st, nd, rd, or th.

    January 1, 2020

    December 25 not December 25th

5. Use numerals with symbols.

    $500   100°C   25 mph

6. Never begin a sentence with a numeral.

    100°C (212°F) is the boiling temperature of water. (incorrect)

    The boiling temperature of water is 100°C (212°F). (correct)

Temperature

Write temperatures in degrees Celsius with Fahrenheit in parentheses. Express temperatures with the ° symbol rather than the word. Use C for Celsius and F for Fahrenheit.

Do not use spaces or periods between the temperature, symbol, and abbreviation.

Bombardier beetles can spray acid as hot as 100°C (212°F).

Contractions

Contractions are not used in academic writing.

Most ants don't have eyes or ears. (incorrect)

Most ants do not have eyes or ears. (correct)

Direct Quotes

When characters talk in a story, use quotation marks to indicate the exact words that the characters say.

"I think I have been cheated," the king told Archimedes.

Separate the speaking verb (*told*) from the direct quote with a comma. If the direct quote is an exclamation or question, follow it with an exclamation mark or question mark.

speaking verb, "Quote."   speaking verb, "Quote!"   speaking verb, "Quote?"

"Quote," speaking verb   "Quote!" speaking verb   "Quote?" speaking verb

Commas and periods always go inside the closing quotation marks. Exclamation marks and question marks go inside closing quotation marks when they are part of the material quoted; otherwise, they go outside.

Punctuating Thoughts

Punctuate thoughts like quotations. Place thoughts in quotation marks when handwriting.

Captain Bowditch wondered, "Who would trust the charts of an uneducated sailor over those written by the First Lord Admiralty of the Royal British Navy? This is my chance to prove that my charts are correct."

Place thoughts in italics when typing.

Captain Bowditch wondered, *Who would trust the charts of an uneducated sailor over those written by the First Lord Admiralty of the Royal British Navy? This is my chance to prove that my charts are correct.*

Names

Titles that precede a name must be capitalized. Do not capitalize titles that follow a name or are not used with a name.

Daedalus worked for King Minos. (title precedes name)

Minos was king. (title follows name)

The names of adults are referenced by their first and last name the first time they are mentioned. After the first time, they are only referenced by their last name.

Henry Ford produced cars that everyone could afford. (first mention)

Ford introduced the Model T automobile. (second mention)

Dates, Locations, Directions

When you add an *s* to a number to make it plural, do not add an apostrophe.

> In the 1400's Leonardo da Vinci drew pictures of flying machines. (incorrect)

> In the 1400s Leonardo da Vinci drew pictures of flying machines. (correct)

When a date includes the month, day, and year, place a comma between the day and year. If the date is placed in the middle of a sentence, place a comma on both sides of the year.

> On December 25, 1802, Nathaniel Bowditch sailed to Boston during an intense blizzard.

Separate a city and state with a comma. When a city and state are placed in the middle of a sentence, place a comma on both sides of the state.

> George Washington Carver moved to Neosho, Missouri, to attend school.

Capitalize *north*, *south*, *east*, and *west* when they refer to a region or proper name. Do not capitalize these words when they indicate direction. Do not capitalize words like *northern* or *northward*.

> Monarchs head south toward warmer weather.

> They travel from North America to Mexico.

> When the new generation of monarchs hatches, they head northward.

Hyphens and Adjectives

Use hyphens when an age precedes a noun. Do not use hyphens when the age is after the noun.

> Twenty-eight-year-old Nikola Tesla moved to New York City to work for Thomas Edison.

> Nikola Tesla was twenty-eight years old when he moved to New York City to work for Thomas Edison.

Titles

Titles of short stories are placed in quotation marks. Commas and periods always go inside closing quotation marks.

> The main character in "The Plant Doctor" is George Washington Carver.

Titles of books are italicized. If a report is handwritten, underline the title of a book.

> Sailors referenced *The Practical Navigator* by John Hamilton Moore to plot a ship's course.

APPENDICES

Appendix III: Critique Thesaurus

Introduction

Story tale, saga, narrative, epic, legend, mystery, tragedy, comedy, romance, novel, yarn, anecdote, myth

Type sad, nature, science fiction, love, adventure, historical, horror, folk, fairy, animal, moral, space, descriptive

Characters players, actors, heroes, personae, participants, figures, villain, victim, protagonist, antagonist, foil

Role main, central, leading, major, minor, subordinate, lesser, supporting, shadowy, background, secondary, foil

Types adventurous, tragic, comic, bumbling, retiring, extroverted, pliant, scheming, sordid, acquisitive, inquisitive, impulsive, sinister

Analysis well- or poorly-drawn, convincing, fully or underdeveloped, consistent, lifeless, too perfect, overly evil, idyllic, static, dynamic, flat, round

Setting

Time long ago, ancient or biblical times, Middle Ages or medieval, modern, contemporary, futuristic, mythical

Place rural, urban, small town, frontier, pioneer, war, space, slums, ghetto, exotic

Mood mysterious, foreboding, tragic, bland, comic, violent, suspenseful, compelling, sad, supernatural, emotional

Conflict

Stages initiated, promoted, continued, expanded, resolved

Intensity exacerbated, heightened, lessened

Analysis over- or under-played, realistic or unrealistic, convincing, contrived, stretched, sketchy

Plot plan, conspiracy, scheme, intrigue, subplot, sequence of events, action, narrative, episode, unfolds

Climax turning point, most exciting moment, dramatic event, high point, crisis, anticlimactic, inevitable conclusion

Theme message, moral, lesson, topic, sub-theme, matter, subject

Literary Techniques foreshadowing, symbolism, quality of language, short sentences, repetition, revelation of subplot to the narrative, suspense

APPENDICES

Appendix IV: Adding Literature

Great literature will be a valuable addition to these lessons. Many of these titles have not been reviewed by the Institute of Excellence in Writing. These selections are provided simply to assist you in your own research for books that may be used to supplement this writing curriculum.

Teachers should read the books before assigning them to their students.

The Diary of Curious Cuthbert by Jack Challoner

How We Crossed the West: The Adventures of Lewis and Clark by Rosalyn Schanzer

My Side of the Mountain by Jean Craighead George

Sea Clocks: The Story of Longitude by Louise Borden

The Wheel on the School by Meindert DeJong

Electrical Wizard: How Nikola Tesla Lit Up the World by Elizabeth Rusch

On a Beam of Light: A Story of Albert Einstein by Jennifer Berne

Kon-Tiki and I by Erik Hesselberg

A Weed Is a Flower: The Life of George Washington Carver by Aliki

Carry On, Mr. Bowditch by Jean Lee Latham

APPENDICES

Institute for Excellence in Writing

Appendix V: Vocabulary

Vocabulary cards are found on the blue page as a PDF download. Print them, cut them out, and place them in a plastic bag or pencil pouch for easy reference. Each week you should study the words for the current lesson and continue to review words from previous lessons. Try to use the vocabulary words in your compositions. For this purpose, you may use any of the words, even from lessons you have not yet had if you would like to look ahead.

For convenience, the following chart shows the words that go with each lesson and where quizzes fall. Quizzes are cumulative and cover all the words listed above them.

Quizzes can be found after the chart. Teachers who do not want students to see the quizzes ahead of time may ask you to tear them from your books and turn them in at the beginning of the school year. This is at the discretion of your teacher.

APPENDICES

Vocabulary at a Glance

Lesson 1	pungent	having an intense odor
	secure	free from harm or threat of danger
	signal	to make someone aware of something
	transport	to move from one place to another
Lesson 2	craft	to make or produce with care, skill, or ingenuity
	efficiently	producing desired results with little or no waste
	instinctively	a strong natural tendency or ability
	intently	very concentrated in attention; focused
Quiz 1		
Lesson 3	aggressively	appearing ready or likely to attack or confront
	caustic	capable of burning away or destroying tissue by chemical action
	generate	to bring into being or to produce
	lethally	in a very harmful or destructive way
Lesson 4	arduous	requiring strenuous effort; difficult and tiring
	intuitively	with an instinctive inner sense
	vital	necessary to the existence, continuance, or well-being of something
	wondrous	inspiring a feeling of wonder or delight; marvelous
Lesson 5	construct	to build or erect something
	glide	to move with a smooth, continuous motion
	resolutely	in a purposeful and determined manner
	surreptitiously	secretively
Lesson 6	conclude	to arrive at a judgment or opinion by reasoning
	ingenious	clever, original, and inventive
	reside	to live in a particular place
	substantiate	to provide evidence to support or prove the truth
Quiz 2		No new words for Lesson 9
Lesson 7	clamber	to climb in an awkward way
	desperately	showing great worry
	germinate	to begin to grow or develop
	vigorously	using force and energy
Lesson 8	alchemist	a person who attempts to turn things into gold
	brag	to boast or show off
	dash	to run or travel in a great hurry
	incredulously	showing disbelief or doubt
Lesson 10	fabricate	to construct from standardized parts
	launch	to set into motion
	momentous	having great importance
	significant	noteworthy or important
Lesson 11	enthralling	capturing and holding one's attention
	ponderous	slow and clumsy because of great weight
	replicate	to make a close or exact copy
	suspend	to keep from falling or sinking by some invisible support
Lesson 12	durable	able to withstand damage
	explosively	in a way that is very sudden and powerful
	monitor	to watch, keep track of
	penetrating	able to pierce or pass into or through
Quiz 3		No new words for Lesson 16

Institute for Excellence in Writing

Lesson 13	dilapidated	in bad condition because of age or lack of care
	mesmerized	fascinated
	reveal	to make clearly known
	speedily	moving quickly
Lesson 14	bob	to move up and down quickly or repeatedly
	cautiously	avoiding danger or risk; carefully
	pen	to write
	resourceful	able to find solutions to problems
Lesson 15	ardently	with intense emotion
	detect	to discover the existence of
	methodically	in a systematic and orderly way
	rancid	having an offensive or unpleasant smell or taste
Lesson 17	accept	to receive something that is offered
	accomplish	to succeed in doing something
	inquisitively	eagerly seeking knowledge
	technical	involving special knowledge that is understood by experts
Quiz 4		
Lesson 18	grieved	with a feeling of sorrow
	instantly	immediately
	plead	to ask for something in a serious and emotional way
	solve	to find the correct answer or explanation
Lesson 19	devise	to invent from existing principles or ideas
	immigrate	to move permanently to a foreign country
	industriously	in an energetically and devotedly way
	potable	fit or suitable for drinking
Lesson 20	alter	to change or modify
	innovative	new, original, and advanced
	persistently	continuing in spite of opposition or obstacles
	unique	unusual
Quiz 5		No new words for Lessons 23, 25, and 26.
Lesson 21	certainly	without doubt
	consequently	therefore; as a result
	furthermore	in addition; use to introduce a statement that adds to the previous statement
	similarly	in almost the same way
Lesson 22	explore	to travel over or through a place to learn more about it
	investigate	to examine in detail
	meander	to take a winding or indirect course
	scrutinize	to examine something very carefully
Lesson 24	achievement	something accomplished by special ability, effort, or courage
	advantage	something that helps make someone or something better
	benefit	something that is good or helpful
	contribution	something given for a charitable purpose
Lesson 27	antagonist	a person who opposes or competes with the hero; adversary
	climax	a decisive moment that is a major turning point in a plot
	protagonist	the leading character, hero, or heroine
	theme	the main idea that is being discussed or described
Final Quiz		No new words for Lessons 28–30

APPENDICES

Institute for Excellence in Writing

Vocabulary Quiz 1 *Answer Key*

craft	instinctively	pungent	signal
efficiently	intently	secure	transport

Fill in the blanks with the appropriate word. Be sure to spell correctly.

1. to move from one place to another

2. very concentrated in attention; focused

3. having an intense odor

4. producing desired results with little or no waste

5. to make someone aware of something

6. to make or produce with care, skill, or ingenuity

7. free from harm or threat of danger

8. a strong natural tendency or ability

1. *transport*

2. *intently*

3. *pungent*

4. *efficiently*

5. *signal*

6. *craft*

7. *secure*

8. *instinctively*

APPENDICES

Vocabulary Quiz 2 *Answer Key*

aggressively	conclude	glide	lethally	substantiate
arduous	construct	ingenious	reside	vital
caustic	generate	intuitively	resolutely	wondrous

Fill in the blanks with the appropriate word. Be sure to spell correctly.

1. to provide evidence to support or prove the truth   1. _*substantiate*_

2. appearing ready or likely to attack or confront   2. _*aggressively*_

3. to live in a particular place   3. _*reside*_

4. capable of burning away by chemical action   4. _*caustic*_

5. inspiring a feeling of wonder or delight; marvelous   5. _*wondrous*_

6. clever, original, and inventive   6. _*ingenious*_

7. to bring into being or to produce   7. _*generate*_

8. to arrive at a judgment or opinion by reasoning   8. _*conclude*_

9. in a purposeful and determined manner   9. _*resolutely*_

10. to build or erect something   10. _*construct*_

11. in a very harmful or destructive way   11. _*lethally*_

12. to move with a smooth, continuous motion   12. _*glide*_

13. necessary to the existence of something   13. _*vital*_

14. requiring strenuous effort; difficult and tiring   14. _*arduous*_

15. with an instinctive inner sense   15. _*intuitively*_

APPENDICES

Vocabulary Quiz 3   *Answer Key*

alchemist	fabricate	launch	penetrating	significant
clamber	germinate	momentous	ponderous	suspend
durable	incredulously	monitor	replicate	vigorously

Fill in the blanks with the appropriate word. Be sure to spell correctly.

1. to make a close or exact copy

2. a person who attempts to turn things into gold

3. to watch, keep track of

4. to climb in an awkward way

5. to set into motion

6. to keep from falling by invisible support

7. to construct from standardized parts

8. using force and energy

9. able to withstand damage

10. noteworthy or important

11. able to pierce or pass into or through

12. to begin to grow or develop

13. slow and clumsy because of great weight

14. showing disbelief or doubt

15. having great importance

1. *replicate*

2. *alchemist*

3. *monitor*

4. *clamber*

5. *launch*

6. *suspend*

7. *fabricate*

8. *vigorously*

9. *durable*

10. *significant*

11. *penetrating*

12. *germinate*

13. *ponderous*

14. *incredulously*

15. *momentous*

APPENDICES

Vocabulary Quiz 4 *Answer Key*

accept	cautiously	inquisitively	pen	reveal
ardently	detect	mesmerized	rancid	speedily
bob	dilapidated	methodically	resourceful	technical

Fill in the blanks with the appropriate word. Be sure to spell correctly.

1. to move up and down quickly or repeatedly   1. *bob*

2. to make clearly known   2. *reveal*

3. to write   3. *pen*

4. to discover the existence of   4. *detect*

5. in a systematic and orderly way   5. *methodically*

6. moving quickly   6. *speedily*

7. to receive something that is offered   7. *accept*

8. avoiding danger or risk; carefully   8. *cautiously*

9. involving knowledge understood by experts   9. *technical*

10. with intense emotion   10. *ardently*

11. in bad condition because of age or lack of care   11. *dilapidated*

12. eagerly seeking knowledge   12. *inquisitively*

13. able to find solutions to problems   13. *resourceful*

14. having an offensive or unpleasant smell or taste   14. *rancid*

15. fascinated   15. *mesmerized*

APPENDICES

Institute for Excellence in Writing

Vocabulary Quiz 5   *Answer Key*

accomplish	devise	immigrate	persistently	secure
alter	enthralling	industriously	plead	solve
brag	explosively	innovative	potable	surreptitiously
dash	grieved	instantly	pungent	unique

Fill in the blanks with the appropriate word. Be sure to spell correctly.

1. to find the correct answer or explanation
2. with a feeling of sorrow
3. to run or travel in a great hurry
4. to move permanently to a foreign country
5. to boast or show off
6. secretively
7. fit or suitable for drinking
8. to change or modify
9. in a way that is very sudden and powerful
10. immediately
11. having an intense odor
12. to succeed in doing something
13. unusual
14. free from harm or threat of danger
15. to ask for something in a serious and emotional way
16. capturing and holding one's attention
17. to invent from existing principles or ideas
18. in an energetically and devotedly way
19. continuing in spite of opposition or obstacles
20. new, original, and advanced

1. *solve*
2. *grieved*
3. *dash*
4. *immigrate*
5. *brag*
6. *surreptitiously*
7. *potable*
8. *alter*
9. *explosively*
10. *instantly*
11. *pungent*
12. *accomplish*
13. *unique*
14. *secure*
15. *plead*
16. *enthralling*
17. *devise*
18. *industriously*
19. *persistently*
20. *innovative*

APPENDICES

Final Vocabulary Quiz   *Answer Key*

alter	benefit	consequently	generate	scrutinize
achievement	certainly	craft	investigate	similarly
advantage	climax	explore	meander	theme
antagonist	contribution	furthermore	protagonist	vital

Fill in the blanks with the appropriate word. Be sure to spell correctly.

1.	something that is good or helpful	1.	*benefit*
2.	in addition	2.	*furthermore*
3.	necessary to the existence of something	3.	*vital*
4.	without doubt	4.	*certainly*
5.	to bring into being or to produce	5.	*generate*
6.	the main idea that is being discussed or described	6.	*theme*
7.	in almost the same way	7.	*similarly*
8.	to take a winding or indirect course	8.	*meander*
9.	to travel over or through a place to learn more about it	9.	*explore*
10.	a person who opposes or competes with the hero	10.	*antagonist*
11.	to examine something very carefully	11.	*scrutinize*
12.	to make or produce with care, skill, or ingenuity	12.	*craft*
13.	something accomplished by special ability, effort, or courage	13.	*achievement*
14.	the leading character, hero, or heroine	14.	*protagonist*
15.	something that helps make someone or something better	15.	*advantage*
16.	a decisive moment that is a major turning point in a plot	16.	*climax*
17.	something given for a charitable purpose	17.	*contribution*
18.	to change or modify	18.	*alter*
19.	to examine in detail	19.	*investigate*
20.	therefore; as a result	20.	*consequently*

APPENDICES

Appendix VI: Review Games

Earning Tickets for the Auction (a semester-long game) ——————————

Gather

raffle tickets (5-, 10-, 25-point tickets printed on colored paper)

Play

Because positive reinforcement is a wonderful motivator, throughout the year allow students opportunities to earn tickets that they can use at an auction conducted at the end of each semester. Give tickets when students win games, incorporate vocabulary words or advanced additions in their writing, and when they do something particularly well. Periodically offer contests for tickets such as "Best Title" or the best of each type of dress-up. Many of the games explained in this appendix include directions for giving tickets.

The Auction (a game to play the last day of each semester) ——————————

Gather

items for auction
a whiteboard and marker
an envelope for each student

Prepare

At the end of the semester, ask students to bring one to three items to auction to class. The items can be new or items from home. Students put their tickets in envelopes. Label each envelope with the student name and number of tickets. Write the students' names and number of tickets on a whiteboard in order from greatest to least. Instead of having students physically use tickets when they buy and sell, add and subtract from the totals written on the board.

Play

1. To begin the bidding, ask the student with the most tickets which item he or she would like to be auctioned first. Bids must begin at 25 tickets or higher. Students who would like the item continue to bid. The highest bidder receives the item, and the bid price is subtracted from his or her ticket total. Once a student has purchased an item, he or she may not bid on another item until everyone has bought one item.

2. Repeat this process, letting the second student listed on the board choose the next item. Then the third student, and so forth. This means the last person will get his or her pick of what is left for 25 tickets.

3. Once everyone has one item, it is open bidding for what is left.

Vocabulary Find the Card

Gather

twelve to sixteen index cards with vocabulary words written on each
a timer
pocket chart (optional for large class)

Play

1. Divide the class into three teams and spread the cards face up on a table. In a large class, display the cards in a pocket chart instead of laying on a table. Allow the students thirty seconds to study the cards.

2. Turn the cards face down.

3. Read the definition of one of the words. The first team must turn over one of the word cards, trying to find the word that matches the definition.

   ✔ If the word matches the definition, that team receives two points and the word card is returned to its spot on the table (face down) so that all word cards remain on the table the entire game. Play continues with the next team and the next definition.

   ✔ If the word card does not match the definition, the word card is returned and the next team attempts to find the correct word for the same definition. Now the correct word is worth three points. If missed again, the next team tries to find the correct word for the same definition for four points. Continue in this way until the correct word is found. Limit the point value to ten. *Variation*: When an incorrect word is turned over, award one point if the team that picked it can give its correct definition.

4. After the first word is found, repeat #3 with a new definition. Continue the process until all definitions have been used.

5. The player or team with the most points wins.

No-Noose Hangman

Gather

a whiteboard and marker
a die (optional)
tickets

Play

1. Choose a phrase and place lines to represent the letters of the phrase on the board. The phrase may be a vocabulary definition or an IEW concept.

Example Phrase

> To remind students what can be written on a key word outline, use the phrase THREE KEY WORDS. On a whiteboard, write a blank for each letter in the phrase.
>
> __ __ __ __ __   __ __ __   __ __ __ __ __

2. Students take turns guessing letters, one letter per turn. If the letter is in the puzzle, place it on the correct blank(s) and give the student a ticket for each time it is used. If the letter is not in the puzzle, write it on the bottom of the whiteboard so no one else will guess it. *Variation*: Let students roll a die and give tickets equal to the number rolled times how many times the letter is used.

3. When a student knows the phrase, he or she may solve the puzzle. It does not have to be his turn. If a student states the phrase correctly, he receives 10 tickets.

4. After a student states the phrase, ask a bonus question about the phrase. If the student answers the bonus question correctly, he receives 5 additional tickets.

Example Question

> In addition to two to three key words, what may you write on each line of a KWO?
>
> *symbols, numbers, and abbreviations*

5. Repeat with several puzzles.

Around the World

Gather

vocabulary cards
tickets

Play

1. Start with two students. Read a definition. The first to shout the correct vocabulary word receives a ticket and moves on to challenge the next student.

2. Continue in the same way. The winner always moves on to the next student. If one student makes it all the way "around the world" (beats everyone in the class), he receives 5 extra tickets.

Vocabulary Pictionary

Gather

two whiteboards (or one large one with a line sectioning it)
two whiteboard markers
a die

Play

1. Divide the class into two teams. Assign each a whiteboard. Call one person from each team to the front of the class. Have each drawer roll the die to determine the number of points his or her team will receive if he or she wins the round. Instruct the drawers to write the number rolled on the top of the whiteboards so it is not forgotten.

2. Show the drawers the vocabulary word you want them to draw. They will both draw the same word. Letters and numbers may not be used.

3. The first team to guess the word receives the number of points rolled on the die. Erase the boards and play again with two new drawers.

Vocabulary Lightning

Gather

vocabulary cards
a timer

Play

1. Divide the class into two or three teams.

2. Choose one or two players from one of the teams to represent the team. Show the representative(s) the stack of vocabulary cards with the word sides up. He or she may not look at the back of the card to see the definition.

3. The representative(s) tries to get the team to say as many of the vocabulary words as possible in one minute. To do so, he or she looks at the first word and gives the team various clues by stating the definition, acting out the word, or describing the picture on the card. He or she may not say things such as what letter the word begins with or what it rhymes with. *Variation:* Do not allow talking—only acting.

4. As soon as someone from the team shouts the correct word, the teacher should place the card on a table and move to the next word. If the representative gets stuck on a word, he or she may "pass" it, resulting in losing a point. For ease in sorting, passed word cards should be placed in a separate stack from the word cards guessed correctly.

5. When the time is up, count the number of words the first team guessed. Subtract the number of words passed. That difference is that team's score for that round. Let other team(s) have a turn in the same way. The team with the highest score wins that round.

6. Play several rounds.

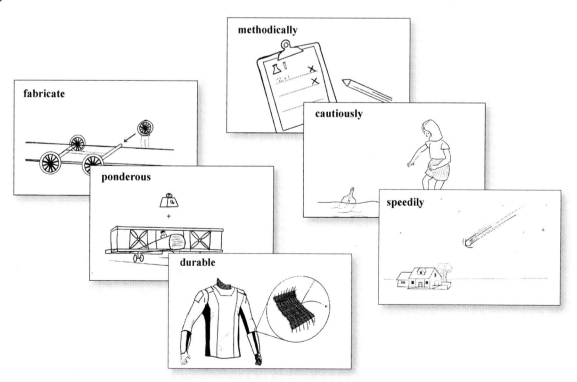

Question Game

Gather

a whiteboard and marker
a die
a list of questions (See suggested questions on pages 329–331.)
tickets

Play

1. Write numbers 1 through how many questions you will be using on a whiteboard and divide the class into three teams.

2. The first team chooses a number, and you read the corresponding question from your list.

    ✔ If the team answers correctly, one of the members rolls the die for points, and you erase the number from the board so that question will not be chosen again.

    ✔ If the team answers incorrectly, you circle the number. That team receives no points and another team may choose that circled number for double points on their turn.

    Three different ways to roll the die for points:

     The simple way is to roll the die once and receive the points indicated.

     A more challenging way is to let a team roll as many times as they choose, adding each roll to their total for that turn. So, if their first roll is a 4, and then they roll a 3, they are at 7 points. However, if they roll a 6 before they choose to stop rolling, they lose all the accumulated points for that turn. In other words, they must choose after each roll whether to roll again for more points or to stop before they roll a 6.

     As added fun, declare 2 means "Lose a turn" and 4 means "Free roll."

3. Play until most questions have been chosen and teams have had an equal number of turns. Each player on the team with the most points receives 5 tickets.

Tic-Tac-Toe

Gather

a list of questions (See suggested questions on pages 329–331.)
a whiteboard and marker
two dice

Prepare

Draw a Tic-Tac-Toe board and number the squares 1–9.
Write the Special Moves on the whiteboard.

1	2	3
4	5	6
7	8	9

Special Moves

A total of 7	=	Take an extra turn.
Double 1, 2, or 3	=	Erase an opponent's mark.
Double 4, 5	=	Erase an opponent's mark and replace it with yours.
Double 6	=	WILD. Go anywhere. You may erase your opponent's mark if need be.

Play

1. Divide players into an X team and an O team.

2. The X team begins. Read a question. If the team answers correctly, place an X in the square of choice. The team then rolls two dice to determine whether they make special moves before the O team plays. If the team answers incorrectly, the O team plays.

3. The O team plays.

4. Play until one team has three in a row or all squares are filled.

5. Repeat until one team has won two out of three or three out of five games.

Two Strikes and You're Out

Gather

eleven index cards (Write strong verbs and quality adjectives on each. Include vocabulary words.)
five index cards (Write banned words students know on each, repeating words if necessary.)
tickets

Play

1. Place the cards in a pocket chart and cover them with numbers or lay the cards face down on a table.

2. Divide the class into three teams.

3. Teams take turns picking a card.

   ✔ If the card chosen is a strong verb or a quality adjective, team members must identify it as such and use it in a sentence. If it is a vocabulary word, they should give the definition. They keep the card.

   ✔ If the card chosen is a banned word, the team receives a strike. When a team has received two strikes, the team is out and may not take any more turns.

4. Play until two teams have been eliminated. The remaining team wins, and each member receives 10 tickets. In addition, give each player on all teams 5 tickets for each strong verb or quality adjective found.

Find the *www.asia* Clause Starters (a variation of the game above)

Gather

seven index cards with *when, while, where, as, since, if, although* written on each
    (After lesson 20, include *because*.)
six index cards with *who, what, why, is, and* written on each (After lesson 20, include *because of*.)
tickets

Play

1. Place the cards in a pocket chart and cover them with numbers or lay the cards face down on a table.

2. Divide the class into three teams.

3. Teams take turns picking a card.

   ✔ If the card chosen is an adverb clause starter, team members must identify it as such and use it in a sentence. They keep the card.

   ✔ If the card chosen is not an adverb clause starter, the team receives a strike. When a team has received two strikes, the team is out and may not take any more turns.

4. Play until two teams have been eliminated. The remaining team wins, and each member receives 10 tickets. In addition, give each player on all teams 5 tickets for each *www.asia* clause starter found.

Preposition Round Robin

Gather

a list of prepositions (A short list is on page 113. The *Portable Walls for Structure and Style® Students* and the IEW Writing Tools App contain longer lists.)
a whiteboard and marker
tickets
a timer

Play

1. Give students one minute to study the list of prepositions. Remove the list from sight.

2. In turn, allow each student ten seconds to name a preposition. As each preposition is named, write it on the whiteboard and let the student take a ticket.

3. Students who are successful remain standing; however, if a student cannot think of a preposition, says a word that is not a preposition, or says a preposition already on the whiteboard, he must sit down.

4. Continue until only one student remains standing. (If two or three students remain and none of them can say another preposition, they tie.)

5. The winner receives 10 additional tickets.

Prepositions

above

across

around

after

by

during

for

from

in

inside

into

. . .

Elimination

Gather

vocabulary cards
tickets

Play

1. Divide the class into groups of three or four students. Try to have an even number of groups.

2. Begin with the first group. Read a definition of a vocabulary word. The first student in that group to shout out the matching word gets a ticket. Continue with the first group until one student has 3 tickets. He or she is the winner and will advance. The rest of the group has been eliminated.

3. Repeat the process with the other groups.

4. Divide winners into two groups and repeat the process with both groups.

5. Finally, repeat the process with the two remaining students. The winner of the final round receives 5 additional tickets.

Simplified Jeopardy!® (an end-of-the-year game) _____

Gather

> prepared cards
> three dice
> a whiteboard and marker

Prepare

> Write several question index cards. Categorize the questions by *Structure*, *Style*, *Mechanics*, or *Vocabulary*. Rank the questions by level of difficulty (1 = easy; 2 = medium; 3 = difficult). Write a question on one side of each card and the category and level of difficulty on the other side.

Play

1. Lay the cards question side down as illustrated.

STRUCTURE 1	**STYLE** 1	**MECHANICS** 1	**VOCABULARY** 1
STRUCTURE 2	**STYLE** 2	**MECHANICS** 2	**VOCABULARY** 2
STRUCTURE 3	**STYLE** 3	**MECHANICS** 3	**VOCABULARY** 3

2. Divide the class into three teams. Teams take turns choosing a question by category and level of difficulty. If the team chooses a Level 1 (easy) question, they may roll one die to determine its point value. If they choose a Level 2, they roll two dice. If they choose a Level 3, they roll three dice.

   ✔ If the team answers the question correctly, they receive the points indicated on the dice. Keep track of points on the whiteboard.

   ✔ If they do not answer correctly, they do not get any points. The missed card should be placed face up as a jeopardy question. This means another team may choose it when it is their turn. Any team that can answer a previously missed question receives double the point value that they roll with two dice. However, if they miss it, they must subtract the points rolled (not doubled).

3. Jeopardy! If a team rolls a total of 5, the question becomes a jeopardy question. This means that if they miss it, 5 points will be subtracted from their point total. However, if they answer correctly, they receive double points, which will be 10 points.

4. Play until time runs out, ensuring each team has had the same number of questions.

? **Questions** (to use with the question games) _____

Style (Dress-Ups)

1. What dress-ups have we learned thus far? How should you label them? *(underline)*

2. If you take a *who/which* clause out of a sentence, what should be left? *(a complete sentence)*

3. What are the banned words? *(think/thought, go/went, say/said, good, bad, big, small)*

4. Where does a comma go with an adverb clause (*because* clause and *www.asia* clause)? *(after the entire clause AC, MC)*

5. Improve this sentence by changing the banned word: *Archimedes went to the king's palace when he was summoned. (Answers will vary.)*

6. Improve this sentence by adding a *because* clause:
   Jack's mother sold the cow. (Answers will vary.)

Structure (Units 2–4)

7. What do we call the time and place of a story? *(setting)*

8. What do we call the problem, want, or need of the main character of a story? *(conflict)*

9. What do we call the event that leads to the conflict being solved? *(climax)*

10. When summarizing a reference, what should each paragraph of a summary report begin with? *(topic sentence)*

11. What is the topic-clincher rule? *(The topic sentence and the clincher sentence must repeat or reflect two or three key words.)*

12. Do Unit 3 narrative story paragraphs have topic sentences? *(no)*

Style (Sentence Openers)

13. What sentence openers have you learned? How do you label them? *(number)*

14. How many -ly adverbs do you need at minimum in each paragraph? *(two: one as a dress-up and one as a #3 -ly adverb opener)*

15. Give six prepositions that can begin a #2 sentence. *(See page 113.)*

16. How do you begin a #5 sentence opener? *(with a www.asia.b clause)*

17. With which is a comma always required, and where do you place the comma: #5 opener or *www.asia.b* clausal dress-up? *(opener; comma goes after the entire clause)*

18. How many words may be in a #6 sentence? *(2–5)*

19. Give an example of a sentence with a #4 sentence opener. *(Answers will vary.)*

? **Questions** (to use with the question games) _____

Structure (Units 5–9)

20. When writing a three-paragraph story from three pictures, how should you begin each paragraph? *(with the central fact of each picture)*

21. When writing a research report (using more than one source text), after you have your sources, what must you do BEFORE you begin making key word outlines? *(choose topics)*

22. Should each note page for a research report have all the notes from the *same source* or all the notes for the *same topic*? *(same topic)*

23. What is a fused outline? *(the outline you make by picking notes from source outlines you made from more than one source; it is the outline you use to write your paragraph)*

24. When you must write without a source text (your own thoughts), how can you get ideas for what to write? *(ask yourself questions)*

25. What are the brain-helping questions that can help you ask questions to think of more details to add to your writing? *(who, what, where, how, why, when, doing, thinking, feeling, saying, before, after, outside) (See page 198.)*

26. What is the structure of a basic five-paragraph essay? *(introduction, three body paragraphs, conclusion)*

27. What must an introduction paragraph include? *(attention getter, background, and the topics of the body paragraphs)*

28. What are some techniques for creating attention getters? *(ask a question, use a vss, use a quote, begin with an intriguing fact)*

29. What must a concluding paragraph include? *(restate the topics, tell what is most something (significant, interesting, . . .) and why, end with a final sentence that repeats one to three words in the title)*

30. What is the purpose of a critique? *(to give and support an opinion about a story)*

31. What should you *not* say in a critique? *("I" or "my," as in "I think" or "in my opinion")*

32. What is the structure of a basic five-paragraph critique? *(introduction paragraph, paragraph for setting and characters, paragraph for conflict, paragraph for climax and resolution, conclusion paragraph)*

? **Questions** (to use with the question games) _____

Mechanics

33.   Which numbers should usually be spelled out rather than written as numerals? *(numbers that can be written in one or two words)*

34.   The first time an adult is referenced, use his or her first and last name. After this, how should he or she be referenced. *(by last name only)*

35.   When used with quotations, do commas and periods always go inside or outside of end quotation marks? *(inside)*

36.   When must you hyphenate ages? *(When used in front of a noun: twenty-eight-year-old Nikola Tesla)*

37.   What must be changed if this is a sentence in a report (academic writing): *Honey bees don't use sounds to communication. (don't should be do not.)*

38.   Where must commas be placed in this sentence: *Yuri Gagarin left Earth's orbit on April 12 1961 and flew in space. (before and after 1961: Yuri Gagarin left Earth's orbit on April 12, 1961, and flew in space.)*

39.   When must you capitalize direction words like north, south, east, west? *(when they refer to a region or proper name: Monarchs in North America fly south toward warmer weather.)*

Vocabulary

Use any definition and ask the student to give the vocabulary word.

What's next **?**

Always prepare yourself for each unit with our teacher-training course.

Teaching Writing: Structure and Style

This powerful and inspiring seminar will transform the way you teach writing to children (and perhaps your own writing as well)!

IEW.com/TWSS2

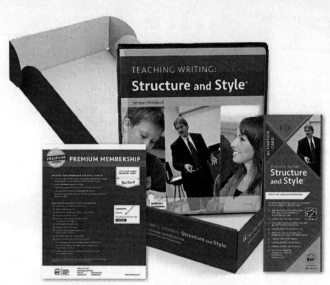

AND Choose a new theme-based book.

Continue with comparable source texts and lessons.

SLIGHTLY EASIER FOR REVIEW

COMPARABLE FOR MORE PRACTICE

MORE CHALLENGING

Fables, Myths, and Fairy Tales Writing Lessons

IEW.com/FMF-TS

Ancient History-Based Writing Lessons

IEW.com/AHW-TS

U.S. History-Based Writing Lessons

IEW.com/USH-TS

Medieval History-Based Writing Lessons

IEW.com/MHW-TS

Modern World History-Based Writing Lessons

IEW.com/WHB-TS

OR Choose the video instruction method on the next page.

Listen. Speak. Read. Write. Think!

IEW.com
800.856.5815